# Because I am a Girl

## THE STATE OF THE WORLD'S GIRLS 2010

## Digital and Urban Frontiers:
## Girls in a Changing Landscape

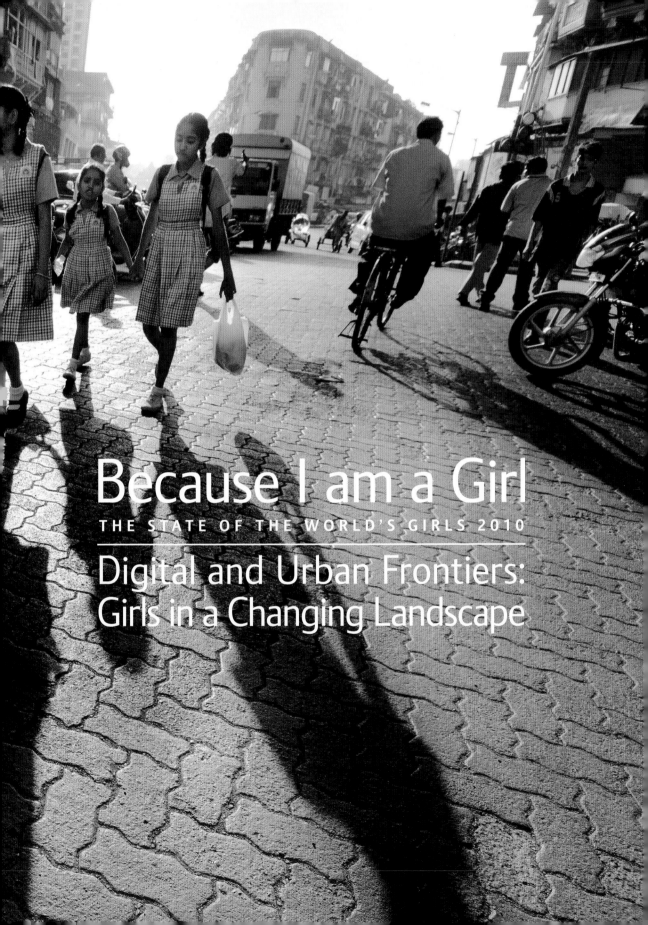

# Because I am a Girl

## THE STATE OF THE WORLD'S GIRLS 2010

## Digital and Urban Frontiers:
## Girls in a Changing Landscape

# Acknowledgements

This report was made possible with the advice and contributions of many people and organisations.

*Global Advisory Panel:*

| | |
|---|---|
| Anja Stuckert | Program Gender Advisor, Plan Germany |
| Annabel Webb | Director, Justice for Girls |
| Ann-Kristin Vervik | Senior Child Rights Advisor, Plan Geneva |
| Carolyn Rose-Avila | Deputy Vice President, Plan USA |
| Cheryl G. Faye | Head of UNGEI Secreteriat, UNICEF |
| Claudia Mitchell | James McGill Professor of Visual Arts-based Methodologies, HIV&AIDS and Social Change, McGill University |
| Cynthia Steele | Executive Vice-President, EMPower |
| Deepali Sood | Head of Global Because I am a Girl Campaign, Plan International |
| Diana Rivington | Director of Equality Between Men and Women, CIDA |
| Elkin Velasquez | Coordinator – Safe Cities Unit, UN-Habitat |
| Francisco Cos-Montiel | Senior Program Specialist, Women's Rights and Citizenship International Development Research Centre, (IDRC) |
| Kathryn Travers | Analyst and Project Officer, Women in Cities International |
| Kathy Hall | Senior Program Officer, Summit Foundation |
| Kemi Williams | Senior Gender and Rights Advisor, Department for International Development (DFID) |
| Linda Raftree | Advisor, Social Media and New Technology, Plan West Africa Regional Office |
| Lisa MacCallum | Managing Director, Nike Foundation |
| Lesley Bulman-Lever | Formerly of World Association of Girl Guides and Girls Scouts |
| Lucero Quiroga | Consultant, Gender Expert |
| Lucia Kiwala | Chief, Gender Mainstreaming Unit, UN-Habitat |
| Nazneen Damji | Programme Manager Gender equality and HIV/AIDS, UNIFEM |
| Noreen Khan | Gender Unit, UNICEF |
| Nigel Chapman | CEO, Plan International |
| Rosemary McCarney | CEO, Plan Canada |
| Ruth Pearson | Professor of International Development, School of Politics and International Studies (POLIS), Leeds University |
| Marie Staunton | CEO, Plan UK |
| Mayra Gomez | Senior Expert – Women & Housing Rights Centre on Housing Rights and Evictions, COHRE |
| Meg Greene | Consultant |
| Mima Perisic | UNICEF Advisor, Adolescent Development, Adolescent Development and Participation Unit Division of Policy & Planning |
| Seodi White | National Coordinator of Women and the Law in Southern Africa Research and Education Trust, Malawi |
| Simon Heap | Head of Research, Plan International |
| Suzanne Williams | International Institute for Child Rights and Development |
| Trine Lunde | Economist, Gender and Development Group, PREM World Bank |

Input was also received from, among others: Lynn Renken and Nythia Gopu (Nike Foundation), Savina Greenickx (StreetChild Africa), Louise Meincke (Consortium for Street Children), Dr Graham Ritchie, Helen Penn and Gabrielle Shaw (CEOP), Susan Schor (ITU), Kulsoom Ali and Michael Quesnell (Nokia Corporation), Kreeta Ryodi and Emma Bluck (Cisco), Akhtar Badshah (Microsoft), Kanwal Ahluwalia (Plan UK).

Steering Group – *Plan International*: Alistair Clay, Alexander Munive, Aimee Suchard, Belinda Portillo, Brad Henderson, Chitra Iyer, Don McPhee, Fadimata Alainchar, Hellen Tombo, Jeanette McKenna, Jon Martin Forland, Kate Fehlenberg, Lydia M Domingo, Ndungu Kahihu, Patrick van Ahee, Rebecca Lake, Rosanna Viteri, Silje Bundeng, Stuart Coles, Stefanie Conrad, Terence McCaughan.

Legal input received from: Kristen Anderson, Ruth Barnes and Erica Hall, Essex Children's Legal Centre.

Thank you to: Emily Lundell (Plan USA), Michael Diamond and Lydia Domingo (Plan Philippines), Hellen Tombo (Plan East and South Africa) and everyone in Plan Egypt, Plan Brazil, Plan Netherlands and Plan Sudan.

Special thank you to: Amos Trust and the Consortium for Street Children for inviting Plan to hold a girl-only session at the Street Child World Cup (2010), to Savina Greenickx from Street Child Africa for coordinating a comprehensive survey of street girls in Ghana, Zambia and Zimbabwe, to Suzanne Williams and Michael Montgomery (IICRD) and the Child Protection Partnership for the research on girls' online protection from Brazil, and to Justice for Girls for the research on adolescent girls and their experience of detention and rehabilitation in the Philippines.

*Girls skipping on a roof in the ruined Haitian city of Port-au-Prince.*

ALEXANDRE MENEGHINI / AP/PA

| | |
|---|---|
| Principal writer: | Nikki van der Gaag |
| Report team: | Feyi Rodway – cohort coordinator |
| | Keshet Bachan – project coordinator |
| | Sarah Hendriks – gender advisor |
| | Sharon Goulds – project lead |
| | Simone Schneider – picture research |

Research: Helen Barley, Jo Holmes, Keren Simons, Laura Margarita Gomez, Rachel McManus.

Primary Research funded by UKAID (PPA Grant).

Special thank you to the families taking part in the 'Real Choices, Real Lives' cohort study and to the Plan staff involved.

All maps in Section 3 courtesy of Maplecroft and GirlsDiscover.org.

Printed in Italy by Graphicom.     ISBN: 978-0-9565219-0-3

**Mixed Sources**
Product group from well-managed
forests, controlled sources and
recycled wood or fibre
www.fsc.org   Cert no. CQ-COC-000015
©1996 Forest Stewardship Council

FSC

Design and production: New Internationalist Publications Ltd

# Contents

TARIQ AND STAN THEKAEKARA

*Girls on the move in
busy Bangalore, India.*

# Foreword

For the first time, more than 50 per cent of the world's population is living in urban areas, a figure that is forecast to rise to more than 60 per cent in 2030. Cities in the developing world are expected to account for 95 per cent of urban growth over the next two decades. Plan's new report, focusing particularly on girls in cities, is nothing if not timely. We need to prioritise housing and urban development or too many of the world's population will be pushed further into poverty.

Cities have the potential to make countries rich, and for many, cities are a symbol of hope for a better life; but in reality, city life can mean exclusion and increased hardship. This is true for the urban poor, particularly girls and young women. The opportunities that present themselves are real, but so are the risks and multiple deprivations associated with the urban divide. Girls with nowhere to live, no family support and no job can end up on the street, in unsafe relationships and unable, through poverty, to take advantage of the education and health facilities that do exist. As this year's report from Plan International demonstrates, rapid urbanisation means that inequality and violence against girls in slums and informal settlements, public spaces and on the streets is growing. Adolescent street-involved and homeless girls in particular are pushed into begging, transactional sex and other forms of exploitation and cruelty. The reality for many girls, like 14 year-old Sala, who has lived on the streets of Accra, the capital

of Ghana, for the past two years, is quite revealing. Sala may have arrived in the city with high hopes, but she found herself on the wrong side of the urban divide. *"As soon as I moved to the city I fell into a group of other schoolchildren who introduced me to sex work. These children are my only friends here."* City life does not have to be like this: there are opportunities that we must help these young women to grasp.

All citizens have a right to their city and we must make sure that all get equal opportunities to exercise this right. Girls and women need to be empowered socially, economically and culturally, and involved in the planning and governance of cities. They need the opportunity to make known the challenges that they face and to be part of the solution, and not to be identified, as street children so often are, as the problem. It is unacceptable that, according to the research in this report, millions of women and girls all over the world feel unsafe in the cities they live in. It is unacceptable that girls and young women must constantly be on their guard in streets, parks and estates, and that rape statistics are a shameful indication that their fear is justified. We need to plan for safer cities that we can all be proud to live in and where girls can feel safe, stay healthy and take advantage of the real opportunities that urban environments, at their best, can provide.

The *State of the World's Girls 2010* focuses on the particular arenas of the city and cyberspace, which are rapidly growing areas where girls will be at risk but where opportunities abound. It also focuses on adolescent girls – girls who are at a particularly vulnerable age and who need to be able to develop the skills to protect themselves, to negotiate these new environments and to distinguish opportunity from threat. We must make it our responsibility to ensure that both cities and the internet are safe and girl-friendly.

The evidence in this report demonstrates what can and must be done and I am delighted that Plan and all the many organisations that have contributed to the 2010 Girls' Report have called us all to action. We must not condemn another generation to life in urban slums, or worse.

As I said at the World Urban Forum earlier this year, the Right to the City is about consultation, inclusion, and empowering people to solve their own problems. It is about fighting slums, not slum dwellers, and fighting poverty instead of fighting the poor! Empowering and including girls and young women is crucial. Their rights and needs have been ignored for too long.

**Anna K. Tibaijuka**
Under-Secretary-General and Executive Director
United Nations Human Settlements Programme
(UN-Habitat)

# Introduction

*"The first night I was on the street I slept under a tree. Then the police came and they just fetched the girls. We thought maybe they just picked the girls to take us somewhere safe. They took us to Albert Park and then they just pointed to one of my friends. Her name was Nutanka, and then they just abused her and when she came out she was naked. They were trying to do something to me but I kept on screaming for other people and they didn't do anything to me. They just put the pepper spray on us and hit us with the* sjambok *[leather whip]. I was 13 or 14, I am not sure. I will never forget what the police did to my friend."*

Precious, South Africa[1]

This year's 'Because I am a Girl' report looks at lives of adolescent girls like Precious in two of the fastest-growing arenas in the world today – cities and new communication technologies. In both, girls should have the right to protection, but this report will show that this right is often violated. For example, one study in Lima, Peru's capital city, found that 41 per cent of girls and young women between the ages of 10 and 24 had experienced coerced sex.[2] This is not just true in the developing world; in the Netherlands, research for this report found that 63 per cent of 17 and 18 year-old girls say they do not feel safe walking around their city at night.[3]

The internet and other new communications technologies blur the line between public and private, and abuse online can turn into real life encounters that put girls at risk. One study in the UK found that adolescents, particularly young girls between 16 and 17 years old, were in serious danger of 'online seduction'.[4] Research commissioned in Brazil for this report found that

79 per cent of girls did not feel safe online.[5]

The dangers for girls in both cities and online are rapidly expanding and yet are little regulated or researched. As a result, they pose massive new threats to girls' safety. These are particularly serious at adolescence, when girls are becoming sexual beings but have not yet developed the skills or the knowledge to protect themselves from harm. It is precisely at this time in their lives that they need the most support. Yet this is also when entrenched gender discrimination – that treats girls as less equal and less important than boys – exposes them to risk.

Adolescent girls are neglected by city planners who could make cities safe for them, let down by the failure to enact or implement legislation that would support and protect them, and exposed by a lack of regulation and enforcement of protection online. Girls are also abused by the very people and institutions that are meant to keep them safe, such as the police. As we will see, this failure is particularly acute when it comes to girls like Precious and Nutanka, who live on the streets.

And yet cities and ICTs also have the potential to offer girls more opportunities than ever before. Increasing numbers of girls are moving, with their families, to cities – where they are more likely to be educated, less likely to be married at an early age and more likely to participate in politics and leisure activities. In 59 countries there are now as many girls as boys going to school – that's 20 countries more than in 1999.[6] And millions of girls and young women now have access to mobile phones and global information systems, putting them in touch not only with their friends but with their peers in different countries.

*Inner city at rush hour in Dhaka, Bangladesh.*

MANOOCHER DEGHATI / IRIN

It is not just the world that is changing; it is also the way that girls and young women see the world and their place in it. This includes the kinds of work that they want to do, their ideas about how women and men should behave, and their dreams for their future. Girls are pushing at the boundaries that limit their lives, and asking for the same opportunities as their brothers.

For the first time in history, there are more people living in cities than in rural areas. And the numbers are growing rapidly – each month, five million people are added to the cities of the developing world.[7] We can estimate that by 2030 approximately 1.5 billion girls will live in cities. This rapid urbanisation means that violence against girls in slums and on the streets is growing as well. Extreme poverty and homelessness push adolescent girls in particular into begging, transactional sex and other forms of exploitation in order to survive. Girls like Sala, who is 14 years old and has lived on the streets of Accra, the capital of Ghana, for the past two years. She says: "Most nights I spend with clients. As soon as I moved to the city I fell into a group of other schoolchildren who introduced me to sex work. These children are my only friends here."[8]

For girls, the new world of ICTs brings old and new, rich and poor, opportunity and danger, up against each other more dramatically, more immediately and perhaps more damagingly than in any other era. Access to new information technologies and the media has exposed young women to new ideas and ways of thinking that open up huge possibilities – but which their families might also perceive as dangerous. The internet creates new intimacies that seem safe, magnifying the power of the peer group and inviting in the stranger. The case of a young woman in the UK who was raped and murdered by a man she met through Facebook illustrates the real and present dangers these types of online solicitations can pose to adolescent girls.[9] One 12 year-old girl from a poor area of São Paulo said: "What Lan Houses [internet cafés] most offer is risk. Porno sites simply pop up." Technology can be liberating for girls, but it may also replace the influence of the immediate family and community to both good and ill effect.

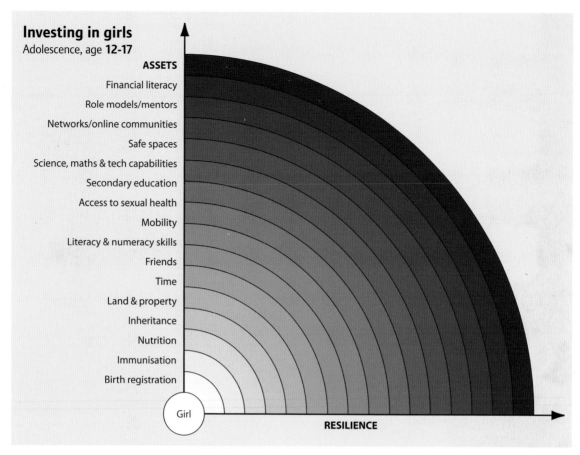

**Investing in girls**
Adolescence, age **12-17**

ASSETS
- Financial literacy
- Role models/mentors
- Networks/online communities
- Safe spaces
- Science, maths & tech capabilities
- Secondary education
- Access to sexual health
- Mobility
- Literacy & numeracy skills
- Friends
- Time
- Land & property
- Inheritance
- Nutrition
- Immunisation
- Birth registration

Girl

RESILIENCE

Adolescent girls need to be able to develop the skills to protect themselves and to distinguish opportunity from threat. Authorities and other 'duty-bearers' must make it their responsibility to make both cities and the internet safe and girl-friendly. As the diagram above shows, in both cities and online, adolescent girls need access to information, to education, to safe spaces and to networks.

We ignore the dangers facing adolescent girls at our peril. Girls are half the world's future: the citizens who will be running our cities and shaping technology in the decades to come. We owe it to them to ease their passage from childhood into womanhood so that they have the skills and the knowledge to build a better and safer future for us all. We owe it to ourselves and to the future of our world to listen to what they have to say. Girls themselves are telling us clearly what needs to be done. As Laura, a street girl from Nicaragua, says: "We all have rights that cannot be trampled on, girls as well. Violence that goes on between men

and women is wrong. You must respect a woman's opinion, as we respect a man's."[10] Or Hasina Hamza, a student from Dar es Salaam, Tanzania, who says:

*"In terms of world leaders, I would like them to know that young people are not simply 'leaders of tomorrow'. We are already leaders, and members of society, today. Our views matter. We need avenues to express them, and for that we need to know that there is guaranteed freedom of expression, as well as solid access to information. When we are treated as full partners in development issues, real change will result."*[11]

Time is running out for the 600 million girls who are adolescents today. Action needs to be taken now. Tomorrow will be too late, because by then the girls in this report will already be women and the critical moment for positive change lost forever.

*Making a living in Freetown, Sierra Leone.*

# Setting the scene 1

## The report series

'Because I am Girl' is an annual report published by Plan assessing the state of the world's girls. While women and children are recognised as specific categories in policy and planning, girls' particular needs and rights are often ignored. These reports provide concrete evidence, including the voices of girls themselves, as to why they need to be treated differently from boys and older women. The reports also make recommendations for action, showing policymakers and planners what can make a real difference to girls' lives all over the world.

The first report was published in 2007 and the last will be in 2015, the final target year for the United Nations Millennium Development Goals (MDGs). For the same period, in our 'Real Choices, Real Lives' study, we are also following a cohort group of girls in nine different countries born in the year of our first report. This year, as the UN General Assembly reviews progress on the goals, we will be measuring the progress of our cohort group and their families against several of the MDG targets which are under review. Does the state of these young girls' lives indicate that the international community will reach its aims or not?

In 2008, we looked at the situation of girls affected by conflict; those growing up 'In the Shadow of War'. The 2009 report focused on economic empowerment: 'Girls in the Global Economy: Adding it all Up.' This year, we look at adolescent girls in two of the most dynamic arenas in the world today – cities and new technologies – and examine the opportunities and the dangers that these present.

*"The government don't do anything for girls on the street, they don't even think about them. They should take them by the hand and say 'I am going to support you, I am going to help you, you are not alone', but no – they look at them as they would any other rubbish."*
Jessica, 17, street girl from Nicaragua[1]

*"Literacy now is not just learning to read and write but learning how to use a computer."*
Rana, 16, Alexandria, Egypt[2]

## New arenas for adolescent girls: cities and new technologies

Today, five years before the 2015 target for the Millennium Development Goals, many millions of girls are still missing out on education, on healthcare, and on prospects for employment.

This year, we have chosen to look at two global arenas of dramatic change – the world's cities, which are expanding every hour, and the global spaces opened up by information and communications technology, where the pace of change is even faster. In both these areas, adolescent girls face bewildering and often conflicting sets of choices as they go about their lives: choices that will affect their own futures, but also the future of the world.

Using case studies, girls' voices, expert opinion and original research, the report highlights the positive and negative aspects of these fast-changing spaces and places. It also looks at what adolescent girls need in order to thrive in them, and makes recommendations to those in authority at international, national and local levels.

JANE HAHN

**15**

Section 1 of the report looks at the opportunities and threats for girls in cities and in new technologies. Section 2 examines in detail how the cohort of girls in the 'Real Choices, Real Lives' study are faring. Section 3 provides statistical evidence to show how girls' lives are changing.

In **Chapter Two**, we look at one of the major changes that our world is experiencing today – the exponential growth of its cities – and ask: what are the benefits for girls and young women and what are their particular needs? What are the coping mechanisms they use to survive when their needs are ignored by those in power and their rights abused by those who want to exploit their sexuality? This chapter looks at the reasons why young women move to the city, what urban life has to offer them, and the mixture of 'push' and 'pull' factors that drive rural-urban migration. For example, a survey in slum areas of Addis Ababa found that one in every four young women migrants between the ages of 10 and 19 came to the city to escape early marriage.[3] And a study in Egypt of street children between the ages of 10 and 18 found that 82 per cent said they had come to the city because of abuse by the family or at work.[4] This chapter shows why urban life offers adolescent girls both the greatest opportunities and the greatest risks. Risks which, for adolescent girls in slums in particular, need addressing urgently.

### DEFINING ADOLESCENCE

The World Health Organisation and other United Nations organisations define adolescence as being between 10 and 19 years old, youth as 15 to 24 and children as 0 to 18. The fact that these categories overlap reflects the fact that young people's lives and their physical and emotional development vary hugely, not just according to age but in relation to their sex, where they live, their family and community, their economic status and many other factors. This report, however, focuses in particular on the adolescent age group from 10 to 19, while not completely excluding girls who are slightly older or slightly younger. It also bears in mind that this is a period of major transitions in a girl's life – from girl

BENNO NEELEMAN

to woman, school to work, dependence to independence. How she is able to deal with these transitions depends heavily on her national, social, economic and political context. All girls are different, but there are some experiences and vulnerabilities that they share and it is these that the report will focus on.

### ADOLESCENT GIRLS IN CITIES – THE FACTS
#### Where cities are working well for girls

As we demonstrate below, adolescent girls in cities are more likely than their rural cousins to go to school, marry later, give birth more safely and have more of a say in their own lives. This not only benefits the girls themselves as they grow into women, but means that cities have a more articulate and vibrant population

*Children at play in Alexandria, Egypt.*

who can take an active part in planning and running city life – and ensure that cities are both safe and girl-friendly.

- In developing countries, school attendance for girls aged 10 to 14 is 18 per cent higher in urban than in rural areas, and 37 per cent higher for young women aged 15 to 19.[5]
- In Bangladesh, 31 per cent of adolescent girls who had migrated from rural to urban areas for work were married by the age of 18, compared to 71 per cent in rural areas.[6]
- Overall, 79 per cent of city births have a skilled attendant compared with 28 per cent of births in rural areas.[7]
- Skilled birth attendants are present at 78 per cent of deliveries in urban settings in Bolivia, 60 per cent in Pakistan, almost 52 per cent in Angola and 47 per cent in Yemen. Skilled deliveries in rural areas in these countries are two to four times lower.[8]
- In urban areas in Benin 25 per cent of pregnant adolescent girls receive HIV counselling and testing, whereas in rural areas the figure is only 6 per cent.[9]
- In the city of Ceará, Brazil, young people were involved in budget setting and in training other youth. As a result of their efforts, an additional $750,000 was allocated to children and young people in 2005.[10]

### Where cities are not working well for girls
Despite the many advantages of living in a city, for adolescent girls city living also means an increased risk of violence and abuse.
- A study of human rights violations in Dhaka, Bangladesh, found that adolescent girls were the most vulnerable group when it came to sexual harassment and rape.[11]
- Many of the benefits of cities do not apply to slums or shanty towns, for example. In these, many girls never start school or drop out before finishing secondary school.
- More than half of the boys interviewed in a Rwanda study and more than three-quarters of the girls, including 35 per cent of those under 10, admitted they were sexually active; 63 per cent

of the boys said they had forced a girl to have sex with them; 93 per cent of the girls reported having been raped.[12]
- Violence against girls and women may be more common in the city than in rural areas: in Brazil 24.5 per cent of female respondents in the city and 15.9 per cent in the provinces reported violence.[13]
- In Pokara, Nepal, 90 per cent of street girls were sexually abused by hotel and restaurant owners and by people in places of work. Junkyard owners, older boys in the group, friends, local people and tractor drivers were also among the perpetrators.[14]
- In Ghana, adolescents in urban areas were significantly more likely to have experienced coerced sex than those in rural areas.[15]
- In the Netherlands, an online survey of girls in cities conducted for this report found that 40 per cent of girls between the ages of 11 and 18 said they did not feel safe walking around their city at night. This rose to 63 per cent of 17 and 18 year olds.

In **Chapter Three**, we focus on one group who are most vulnerable in the city – adolescent street girls. Although accurate estimates are difficult to come by, numbers of street children are rising. Girls apparently constitute fewer than 30 per cent of street

*Girls at work in Accra, Ghana.*

children, but this may be partly because they are less visible, which makes them more vulnerable. Of all those living in the city, it is street girls, particularly adolescents, who are most at risk. A study in India, involving more than 1,000 street girls aged between 5 and 18, found that 68 per cent reported they had been physically abused. Almost half the girls told the researchers that they wished they were boys.[16] Adolescent street girls face sexual harassment and abuse and often have to rely on street boys or older men to protect them. A survey by Child Hope found that 95 per cent of girls living on the streets of Ethiopia experienced sexual exploitation.[17] Street girls can find no refuge with the authorities or the police, who are as likely to abuse them as protect them. Justice systems and prisons also treat them harshly, sometimes imprisoning them because they are girls on the street rather than because they have committed a crime. Research in the Philippines commissioned for this report found that girls were arrested simply for being on the street and breaking curfew.[18] This chapter examines what happens to adolescent street girls in cities. It also looks at the strategies they use to survive and protect themselves; for being a street girl also means being resilient.

### AN IDEAL CITY FOR GIRLS IS...[19]

- A city where girls' rights (economic, social, political and cultural) are guaranteed
- A city where girls have equal access with boys to all services
- A city where no girl is so poor that she has to sell her body to survive
- A city where every girl has access to decent shelter, education, employment, transport and health services
- A city where girls are free from violence, at home, at school, and in the street
- A city where girls are not discriminated against or harassed
- A city where girls have equal access with boys to technology
- A city which notes that girls' needs are different from boys' and from each other
- A city which documents and takes account of adolescent girls' needs in its political and planning processes

- A city where all girls can participate in cultural, political and other activities
- A city which prevents and punishes violence against girls
- A city where the state and local government guarantee girls' access to justice.

In **Chapter Four**, we look at how girls are operating in the fast-moving world of communications technologies (ICTs) – the internet and email, instant messaging, social networks and mobile phones. ICTs are critical for girls' empowerment. Because this arena is growing and changing, girls have a unique opportunity to influence

*A rickshaw ride in India.*

the formation of ICTs and to challenge gender discrimination through these technologies. We explain how and why boys and young men have greater access to these technologies than girls and young women and how they use them differently. In Indonesia, for example, girls and young women aged 15 to 24 are half as likely to use the internet as boys the same age.[20] We also reveal how ICTs are an arena where sexual predators can operate with impunity, and how adolescent girls and young women have become prime targets for new methods of abuse, including trafficking, via the internet and other communications technologies. In China, for example, 44 per cent of children said they had been approached online by strangers.[21] We look at the new phenomenon of cyberbullying, which is most prevalent among adolescents and teenagers and where girls are more likely to be the victims – in one study in the US, 41 per cent of adolescent girls between the ages of 15 and 17 said they had experienced bullying via the internet or mobile phone, compared with 29 per cent of boys.[22] This chapter will look at how adolescent girls can be both informed and empowered online.

### ONLINE FACTS ABOUT GIRLS IN BRAZIL
The International Institute for Child Rights and Development through the Child Protection Partnership undertook research in Brazil for this edition of 'Because I am a Girl' (see Chapter 4). For this research, they interviewed 44 girls and conducted a national online survey. These facts are extracted from their report, which shows that most girls have a mobile phone and access to the internet, and that virtually all the respondents think online dangers are greater for girls than for boys.
#### The good news
- 84 per cent of girls have a mobile phone
- 60 per cent say they have learned about online dangers
- 82 per cent have used the internet, with 27 per cent indicating that they are always online
- The more awareness and knowledge about ICT use that girls have, the greater degree of security they feel online

#### The bad news
- 79 per cent of girls said they did not feel safe online
- Almost half the girls who responded to the survey indicated that their parents know what they access online
- Only about a third of the girls know how to report a danger or something that makes them feel bad online
- Almost 50 per cent of girls say they would go to meet someone in person who they had met online.

*Travelling with a mobile phone in Singapore.*

Finally, the report asks those with power to make decisions about adolescent girls' lives – to confront, challenge and address the threats that girls and young women face in our fast-changing world. It shows the importance of investment, both public and private, in order to build girls' capabilities and assets so that they can better protect themselves. It argues that the laws that are meant to protect young women must be enforced. It emphasises the need to protect and promote girls' rights in cities and online. It makes specific and targeted recommendations for those responsible for our cities and those who provide services, be they private sector, non-governmental or international organisations. And it calls for support for girls and young women as they claim their place in the new millennium.

## BUILDING GIRLS' ASSETS

The word 'assets' is often used in development. In the context of girls, we are talking about social, political, economic and human assets – for example, ensuring that a girl has enough to eat, good healthcare and education, and a strong social support system that enables her to make choices in her life, achieve her goals and build the resources she needs to do this. Other assets include a supportive family, a network of friends, role models/mentors and access to online communities and networks.

We urge those who have a duty and a responsibility to invest in girls, to protect them, to plan for them and to ensure that they are able to participate safely in the exciting and dynamic developments that are taking place in cities and in the rapid expansion of new technology. This is an issue that involves us all, from street girls to civil society organisations, from mayors to ministers, from parliamentarians to the police. As Tala, a street girl from the Philippines, said:

*"The government must work together. We must all work together because nothing will happen if we don't have unity."*

*Young women in a street market in Bangalore, India.*

# 'Real Choices, Real Lives' –
## The Plan cohort turns four

In 2007 we set up a cohort study – 'Real Choices, Real Lives' – to follow a group of girls from birth until their ninth birthday. Their stories help illuminate the decisions and choices families worldwide face as their daughters grow up, and are a vivid reminder that the facts and figures contained in the report are about real people – real girls and their families.

This year, because the focus of the report is on adolescent girls in new and changing places – both urban space and the growing world of new technologies – we interviewed not only the parents of the girls taking part but also older siblings, cousins and neighbours. The purpose was to gain a better understanding of how teenage girls experience their place in today's world.

We found that although the vast majority of the girls taking part in Plan's 'Real Choices, Real Lives' cohort study live in rural areas, the dramatic changes described in this year's 'Because I am a Girl' report are nevertheless impacting on their families. This is particularly so in Latin America (Brazil, Dominican Republic and El Salvador) and in West Africa (Benin and Togo). As family members move to cities, the study clearly shows both the 'push' factor of rural poverty and the 'pull' factor of opportunity that city life represents. It also shows the impact that the exodus has on family members left behind.

The death of Yassiminatou, one of the little girls from Togo, shows us how overpowering the sheer struggle for survival is for the very poorest families. Yassiminatou's family took her to a local traditional healer but she died after a short illness, before they could take her to the health centre. It brings the total number of deaths in our small survey to five in four years. Many of the little girls in West Africa, in particular, struggle constantly with illness and disease. The impact of poverty and poor nutrition is all too clear.

Gastine, also from Togo, was luckier than Yassiminatou – access to a trained health worker saved her life.

### Gastine's Story

Gastine recently turned four. She lives with her mother, Bella. Gastine's father lives in the local town, so Bella is raising her children largely on her own. Bella says: *"Gastine will be my last child. I have a lot of children and the problem is to feed them. I grow maize and yam and three days each week I walk two hours to the fields and two hours back, to till my fields. On Monday and Wednesday, I make and sell local beer and maize cakes."*

Gastine has suffered from malaria several times in her short life but, crucially, has

Gastine

had access to free treatment provided by a trained healthcare worker who lives in the local community. Gastine's mother is able to look ahead: *"When she is older she will go to school. I want her to be a teacher, not working on the land like I do."*

The fate of these two little girls demonstrates how important it is that their families break out of the trap of poverty, and how vital it is that we invest in them and their communities. The cohort families in Togo spend more than 90 per cent of their income on food. For them, health and education are 'luxuries' they cannot really afford.

The experiences of the 20 Togolese families in the study demonstrate the pull of the city among rural communities desperate to leave their poverty behind. Twelve of them have a close family member – mother, sister, brother – who has already moved. Many others talk of moving to their nearest city to find work and better educational opportunities for their children. Forty-two per cent of Togo's people already live in an urban area. Massama's father, for example, would like her to become a teacher, but there is no secondary school in their village so he too is thinking about moving to the nearest town. For many of the families the nearest town is Sekode. Situated by the main north-south road running through Togo, it is on one of the major child-trafficking routes in West Africa – a potential risk to balance against the educational benefits. Many of the teenage girls we talked to spoke of the pressure to leave their villages and earn money elsewhere. They also spoke of the

Noelia and her grandmother

misery they suffered. Abide, aged 15, went to Nigeria:

*"I was working as a maid 18 hours a day for 5,000 cprs [$10] per month. I tried to come home every year... on the way to Nigeria we had to hide from the police as child trafficking is now illegal."*

In El Salvador, two of the girls taking part in the study are being raised by their grandmothers, as their parents have migrated to the United States and to Italy. Others are being raised by their mothers alone because their fathers have left to work in cities abroad. In the Dominican Republic the mother of Noelia has gone to work in the capital San Domingo and speaks for many mothers when she expresses how much she misses her daughter and how much of her childhood she will never see. "My mother knows her better than I do," she comments.

The information from our researchers in the nine cohort countries has again provided a vivid illustration of the analysis provided by the report as a whole. It keeps us aware of the real human costs of poverty and lack of opportunity. The young women we talked to in Brazil spoke for their younger siblings and all the children whose parents had gone to look for work elsewhere when they told us: "When any member of the family leaves, the changes are for the worse..." and "when

Massama and her family

Doreen,
Philippines

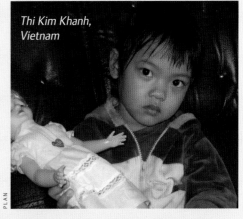
Thi Kim Khanh,
Vietnam

one member of the family is absent, there is a lot of sadness..."

The cohort study also supplies revealing information about girls and new technology. A small number of the teenage relatives of the girls taking part in the study have access to information technology. Mobile phones feature most prominently in their lives. Access varies from country to country – in Togo, for example, none of the families taking part in the study had heard of the internet and none had regular access to mobile phones. In Brazil, where many in our cohort live in urban slums, all of the teenagers, girls and boys alike, have access to the internet, either at school or at an internet café. However, a larger proportion of boys interviewed appeared to have regular access to mobile phones.

Talking to a focus group of Brazilian mothers and daughters, it became clear that girls are held back by parental fears for their safety. Girls commented: "We want to take a professional course... our mothers don't let

us take a course outside the community... they are afraid of sexual harassment." This desire to protect girls will hold them back from school, from internet cafés, from college and from fulfilling their potential.

For the adolescent girls, increased access to information is in itself contributing to increasing urbanisation. Young people are keen to move to urban areas, where they expect to have better prospects. One of the teenage girls from Brazil explained that "on television we see the changes, but in our own homes the story is very different".

The parents in the survey may fear for their girls' safety but they continue to express their hopes and dreams for their children. Many desire equality of opportunity for their daughters and want them to stay in school "to become a doctor, a lawyer or a teacher". Attitudes are changing, sometimes ahead of practice, but by the time the cohort's four year olds are adolescents we must make sure these dreams are closer to fulfilment.

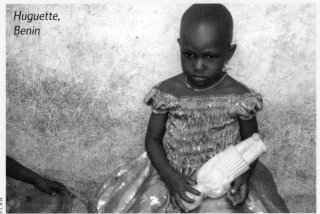
Huguette,
Benin

Soumeyatou,
Togo

# Bright lights and big hopes: adolescent girls in the city

"*I am going to talk about the challenges that we girls in the ghetto get. First we are raped and there is no action taken against the men who raped us. Second, early pregnancy. Boys say: 'You are beautiful, can I sleep with you?' Third, dropping out of school. So the challenges girls face in the ghetto are many. That is why we created Safe Spaces to talk about our challenges.*"

Linda Nyangasi, one of the young leaders of the Safe Spaces project in Kibera, a slum in Nairobi.

"*My mother used to listen to my brothers and not to me. I used to be afraid and never imagined I could do what I can do now. Now they listen to me as well and treat me the same as my brothers. I am the secretary of the school parliament. I want to be a child doctor. I want to distribute all the experience and knowledge I have to other girls around the world.*"

Asalaa, 12, from Alexandria, Egypt. She has benefited from training programmes that she would be unlikely to get in a rural area.

## Summary

In this chapter, we look at one of the major changes that our world is experiencing today – the exponential growth of its cities – and ask: what are the particular needs of adolescent girls in this context? We look at the reasons why young women move to the city and what urban life has to offer them. We show the many opportunities that the city opens up for them, which are not available or possible in a village. But we also reveal how violence is a growing threat for adolescent girls in cities because of their age and sex. We argue that they must be supported to develop the skills to protect themselves, and to distinguish opportunity from danger. We showcase models of good practice; for example, urban planning that takes young women's views into account and initiatives aimed at building safer cities for girls and women. We look at the difference for girls living in poorer and richer housing areas. Finally, we call for investment, not just in young people in cities as a generic group, but in adolescent girls specifically. We must listen to what they have to say. They have a crucial part to play in building the safe and sustainable cities that we will need for the 21st century.

## 1. Introduction: the global context of urbanisation and youth

"*We have achieved things that the teachers didn't think we would be able to achieve as girls. They never had these kind of opportunities at our age. My parents too are astonished at the change they see in me.*"

Rana, 16, on the leadership training she had from Plan in the city of Alexandria, Egypt.

For the first time in history, we are now officially an urban planet. More people now live in cities and towns than in villages.[1] Each week, three million people are added to the cities of the developing world.[2] The urban population of Africa and Asia will double in less than a generation.[3]

Despite common perceptions, not all cities are expanding due to rural-urban migration. In fact, 60 per cent of urban growth, particularly in mega-cities of over 10 million, occurs due to natural population growth.[4] Cities also grow because rural land around the perimeter gradually becomes urban as people move in. And in some countries the economic crisis has also brought about a reversal in this trend as people leave cities to return to villages.[5] While many millions migrate, most young people living in a city today were born there.[6]

What statistics cannot reveal is the diversity of experience of living in a city. As we will see, life for an adolescent girl in one of the world's growing number of mega-cities of over 10 million is very different from living in a small town, let alone in a village. And one of the most important factors shaping that experience is whether she is rich or poor.

The cities' richest inhabitants are increasingly isolating themselves in gated communities and using private services. Then there are the middle classes, who benefit most from the amenities and services provided in a city, and for whom they are generally provided.[7] And finally, there are the most marginalised – the urban poor – who constitute up to half the urban population, especially in developing countries. They have little access to the benefits of a city, and may live in slums or shanty towns. Father Bruno Sechi, co-founder of the National Movement of Street Boys and Girls in Brazil, says: "The first and greatest violence is the systematic exclusion of a great number of people by society. From this violence other violence directly and indirectly flows. Where you exclude, you must establish instruments to control those who are excluded so that they don't invade the peace of those who have access to opportunities and wealth."[8]

As Women in Cities International have stated: "It is important to recognise that cities are not homogenous; rather they are experienced in different ways by the diversity of their residents. Not only is the experience of the city shaped by one's gender, but it is

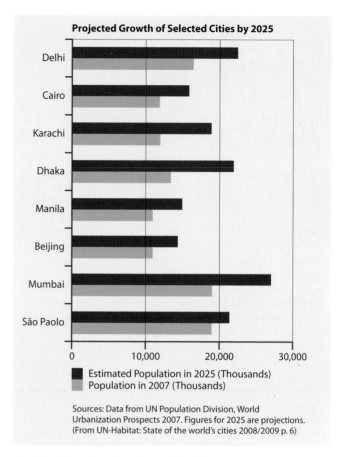

**Projected Growth of Selected Cities by 2025**

■ Estimated Population in 2025 (Thousands)
■ Population in 2007 (Thousands)

Sources: Data from UN Population Division, World Urbanization Prospects 2007. Figures for 2025 are projections. (From UN-Habitat: State of the world's cities 2008/2009 p. 6)

further shaped and re-shaped by additional factors, including age, ethnic background, religion, marital status, sexual orientation and disability."[9]

This fact has been recognised in many cities, which have special programmes for women, children and those with disabilities or from particularly disadvantaged groups. However, there are only a few that recognise the particular needs of adolescent girls, especially those who are most marginalised, and therefore most deprived of its benefits. And yet we know that investing in girls can break the cycle of poverty that is often handed down from generation to generation.[10]

### A GIRL'S RIGHT TO THE CITY

Women and girls should have as much right to the city as men and boys; to freedom of mobility, to use public spaces, to go to school, to engage in politics and to participate in the benefits of urban life without fear.

In response to the growing concentration of the world's population in urban centres and to increasingly fragmented cities, a new concept has emerged as the backdrop for affirming the entitlement of all city dwellers to its privileges and opportunities, spaces and services – the idea of the 'right to the city'. This stems from the premise that all city dwellers should be able to benefit fully from city life in ways that are accessible, appropriate, affordable, safe, adapted and equitable for all, regardless of age, gender, race, religion, sexual orientation or any other factor.

UNESCO and UN-Habitat state that the assertion of one's right to the city can serve as a vehicle for social inclusion. The right to the city includes the following:

- Liberty, freedom and the benefit of the city life for all
- Transparency, equity and efficiency in city administrations
- Participation and respect in local democratic decision-making
- Recognition of diversity in economic, social and cultural life
- Reducing poverty, social exclusion and urban violence.[11]

These principles are particularly important for women and girls, whose ability to access the city is more limited. Urban environments, governance structures, services and spaces must be re-thought and designed or adapted with the particular needs and experiences of girls in mind. Adolescent girls must be actively involved in all stages of this re-thinking process to ensure that their voices are included and reflected in how cities are organised and run.[12]

Young people under 25 already make up half the world's urban population, and the numbers living in cities are growing fast.[13] They all should have their needs and rights recognised and live in a city free from violence, with adequate housing, safe water, transport, and access to healthcare, technology, networks, education and skills training.

The diagram below shows how the population of young people is projected to grow in cities all over the world.

Life in the city has much to offer adolescent girls. They are more likely to be educated and find work, and less likely to marry young in a town than in a village. They have more opportunity to interact with boys and to work towards equality.

But millions of adolescent girls are not able to access these positive sides of city life. Because they are at the point in their lives where they are maturing sexually, they are especially vulnerable to violence and sexual exploitation, in particular if they are homeless, live on the streets or live in poorer parts of the city, especially slums.

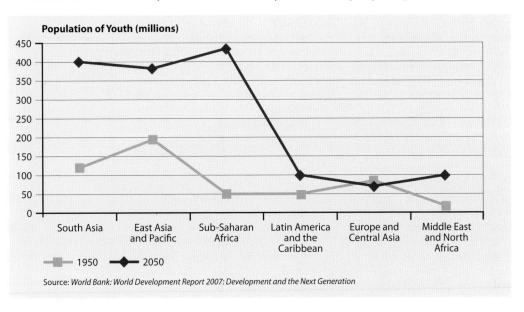

**Population of Youth (millions)**

Source: World Bank: World Development Report 2007: Development and the Next Generation

## GIRL HOMELESSNESS IN CANADA – A NATIONAL CONCERN[14]

Despite a context of economic prosperity and relatively progressive social policy in Canada, teenage girls who live in poverty, a disproportionate number of whom are indigenous, are very often denied access to the most basic human rights. They are criminalised for the oppression they face and encounter additional abuse in state-run facilities, leaving them vulnerable to becoming homeless. The United Nations Special Rapporteur on the Right to Adequate Housing recently found: "Homelessness in general and that of young women and girls in particular has become a national concern in Canada."[15] Teenage girls constitute between 30 and 50 per cent of homeless youth in big cities across Canada.[16]

Many girls leave their homes to escape sexual and physical abuse by male family members, which is not properly dealt with by the criminal justice or child welfare systems. For indigenous girls, the impact of historical and current colonial social policies is also a driving force behind girls' trajectory into homelessness.

There is virtually no girl-only housing in Canada for girls who are homeless and escaping male violence. Instead, girls who are often dealing with the emotional and physical traumas of male sexual and physical violence are expected to go to co-educational shelters and group homes which they share with young men and adult male staff. Many girls try to survive outside of state care as a result.

When Canadian governments fail to provide safe accessible housing to Canadian girls, exploitive adult men step in to fill the gap. Before long, homeless teen girls are 'trading' sex with older abusive men in exchange for a place to stay. Many of these adult men subsequently reveal themselves as drug dealers and pimps who eventually 'turn out' girls, under threat of force, into selling sex and/or drug dealing. In a 2007 survey of 762 homeless youth aged 12 to 18 it was found that 57 per cent of the girls had been sexually abused.[17]

On the street, teen girls in Canada endure frequent and severe male sexual and physical violence (including rape and murder), commercial sexual exploitation, police harassment and brutality, criminalisation and imprisonment and serious, sometimes fatal, health disorders such as HIV and Hepatitis C. They survive in grossly inadequate and dangerous living environments such as squats or adult rooming houses that are often infested with bed bugs, cockroaches and rodents, inhabited by violent men, or toxic with environmentally hazardous chemicals, building materials and pesticides.

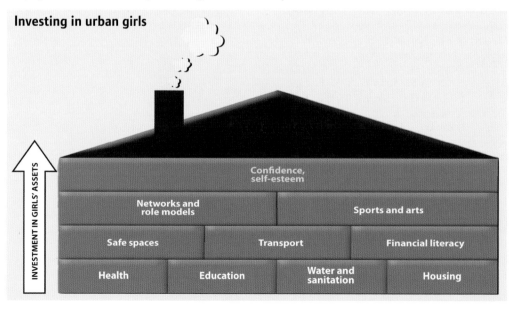

**Investing in urban girls**

INVESTMENT IN GIRLS' ASSETS

| Confidence, self-esteem | | |
| Networks and role models | | Sports and arts |
| Safe spaces | Transport | Financial literacy |
| Health | Education | Water and sanitation | Housing |

## Justice for girls

There is little recognition at any level by those who run our cities that adolescent girls have different requirements and different vulnerabilities than boys, older women and younger girls. We will show how, in order to keep safe, they need secure transport, adequate lighting, and affordable and decent housing. To mature into responsible adults, they require education and health services targeted at their needs and, when they are the right age, the possibility of decent work.

With cities mostly built, planned and run by men, the requirements of women and girls are often ignored – and those of adolescent girls particularly so. Adolescent girls have huge energy, ideas and enthusiasm, as some of the projects we will showcase reveal. But, as UN-Habitat points out: "Young women and girls have traditionally had little say in how cities are developed, how services are delivered, and how governance structures are run."[18] Giving them a say will not just make cities safe for girls: they will make them better places to live for everyone.

The issues about adolescent girls in cities that this report raises are not going to go away; on the contrary, they will become more urgent with each passing day. By the middle of the 21st century the majority of countries in the developing world will be mostly urban.[19] The issues must therefore be addressed with the speed that they deserve. We owe this, and much more, to the millions of adolescent girls who live in cities and the many more who will live there in the coming decades. The United Nations notes that: "The future of cities depends on the future of young people. In particular, it depends on what policymakers can do to equip young people to break the cycle of poverty. This in turn depends on involving young people in the decisions that affect them."[20]

## Adolescent girls in slums

*"Both men and women in slums face problems associated with poverty, poor living conditions and lack of social safety nets. But research shows that women and girls are by far the worst affected."*
Anna Tibaijuka, Executive Director of UN-Habitat[21]

*Living in a Bangladeshi slum.*

According to UN-Habitat, a 'slum household' is a group of individuals living under the same roof in an urban area who lack one or more of the following: durable housing, sufficient living area, access to safe water, access to sanitation and secure tenure. Not all poor people live in slums, and not all people who live in areas defined as slums are poor. However, slum dwellers constitute the majority of the world's urban poor.[22]

Slum dwellers are no longer a few thousand in a few cities of a rapidly industrialising continent. Vast urban slums are now the reality of daily life for around 828 million people: one out of every three city dwellers, almost a sixth of the world's population.[23] The majority of slum dwellers live in Asia, and more than 70 per cent of Africa's urban population live in areas that can be defined as slums,[24] although aggregate statistics hide deep inequalities and gloss over concentrations of harsh poverty within cities.[25] The pace and scale of slum growth is changing rapidly. There are now more than 250,000 – Delhi now has 'slums within slums' and in Cairo and Phnom Penh urban squatters on rooftops have built slum cities in the air.[26]

Slums are also vibrant places: "Slums are filled with entrepreneurs," as Judith Hermanson of InterAction points out:[27] "Slums are creative places, full of people who have made a living in very difficult circumstances."

However, the majority of the world's slum dwellers are likely to die younger,

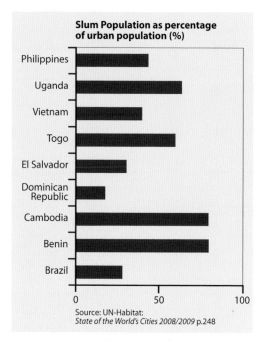

**Slum Population as percentage of urban population (%)**

| | |
|---|---|
| Philippines | |
| Uganda | |
| Vietnam | |
| Togo | |
| El Salvador | |
| Dominican Republic | |
| Cambodia | |
| Benin | |
| Brazil | |

0    50    100

Source: UN-Habitat:
*State of the World's Cities 2008/2009* p.248

experience more hunger and disease, attain less education and have fewer chances of employment than people who live in other parts of the city.[28] The majority of them are young.[29] While there are few statistics which disaggregate by gender and by age, there is some evidence that there are more girls than boys in slums.[30] We know that women and girls now represent 55 to 70 per cent of slum dwellers globally. Evidence shows that woman-headed households, of which there are many in slums, are likely to be the poorest of the poor.[31]

On the other hand, adolescent girls living in slums may have access to projects that they would not have elsewhere. Raouda, who migrated to the city of Alexandria in Egypt, says: "In Upper Egypt [rural areas] there are not the same opportunities for girls and women. There are cultural activities and discussions here that we can join, from literacy classes to awareness about practices such as female genital mutilation. I hope that my daughters who are born in the city have more chances in life than I did."

Very little research has been done looking specifically at how adolescent girls fare in slums. As they enter a phase of their lives where their bodies are maturing, they have particular needs for education, support and information. At the same time, they are at increased risk of harassment, sexual violence and rape. These issues have been left largely unaddressed by academics and advocates alike and there is limited data on adolescent girls and the poverty of urbanisation.

## 2. Streets of gold? Why adolescent girls move to cities

*"For me, a 'better life' means having goods you would never get when staying in your village. In their villages, [children] always eat the same kind of food, and that's not good. My living conditions are tough, but at least I earn 500 cfa a day, a sum that I would never get within three months, if I stayed home [in the village]."*

Young girl in Mali[32]

*"Well, it's very difficult here; here there are no jobs. She will have to go to the city. She'll have to work there, to look for employment so she can study."*

Mother of Maria, a young woman in Peru[33]

Many adolescent girls leave the village in search of education or work and the many opportunities a city has to offer. Some think they are moving permanently; others only for a short time. This section explains the reasons why girls leave.

We know that young people are more likely than older people to move from

*Collecting water in Mumbai, India.*

MARK HENLEY / PANOS PICTURES

# GIRLS' LEGAL RIGHTS IN THE CITY [34]

Girls who move to the city are vulnerable to a number of human rights violations and it is primarily the obligation of governments to ensure that their rights are protected. International human rights standards can be used to provide guidance on domestic legal frameworks and other measures to ensure that the city is an environment in which girls can survive, develop and thrive. The UN Convention on the Rights of the Child (UNCRC Article 19) is perhaps the most significant instrument that can be used to address violations of girls' human rights in the city. However, other instruments, including the International Covenant on Civil and Political Rights (ICCPR), the International Covenant on Economic, Social and Cultural Rights (ICESCR), and the Convention on the Elimination of all Forms of Violence Against Women (CEDAW) are also important.

## The right to adequate housing

The right to adequate housing is a key component of the right to an adequate standard of living, which is recognised in a number of international instruments, including Article 11(1) of the ICESCR, Article 27(1) of the UNCRC, and in a number of other conventions and commitments. Ensuring that girls have adequate housing is key to preventing violations of other fundamental human rights, including the rights to health, education, security and protection from violence.

Adequate housing, according to international standards, includes more than just having a roof over one's head. It also includes the right to live somewhere in peace, security and dignity. According to the UN Committee on Economic, Social and Cultural Rights, the right to housing includes the following key components: legal security of tenure (including legal protection against forced evictions); availability of services, materials, facilities and infrastructure, including, for instance, access to safe drinking water, food storage, sanitary facilities, energy for cooking, heating and lighting, refuse disposal and emergency services; affordability; habitability, including protection from the elements; accessibility; location which affords adequate educational and work opportunities and access to services, like medical facilities; and cultural adequacy.

According to Article 27(2) of the UNCRC, parents have the primary obligation to ensure that children have the conditions that are necessary for their development, including access to adequate housing. However, where parents are not able to provide safe, secure accommodation for children in their care, governments must give them the necessary support to ensure that their right to adequate housing is protected. Where children either do not have parents or carers, or cannot live with their parents, Article 20 of the UNCRC places an immediate obligation on governments to ensure that alternative care is available to children including, for example, foster care.

## The right to protection from violence, abuse and exploitation

Governments have an obligation to protect girls from all forms of violence, exploitation and abuse. The most important instruments on the rights of girls to protection from violence, abuse and neglect are the UNCRC and CEDAW. While there is no specific international instrument relating to girls, children's rights and women's rights standards can be used to set out a framework of action for governments to use in aiming to protect girls who have moved to cities to escape from violence.

According to Article 2(1) of the UNCRC, governments must ensure that the Convention's rights are available to each child, without discrimination. Governments must address the gender dimensions of violence against children and employ measures to ensure that girls are not disproportionately affected by violence.

Article 2 of CEDAW places an obligation on governments to take all appropriate measures to eliminate discrimination against women. According to the UN Committee on the Elimination of Discrimination Against Women, gender-based violence is a form of discrimination. It includes physical, sexual and psychological violence in the home, the community and by the State. Governments are obliged to take a range of measures to address violence against women (including girls), as set out by the Committee. These include legal measures (such as penal sanctions and civil remedies); preventive measures (such as public education and information programmes); protective measures (including rehabilitation and support services for girls who are victims of violence); and monitoring the extent, causes and effects of violence. The UN Declaration on Violence Against Women further entrenches and elaborates the international commitment to addressing gender-based violence.

the village to the city – one study of 29 developing countries showed that young people are 40 per cent more likely than older generations to migrate. Migration rates peak between the ages of 15 and 24, as young people grow up and begin to take risks, search for jobs or further education or simply want to earn more money than they can in their home village. Many are encouraged in this by their families, but others are escaping abuse or the threat of abuse in the village. Gina Crivello of Young Lives, a 15-year research project into child poverty, notes that in Peru: "For poor rural households, the city was often imagined as a place of opportunity where children could do well in life by becoming 'professionals'. The countryside, on the other hand, was often described in terms of suffering, hardship and stagnation. While there were many positive aspects of living in the village, such as greenery, animals, vegetation and safety, opportunities for escaping poverty were considered to be concentrated in the cities."[35] In West Africa, reasons such as family and social pressure, the ambition to 'become somebody' in a world perceived to hold a basket of opportunities and rights that can only be accessed elsewhere, are behind many current female migrations. Those who migrate hope that they will be able to earn money, prove themselves and then return in glory to their families.[36]

Girls and young women may also leave simply in search of the unknown – adolescence is a time of change and transition, of exploration and excitement, and leaving your family and the life you have known is in many cultures part of the move into adulthood.[37] The sheer volume of people moving about has increased and the expectation is that migratory patterns will continue to change, moving progressively from permanent to circulatory migration. Adolescent girls may find themselves moving between town and country or even across borders, avoiding permanent migration but spending much of their time away from their original home. This mobility will be dependent on the requisite skills and training.[38]

It is, however, more difficult for an adolescent girl to leave than a boy the same age. Her parents may be afraid that

something will happen to her, or simply that she will be exposed to influences that they consider undesirable; while for a boy, leaving home for the city may be seen simply as part of growing up. As this young woman from Morocco said: "I am a girl. I can't go working in other cities. My brothers could never tolerate it."[39]

Many young people leave because they feel they have no choice. If the village provided as many opportunities as the city, they would not have to leave.

N'deye Faye, age 19, from Senegal, has been involved in a savings project. She says: *"In our village, N'Goundiane, the dream of all young girls is to work as a maid in a large city, especially Dakar. My aunt, with whom I lived, was always against this. When the Plan project arrived, I was finally able to obtain what had been missing: financial capital. I was able to borrow, and with that money, to buy cloth and other things necessary to make attractive outfits and clothing that I sold. I have a very faithful group of customers, because I do good quality work. In summary, I borrow, I work, I make profits, I reinvest in my work. I no longer think of Dakar and my former dream. Now I feel good in N'Goundiane, where I have an activity that works well and makes me money. In addition, it's generally true that a woman stops working after she marries. But my skill of sewing I'll have for my whole life. Even better, I can still improve myself in the future. It happens that from time to time I go to Dakar to shop or to visit members of the family. I'm proud to be staying in the village. I'm not envious of anyone. The project has changed my life."[40]*

While the traditional image of a migrant is a man looking for work, today, women account for almost half the world's migrant population.[41] The International Organisation for Migration (IOM) states that: "Gender is perhaps the single most important factor shaping migrants' experiences – more important than their country of origin or destination, their age, class, race or culture."[42] And yet, as the IOM points out: "Despite growing evidence about the gender-specific aspects of migration, most migration-related policies and regulations

are not gender specific."[43] They are even less likely to take account of both gender and age, although adolescent girls' needs, expectations and risks in moving to the city are different from those of older women, younger girls and even boys their own age.

The decision to migrate can be a complex combination of 'push' and 'pull' factors, as we show below.

## Pull...

Adolescent girls may migrate in search of the promise of a better life – in South Africa, Johannesburg is often called *Eboli* – City of Gold. They hope to find education or work. Some go to be reunited with relatives, to seek opportunities for leisure and entertainment, or simply because they have heard reports from peers of positive city experiences.[44] They may think that in the city there will be safety in numbers, a greater acceptance of difference, including difference of sexual orientation, and more potential and choice about their own lives.

One study of adolescents who migrated from the village to the city in Burkina Faso noted the attraction of television and

fashion: "Most of the adolescent migrants aspired to look smart and when they first came to the capital, some got blinded by the bright city lights and the abundance of fashionable clothing and accessories. Living in the city provided them with the opportunity to follow radio and TV programmes on a regular basis... or to go to video clubs showing action-, vampire- and sometimes [Nigerian] Nollywood movies, usually dubbed in French. Their ideas about which 'looks' were smart changed, but their small incomes of 3,000 to 7,000 francs per month – between one-tenth and one-fourth of the formal minimum wage – soon made them realise their limitations. Their ability to assert particular identities was circumscribed by their rural origins and poverty."[45]

Other girls come to the city because they hope for more tolerance in the city than they had in the village.[46] Girls like Radha, now 28, who ran away from her home in Kerala, India, when she was 15 because her parents wanted to get her married. Radha was present at the launch of the first helpline for lesbian women in Chennai in February 2009. She and her lesbian partner, she says,

*Girls learn to sew in Senegal.*

"suffered a lot as we didn't get support or counselling 10 years ago. Today's lesbians will benefit from the helpline."[47] However, as the laws on sexual orientation become ever more stringent in some countries, this remains a major challenge even in cities, particularly in Africa.[48]

### BRIGHT LIGHTS AND ASPIRATIONS – 'REAL CHOICES, REAL LIVES' COHORT STUDY

More than half of the families taking part in the 'Real Choices, Real Lives' cohort study would like to see their daughters pursue careers that involve further education and training to become midwives, nurses and teachers. Post-secondary education is not widely available in the rural villages in which most of the families live. Therefore the parents' aspirations for their daughters will inform the decisions they make about moving to cities. In Brazil, at least half of the families interviewed already have older daughters who have left home, the vast majority to either improve their educational prospects or to work. The sister of one of the girls taking part in the study explains: "I want to finish high school to work, and maybe go to the university, and here in Codo there isn't one..."

In Benin, a third of all the families taking part in the study are separated by seasonal or long-term migration to nearby or capital cities.

The teenage members of an older focus group, neighbours and friends of the families in the study, whom we interviewed in Uganda, were clear that they are motivated to move to cities and gave the following reasons:

- To send money back home and support their elderly parents
- To live a more exciting life than in the village
- To reduce family expenditure at home
- To raise money in order to build a house in their village of origin
- To pay school fees of their siblings
- To ultimately help other family members to get jobs in the city/town.

In Brazil, at least half of the girls' parents were considering moving to a city, and 75

per cent indicated that their fathers had left home at various times to work. One girl related: "My father has left. He spent three years away from home to work. The family was sad; he didn't even see my brother when he was born, and then my brother died and my father couldn't even come home to see him..."

Teenagers we interviewed were very clear about the impacts of migration on those left behind. In the Philippines, they observed that when mothers move away for work, their daughters tend to marry soon after graduating from secondary school. Despite the potential benefits for the family, as parents or siblings working away send money home, the majority of the Brazilian teenagers also felt that migration to cities had a negative impact on family members who remained: "When any member of the family leaves, the changes are for the worse..."

*Advertising mobile phones in the Philippines.*

The reality of city life does not always match up to adolescent girls' expectations. As a study from Burkina Faso notes: "Comparing adolescent girls' situation to that of boys demonstrates that their opportunities as migrants were very different. Since girls were rarely paid on a regular basis, they could not easily save up money. Instead, they emphasised the status and skills they gained such as clothes, things for their trousseau and, in particular, urban cooking skills – things that would help them find a good husband, and preferably one who appreciated their urban skills: that is, a migrant. Thereby they reiterated adult notions of rural girlhood, namely that adolescent girls are ready to marry and that they in fact do not think about much else."[49]

In addition, the risks an adolescent girl faces in trying to realise her aspirations are often disproportionately higher than for an adolescent boy. As we will see later in the chapter, there are many aspects of city life which are hugely problematic for an adolescent girl.

### ...and push

*"I dream, always dream that the city isn't like it is here, here it's always suffering… well, as I see it, there can't be that much suffering [in the city], because they don't get wet, they don't get sunburned, they have their secure jobs, they have their daily schedule, and in contrast, here it's back-breaking."*

A rural mother's hopes for her children in Peru[50]

For many adolescent girls, the lure of the city is matched by the need to escape from the village. One study in Egypt of street children between the ages of 10 and 18 found that 82 per cent of children said they had come to the city because of abuse by the family or at work; 62 per cent cited parental neglect; and 62 per cent "came from broken families due to divorce, separation, the death of one or more parents, imprisonment of a parent or both, or extreme sickness of a parent or both".[51]

Violence, abuse, or family breakdown are other 'push' factors for young women leaving the countryside.

Adolescent girls may also be escaping various forms of gender discrimination. For example, one study in Accra, Ghana, showed that young women, disinherited by their fathers because of inheritance laws that favour boys, moved to the city as they were unable to support themselves in the village.[52]

Rukshana, who now lives on the streets of Mumbai with her 11 year-old sister Deepa, also left because of inheritance disputes: *"Our village is in Murshidabad, West Bengal. My two brothers live in the village. Both are married. My younger brother loves me a lot. But how can I live with them? He has five children and no house. When my father was ill, he asked his brother – my uncle – to leave all his land in his children's names. You know what my uncle did? He put it all in his name. My father died and my uncle removed us from our house. He is the one who threw us into problems. He brought us to Kings Circle in Mumbai, made us work and didn't give us anything to eat. We almost died of starvation. My mother cried a lot. She told me: 'My daughter, do honest work to eat. Don't go on the wrong path.' Since then I have worked hard and come up. There is no question of going astray."[53]*

Her mother later died in the city when Rukshana was 13, leaving her to look after her little sister.

Escaping forced or early marriage is another reason many adolescent girls leave their village. Shimu is one of thousands who did so. She now lives in Dhaka, the capital of Bangladesh. She left her village to avoid marrying a man that her parents had chosen for her at a very young age. She says that "living in the city has allowed [her] to make a break from traditional networks". True, she sometimes feels lonely and doesn't know what to do. But she does know that she doesn't have to do what her relatives and elders tell her. She prefers living in Dhaka because "here I can earn a living, live and think my own way". In her village none of this would have been possible.[54]

Shimu is not alone. A survey in slum areas of Addis Ababa found that one in every four young women migrants between the ages of 10 and 19 came to the city to escape early marriage.[55] This 17 year-old said:
*"My parents were trying to marry me, but I didn't want to get married. So I ran away and came here. My mother has said that I'm not her daughter any more, but I didn't want to get married. I wanted to study – that's why I came."*

She is now at school.[56] In Ghana too, a study found that younger women migrated to the city to run away from the possibility of being married off by their parents.

"With no hope of continuing their education, families often force their girls to marry, often at a young age. In defiance, girls sometimes escape with their friends and join the trek into Accra."[57]

Female genital cutting and other harmful traditional practices are also generally less prevalent in the city than in urban areas, as the chart below shows.[58]

There may, however, also be a counter movement as families try to protect their daughters in the city by clinging even more fervently to the old ways.

### NEW CHANCES: RESISTING HARMFUL TRADITIONS IN THE CITY

The incidence of female genital mutilation or cutting in Egypt is lower in the city than in rural areas, and is slowly falling. But mothers find it hard to resist pressure from older relatives who bring village traditions with them when they move to the town.

"I have come here on condition that it is a secret. I don't want anyone to know my name. If you can promise me no one will find out then I will tell you my story…"

We are in a slum area in south Cairo and the woman's nervousness reflects the continuing difficulty of talking about something like female genital cutting (FGC).[59]

Even though the government in Egypt has banned FGC, 85 per cent of girls and women in cities and 96 per cent in the rural areas[60] are still being cut in this way. This woman, whom I will call Samar, recalls:

"I was nine years old and I had no idea what was going to happen until I saw the razor. My mother and two other women held me down while the barber did his work. He was very rough. The pain was terrible, and the bleeding. I got an infection from the dust they put on the wound, which is supposed to stop such infections but in fact makes them worse. Afterwards I had urine problems but I never connected them to the cutting until much later."

Time after time the women who tell their stories talk of their suffering during and after FGC. And time after time they also

tell of their determination not to have their daughters cut. The women I met said that although it was sometimes their husbands who insisted on cutting, more often it was the older generation of women who were most determined to have it done.

"For our first daughter, my mother-in-law said that if we did not do this to her, she would be a bad girl. At least I managed to have it done by a nurse instead of the barber, which was something. But my daughter kept asking me: 'Mummy, why did you do this to me?' It was terrible. I told her it was her religious duty.

"But for my second daughter I do not want to have her cut. I will ask the doctor and the imam and if they say no then I will somehow persuade my husband and my mother-in-law. My sister had such a bad time with her cutting that she has refused to do this to her daughters. But my youngest daughter is very confident and speaks out a lot and my mother says this is not a good thing and it is because she has not been cut."

This generation gap also reflects the gap between town and village. Forty-eight per cent of women in rural areas say

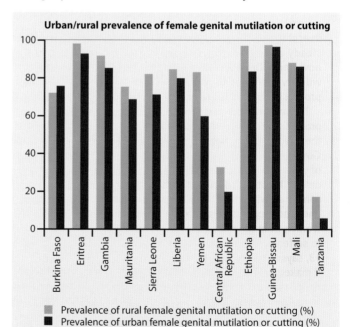

**Urban/rural prevalence of female genital mutilation or cutting**

■ Prevalence of rural female genital mutilation or cutting (%)
■ Prevalence of urban female genital mutilation or cutting (%)

Source: Population Reference Bureau – update 2010 –
'Female Genital Mutilation/Cutting: Data and Trends'
http://www.prb.org/pdf10/fgm-wallchart2010.pdf

they support the practice, compared with 25 per cent in urban areas.[61]

Government television programmes on the dangers of FGC; contact with those in authority, such as doctors and imams who are prepared to speak out against the practice; and women themselves who, once convinced, influence their neighbours, can all help. Plan works with local Community Development Associations on raising communities' awareness of gender equality, including issues around FGC, to build both the knowledge and the confidence that can begin to bring about change.

Education is another important reason why fewer girls in the city undergo FGC, as one of the mothers told me: "We are more educated here in the city, our children are part of the internet generation and things will change even more for them. My girl talks to me in a way that I would never have been able to talk to my mother. When I had my first period I thought I was dying because my mother never told me about these things."

The statistics back her up: while 98 per cent of women with no education are cut, this drops to 87 per cent of those who have completed secondary or higher education – and is dropping each year.[62] Government surveys estimate that over the next 15 years there will be a steady decline. By the time girls who are now under three are 18, the percentage will have dropped to 45 per cent. Slow progress, but this is still progress.

Today's mothers are the vanguard of protection. But their main hope lies in the future, with their own daughters. Government surveys show that 46 per cent of young women aged between 15 and 19 believe that the practice should be stopped, compared with 28 per cent of older women. These are hopeful signs that fewer young women from the next generation will have to suffer as their mothers did. Sahar, aged 13, says: "When I see one of my friends cut it makes me even more determined not to do it." And Leila says: "When my girls are mothers they will be very different from me. I want to give my daughters the chances in life that were denied to me."

Nikki van der Gaag talked to community members in a Plan-supported project in Egypt.

NIKKI VAN DER GAAG

*The Arabic translation reads: "Do not kill your children's innocence".*

One study in Addis Ababa found that both girls and boys gave a mixture of these push and pull factors as their reasons for moving to the capital. On the pull side, education and work opportunities came high on the list for both sexes, as did joining family members. Boys were more likely to cite family problems and girls the threat of marriage.[63] The aspirations of both girls and boys were in fact quite similar – education, economic opportunities and security.

There are many other reasons why adolescent girls leave their villages. Girls may be forced to leave due to wider circumstances, such as war and conflict, climate change, natural disasters, rural underdevelopment, the collapse of rural economies and the uncertainties of

### Reasons for migration to Addis Ababa, by sex[64]

| Reason given | Boys (n=94) % | Girls (n=306) % |
|---|---|---|
| Educational opportunities | 41.5 | 43.9 |
| Work opportunities | 25.5 | 25.5 |
| Poverty in the rural area | 20.2 | 22.1 |
| Family problems | 26.5 | 18.6 |
| Threat of marriage | 1.1 | 18.6 |
| Joining family members | 24.5 | 24.1 |

*Total percentages may be over 100 as more than one reason was possible

subsistence farming. This teenage girl from Bomi Country, Liberia, said: "If the war starts again, Monrovia [the capital city] will be the best defended place, so I want to move there so I will feel safer."[65]

It is not just young women from the South who leave home for the city. Nicole, featured in the box below, left her small town for the bright lights of Toronto when she was just 15 because of abuse by her stepfather. One study in Canada indicated that more than 70 per cent of street youth leave home because of physical or sexual abuse.

### NICOLE'S STORY [66]

*"I grew up in a small town. My mom and dad split up when my sister was just a baby. When I was a kid, money was tight... It was a rough time. But my mom and I were close. I remember saying: 'I don't want to get old and if I do, I'm not going to leave you.'*

*School was fun till they tried to change me. I was 13 then and when you're 13 you start doing your own thing and finding out who you are. I was dressing in baggy clothes and getting into trouble at school. My mom had just met my stepdad. He didn't like me and used to beat me up. Once he banged my head again and again on the table. I told my real dad about it but he pretty much said it's my stepdad's house and he can do what he wants. It was his word against mine. I felt like I was on my own and I had to take care of myself.*

*My stepdad kept saying that all my friends were stealing so I must be stealing too. Then I went out and did a stupid thing. I became a tag-along in an auto theft. That was the first and last time I got into trouble with the police. My mom and stepdad came to the police station and said: 'She can stay in jail and learn a lesson.' After that it was: 'You're going to a foster home. We're gonna send you away to these places for good.' My stepdad said: 'They will beat you and rape you at a foster home and you won't be able to do anything about it.'*

*I ran away in July 2002. My boyfriend Mike gave me a ride to Toronto. I was 15 when I ran away, and Mike was 23. My parents didn't know about him. It was two years before I saw my mom again.*

*During the first five months food banks were my best friends. I don't think I'll ever forget the pain of hunger.*

*I was feeling guilty for a while after I ran away from home until I spoke with my stepdad. He was like: 'Oh, this is what you wanted and now this is what you get.' Once I heard that, I thought: 'Well, I don't really care'. I'll admit, if my stepdad wasn't there, I'd still be at home. But I'm out here for a reason. I'm not regretting it any more.*

*I learn from my mistakes. We all know what we have to do to help ourselves. And we need to find the strength inside to ask for help. Go to anyone you trust. Talk about it."*

Nicole spoke to Noreen Shanahan.

## 3. The best recipe? The benefits of city life for adolescent girls

*"At the beginning of the 21st century, the best recipe for a life without poverty is still to grow up urban."*

> Growing Up Urban, State of World Population 2007, Youth Supplement, UNFPA

*"I became more of a social person and like to stay with the group and participate with them positively. I also learned to work with a team."*

> Sarah, from El Marg, a poor town outside Cairo, was able to join a jobs training programme and is now working.[67]

Girls come to the city full of dreams and aspirations about how their lives will improve. Statistics show that they are right to dream.

For example, a girl is much more likely to go to school if she lives in a city – in developing countries school attendance for girls from 10 to 14 is 18 per cent higher in urban than in rural areas, and 37 per cent higher for young women between 15 and 19.[68] This gap is also there for boys, but it is less stark.

An older adolescent girl is also more likely to find employment in the city than in a village, as the following section shows. She is less likely to be married at an early age – for example, in sub-Saharan Africa and

South Asia, 50 per cent of young women in rural areas are married by the time they are 18, which is about twice the rate of young women in cities.[69]

There are many reasons for this. Some are simply about the different aspirations and understandings of city dwellers – the people girls live with in the cities such as parents, relatives, guardians and boyfriends have aspirations and expectations that are radically different from their rural peers and this translates into a powerful influence on girls. Some are practical – schools may be more plentiful and closer to home, or there is less work for girls to do in the home in the city, because there is no land to work on. Once a girl makes the city her home, she then faces the same opportunities and threats as other girls her age.

## PLAYING SPORTS, BUILDING CONFIDENCE

Sport is good for girls, especially those in cities who are less likely to lead active lives than their rural counterparts. UNICEF notes: "Girls who participate in sports tend to be healthier – emotionally and physically – and less likely to smoke or abuse drugs or alcohol. There may also be a link between decreased incidences of breast cancer and osteoporosis in women who have been physically active throughout their lives. In addition, adolescent girls who take part in sports tend to delay becoming sexually active until later in life.[70] This may in part be because participation in sports encourages adolescent girls to develop a sense of ownership of and strength in their own bodies instead of seeing them simply as a sexual resource for men. "Before playing football I was fearful," said one girl. "Now I am not because I am used to mixing with people and I know what is good and what is bad." Through football, another young Kenyan said, "I have learned how to have my own principles and not be blown and tossed around by the wind."[71]

There are a number of projects working with adolescent girls to build their

A girls' football match in Brazil.

LEO DRUMOND

football skills – for example, the Mathare Youth Sports Association Football Programme (MYSA) for Girls. One of the girls taking part noted: "When I started playing for MYSA my father would say that there is no football for girls, and he would beat me up. So whenever I wanted to go and play, my mother would cover up for me by saying that she had sent me somewhere. Then when I went to Norway, he started liking it."[72]

Plan spoke to some of the girls who came from seven different countries to the Street Children's World Cup in South Africa in March 2010, and found that many of them felt playing football had given them a new approach to their lives. Jessica, aged 15, from Nicaragua pointed out: *"I think football has helped me not to think about the bad things that have happened to me… I have become more involved with football than my past. I'm trying to leave the past behind and live a new life."*[73]

## Building capacity: finding jobs in the city

*"I like working [in a restaurant]. The hard work only really starts at 4pm, and I have learned a lot. In my spare time I watch TV and text my friends. I don't want to get married until I have finished college."*
Irene, 17, Masbate, Philippines[74]

*"Over the next 10 years, 1.2 billion young women and men will enter the working-age population. They will be the best-educated and best-trained generation ever, with great potential for economic and social development, if countries can find uses for their skills, enthusiasm and creativity. Otherwise they will be condemned to poverty, like many of their parents are."*
UNFPA[75]

It is not surprising that some young women come to the city in search of employment. Some are sent by their families, others come of their own volition. Some will find formal paid work, but this varies enormously from country to country and even from city to city. Young people in general are more than three times as likely as adults to be unemployed – of the 1.1

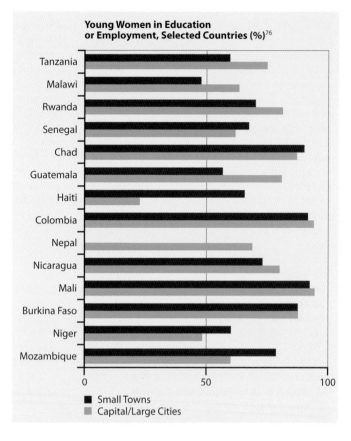

**Young Women in Education or Employment, Selected Countries (%)**[76]

■ Small Towns
■ Capital/Large Cities

billion young people between the ages of 15 and 24, only 3.8 per cent, or 548 million, are employed.

In general, apart from agricultural work, cities offer young women more employment opportunities than rural areas. There also appears to be a difference between cities and small towns, as the chart (above) shows.

Many older adolescent girls in cities, particularly in Asia, find themselves working in factories in export-processing zones or in call centres. In Indonesia, for example, export-oriented sectors employ more than twice the national average of young people. Young women are particularly likely to be employed in these industries; case studies in Bangladesh showed that many young women preferred working in factories to their other choices: agriculture or domestic service.[77] This is true elsewhere too. Cho Cho Thet is 15 and works in a garments factory in Rangoon, Burma. She works for 14 hours a day, seven days a week and is paid $35 a month. She is given free accommodation and meals of rice and vegetables. But she says she still prefers this to working in the fields. "Working under a roof is better than working in the rice field under the sun or the rain. I don't feel tired at all here."[78]

## Girls and child labour in the city

Child labour is an issue for many adolescent girls in the city. A research study commissioned for this report by Justice for Girls found that it was common in the cities of the Philippines. Their report noted: "Many girls do not make a monetary income; rather, their labour is exploited in dangerous, labour-intensive jobs simply in exchange for food. For example, 13 year-old 'Lisa' has a job working at weekends cleaning the public toilet in exchange for food to feed herself. Other girls reported doing similar forms of child labour, including selling things at local malls for up to 10-12 hours per day for food, and no pay.

Often, the work that is available to girls exposes them to conditions that are hazardous to their health, ranging from extreme exhaustion, physical and sexual violence, exposure to harmful environmental toxins, and psychological stress. Many girls report work-related health conditions including asthma and respiratory diseases that either plague them while they work, increasing stress and reducing their income, or simply prevent them from working altogether. "Sometimes I can't work because of my asthma," says Charrie-Mayof, a tricycle-driver on the streets of Cebu.

Some girls helped their families at home by assisting their parents in their work. One girl reported that after school she helped her father peel garlic until midnight. Another girl reported that she assisted her mother as a laundry woman.

Many girls end up in the illicit street economy, coerced and trafficked by adults into commercial sexual exploitation, selling drugs or acting as accomplices.

But having paid work also gives older adolescent girls and young women more confidence. In one survey of Bangladeshi garment workers, 90 per cent of young female respondents had a high opinion of themselves, compared with 57 per cent of female workers in non-export industries.[79] Contributing to the family income gives young women more say over the decisions about their lives, such as when and who they marry. In one study in Bangladesh, young women's wages contribute up to 43 per cent of household income.[80]

### THE LAW ON GIRLS AND THE RIGHT TO PROTECTION FROM HAZARDOUS OR EXPLOITIVE WORK[81]

Governments have an obligation to protect children from economic exploitation and from performing hazardous work. 'Hazardous work', according to Article 32 of the UNCRC, includes work that: interferes with a child's education; is harmful to the child's health; or is harmful to the child's physical, mental, spiritual, moral or social development. In accordance with Article 32, governments must take a range of measures to prevent children from becoming involved in hazardous or exploitive work. These measures include providing for minimum ages for admission to employment; providing for appropriate regulation of hours and conditions of employment; and providing for appropriate penalties and sanctions.

Various International Labour Organisation (ILO) Conventions and instruments also prohibit hazardous child labour. The ILO Convention Concerning the Prohibition and Immediate Action for the Elimination of the Worst Forms of Child Labour 1999 requires parties to prohibit and eliminate the 'worst forms' of child labour. This includes:

• All forms of slavery or practices similar to slavery (for example, the sale and trafficking of children, debt bondage and compulsory labour)
• The use, procuring or offering of a child in prostitution, or in pornography
• The use, procuring or offering of a child for illicit activities, including the production or trafficking of drugs
• All other work that is likely to harm the health, safety or morals of children.

Governments are obliged to criminalise acts that are involved in the use of children in any of these types of child labour. A range of non-penal measures aimed at eliminating the worst forms of child labour must also be undertaken. In designing and implementing such measures, according to the ILO Convention, governments must pay attention to groups of children who are at a particular risk of becoming involved in the worst forms of child labour.

# My ideal city

The ideal city, in the words and drawings of young girls from White Nile State in north Sudan. The girls took part in a session about girls' rights and city life organised by Plan programme staff.

Amal, 12 years old
*"A society that is free of FGM [Female Genital Mutilation] and early marriage in which there is self-determination."*

Fareeda, 14 years old
*"My dream about an ideal city – there should be development and progress, all community services must be complete, such as attractive schools, nice hospitals and pure water sources"*

Afaf, 13 years old
*"I love the FLAG at my school, because it stands for freedom and I dream that our entire teachers are good model."*

Afaf, 13 years old
*"Families should take care of both girls and boys equally."*

Faiha'a, 12 years old
*"I dream of a society that encourages us to complete our learning. Without discrimination!"*

Tawasoul,
12 years old
*"A city that does not discriminate between girls and boys and gives us all our rights."*

Longer-term, the effects of such work are unclear, as this World Bank report notes: "Once married, young women tended to leave wage employment, and most young women expect to work only three or four years. Aside from the short tenure, many of the jobs were tedious, low-skilled, had limited upward mobility, and were managed in traditional patriarchal ways. Young women experienced greater autonomy as they migrated to urban settings but were sometimes stigmatised for having a more Western, individualistic lifestyle. Nevertheless, what is clear is that these young women in Bangladesh and Malaysia have broken some new ground and in the process contributed economically to their families and societies.'[82]

### JOBS FOR THE GIRLS – TRAINING AND EMPLOYMENT OPPORTUNITIES IN EGYPTIAN TOWNS

El Marg is a city of immigrants from rural areas; 30 years ago it too was just fields and villages. Now it is a slum town, an outpost of Cairo that houses some half a million people. Many areas are still without electricity or water or sewerage and rubbish is piled in the streets. A market sells the vegetables that the inhabitants can no longer grow; a woman

carries an enormous cabbage, like a huge flower, on her head, and in one corner goats stare warily from under a makeshift shelter.

"It is difficult for young people to find work here," says Sameh, one of the facilitators of the Forsa programme, which gives three months' training to young people and then finds them work at the end. "This is why Forsa is so useful. In Arabic it means 'opportunity'."

The programme targets three categories of young people – those who have dropped out of school, those who have been to college but can't find work, and those who are working in jobs which do not suit their skills. Most come from poor families. Recruitment is done via posters and roadshows – but also via Facebook. The programme here is run by Plan, but the idea is the brainchild of the CAP Foundation, a public-private partnership which aims to alleviate poverty through linking learning and livelihood needs of working children and disadvantaged youth.[83] The courses were first successfully trialled in India and because of their success have now been exported to Egypt. The diagram (above) shows the CAP model.

Forsa training has already been carried out successfully in East Cairo, where 90 per cent of the graduates found jobs. Marwa, aged 19, was part of this programme. She says: "Before joining Forsa, I was afraid to deal with people

*Country meets city on the outskirts of Cairo.*

NIKKI VAN DER GAAG

as I am rather shy. After joining Forsa, I began to overcome my shyness and fear and started to be open to all. I acquired a great deal of self-confidence. I made a lot of friends throughout the course, with whom I speak a lot and without any fears or worries."

Cultivating the desire to learn and the confidence to speak out is especially important for girls in a society where women are not valued in the same way as men and where only 22.9 per cent of women are officially in the labour force.[84] In El Marg, the primary schools are enormous and there are often 60 or 70 children in a class. Some primary schools have to operate a three-shift system, with children attending for only a third of each day, in order to accommodate the numbers. Not surprising, then, that drop-out, especially for girls, is common. The only secondary schools are in the centre of town, so once again this means girls who live nearer to the outskirts are unlikely to finish their education.

Ola, who is still at school, says: "We are the youth; we are the future of this country, but when I analyse the situation I feel there is a lack of opportunities for jobs for young women. The government must think about young women and give us the same opportunities as boys."

Nikki van der Gaag talked to participants in the Forsa programme in El Marg, Egypt

## The informal economy: where most adolescent girls in cities work

The International Labour Organisation estimates that approximately 85 per cent of all new employment opportunities in developing countries are created in the informal economy, which is where the majority of adolescent girls and young women are likely to find work.[85] This is particularly true in slums. "In fact, slums tend to form the epicentre or principal source of informal labour, and within slums most economic activity is informal," according to the United Nations Settlements programme.[86]

In sub-Saharan Africa, 84 per cent of women's employment in the non-agricultural sector is informal. In many countries, more young women work in the informal sector in small cities than in the capital. For example, in Kenya, 58 per cent of young women employed in Nairobi and the country's other large cities work in the informal sector, compared with 73 per cent of their counterparts in small cities and towns and rural areas. In Peru, 50 per cent of young women in large cities work in the informal sector, while the figure for smaller cities is 64 per cent.[87]

However, what these general statistics fail to reveal is the particular situations of adolescent girls who are poor, or from a minority group, or live in a slum. Having a health centre in the next street is of no use if you cannot afford to pay the fees, and having a school within walking distance is only useful if you have money for books and uniforms. The picture for these groups is very different, as we will see in the next section.

### MAKING A LIFE IN THE CITY – RAKY, WATER SELLER

Raky is 15 but looks younger. She has a ready smile and a quick wit. Along with her older sister, Daba, she sells plastic bottles of iced water to passengers on the buses that stop along the side of the busy highway on the outskirts of Dakar, Senegal.

"I take two bottles at a time and walk the 15 minutes from my house to the road," says Raky. "I sell them for 100 CFA francs each [about 20 US cents]. On a good day I sell 50 and make 5,000 CFA [$10]. My sister does the same. Someone brings the empty bottles to our home from a factory in Dakar and we pay 25 CFA [five cents] for each." With the cost of ice and water, she probably makes just a few pence per bottle. But this helps the family income. "I give my money to my mum but I can also use it for things I need like clothes and transport. I have enough for my needs."

Raky lives in a compound with her mother, Mbengue, her father, her older sister Daba, and her three younger siblings, Ndaye, Fallou and three year-old Yacine. The family moved here four years ago and Raky has been a water seller for two years.

Mbengue says she doesn't approve of children working too young, but some work can help to link childhood to adolescence. It teaches them respect, which Mbengue thinks is very important. She also believes it is just as important for girls as for boys to learn independence and to have the ability to make their own living. For this they need education and training, but also the ability to make their own decisions in life. "I don't tell my children what to do," she says. "It is up to them. I don't impose my ideas on my daughters. But I don't believe in girls staying at home and doing nothing. That is the worst thing. I came from a poor family and learned at a young age that a

Raky and her mother

NIKKI VAN DER GAAG

woman as well as a man needs some kind of economic activity to survive."

Raky has been lucky: she was introduced to the African Movement for Working Children and Youth by a local volunteer who came to her house and suggested that she learn to make clothes and at the same time attend classes to improve her reading and writing. So now Raky sells water from 10am to 2pm. After lunch and a rest, she then walks the 30 minutes to a centre where, along with 32 other young women, she studies and learns the art of dressmaking. On some days, she also has lessons at a tailor's shop. Although she doesn't yet dare to speak it, she understands French and has been elected to represent the Dakar branch of the Movement and travels regularly to Dakar and elsewhere for meetings.

Asked how she sees her future, she says she wants to be a famous dressmaker. Her mother agrees. Smiling proudly, she says: "I want her to make a name for herself as a dressmaker, but also to be able to travel and meet people and make a life for herself."

## 'A difficult life' – domestic service

Many adolescent girls from slum areas end up doing domestic work for richer families. This is where the urban divide shows itself most clearly. The employer is often an educated, middle-class woman who thinks she is helping a girl by taking her off the streets or out of poverty. Once employed in a household, the girl becomes invisible, swallowed up in the wider household, and therefore at risk of all kinds of abuse, from long hours with no breaks to sexual abuse by a male member of the family. She also misses out on education. One nationwide study in India showed that 81 per cent of domestic workers were girls, and in fact the figure was highest for the youngest age group, between five and 12 years old.

The research for this report by Justice for Girls in cities in the Philippines[88] (see page 83) also found that: "Girls are trafficked from rural to urban areas to work as domestic 'house helpers' where, if they are paid, the wage is grossly disproportionate to the slavery-type working conditions to which they are subjected. 'Jendy', in a rehabilitation centre for stealing a cell phone from her employer, reported he made her work from 5am to 10pm, seven days a week and that she earned less than $100 per month."

The report also notes that: "Violence by employers in domestic settings is common. Vangie and Sancia, both in a rehabilitation centre for false accusations of qualified theft from their employers, discuss the abuse they experienced as house helpers: 'I was made to do everything. I wanted to leave. I did not like my employers. When his wife was drunk she would slap me. He would verbally assault me. Calling me names like 'devil worshipper' and cursing me to be dead' (Vangie). 'He got angry with me, held me down and slapped me' (Sancia)."

Justice for Girls notes: "Domestic child labour, in addition to being a human rights violation in and of itself, sets up girls' vulnerability to abuse by employers, organised crime syndicates or other employees and false accusations from exploitive employers that see them criminalised for the crime of 'qualified theft'. Qualified theft is treated more severely than simple or petty theft (snatching, shoplifting)

because it carries with it the moral weight of an assumed 'trust' relationship."

In another study, Themba, aged 16, from Zambia, explains how she came to be working as a maid: "My mum left us with Dad and went to live in Lusaka after a quarrel. Dad got sick and I started looking after him until he died. Mum came back and took us to Lusaka. While in Lusaka, life became difficult and I started working as a maid to support my mum and my siblings. One day, when I came back home, I found my young brothers alone; they told me that Mum had been gone for a long time."[89] Themba and her brothers are now in a centre for street children where, she says, "life is good because they give us support as parents and teach us how to live and work with people". Themba was lucky; often domestic work not only takes girls out of school, but places them in situations where they have very little time off and very little social support, which puts them at risk of sexual harassment and trafficking (see section page 73).

## "Your own place in the world" – housing and homelessness

*"If the time comes that I have my own family, I will have a house by then. I will do everything so that my children will not experience how it is not to have a home."*
Lean Joy, 17, Manila, Philippines[90]

*"On the street, no one respects you. Here, you have your own house, it's yours and they have to respect you. Here, even if you don't have a thing to eat, you have your own place in the world."*
Woman from Mahila Milan, Mumbai, India[91]

Living in the city will often mean living in a slum area, desperately trying to put a roof over your head. However basic and inadequate the roof, "your own place" is of prime importance.

Young women living on their own find it very difficult to pay for adequate housing. In Ghana, research revealed that groups of young women pooled their resources to rent a shack on a weekly or monthly basis, living 10 to 30 in a small room.[92] The same is true in many cities around the world: in the Philippines, such accommodation is known as a 'bedspacer'.[93] They know that any accommodation, however poor, is safer than living on the streets. Secondary school girls who come to the cities may rent a room and find a 'boyfriend' who will protect them, exchanging accommodation for sex.[94]

Even if girls manage to gain housing within cities, their housing tenure is often insecure, and girls, along with their mothers, may be forcefully evicted from their homes. Forced evictions are often characterised by violence, particularly against women and children.[95] The rapid expansion of urban slums has led governments around the world to use callous methods to 'clean up' cities and erase the urban poor from the sight of city centres. The most vulnerable in slums, including women and girls, are often susceptible to forced evictions by governments and other actors, and too often face gender-based violence before, during, and after eviction.[96]

We know that overcrowding in slums is a major issue for adolescent girls. Aoife Nic Charthaigh of Interact Worldwide points out: "The very fact of living in confined conditions exacerbates the lack of safe spaces for girls: places to access peer support away from prying eyes and ears. When land is scarce there tend to be few designated spaces for young people, and girls are often crowded out of this space. Without this peer support network, girls lose out on opportunities to share experiences and develop coping mechanisms – leaving them more isolated and vulnerable to exploitation."[97]

## Adolescent girls have different needs: access to healthcare

*"We need to show [girls'] potential to contribute to good sexual health in their environment – for example, through informing peers or other people around them."*

Sophie, young woman from Benin[98]

Once they come to the city, adolescent girls often find they have access to better services and better healthcare, including sexual and reproductive health services – provided that they can pay for it. They are also more able to access information about health. For example, young people in cities generally know more about contraception and use it more than their rural peers. In one study, over 37 per cent of women in urban areas said they used condoms to avoid AIDS, compared with only 17 per cent of rural women. And 87 per cent of urban girls and women said they had 'ever used' a condom as opposed to 57 per cent of rural girls and women.[99]

Adolescent girls in slums, however, face a number of health hazards common to all slum dwellers – lack of opportunity,

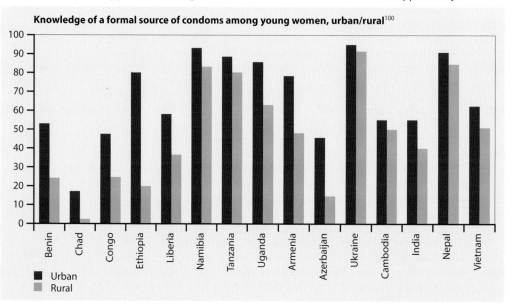

**Knowledge of a formal source of condoms among young women, urban/rural**[100]

- ■ Urban
- ■ Rural

overcrowded housing, poor sanitation and unsafe water supplies which reduce slum dwellers' life expectancy.[101] Studies have shown that children living in slums are more likely to die from pneumonia, diarrhoea, malaria or measles than those living in non-slum areas, because many of these diseases are linked to poor living conditions. In addition, as Rutti Goldberger, Asia Programme Manager for Interact Worldwide, points out: "An adolescent girl may not want to visit a centre that is easily identified as providing sexual and reproductive health services if she thinks her whole neighbourhood will know/think that she is sexually active, and will not want to discuss confidential and sensitive issues with a counsellor that knows her family."[102]

Adolescent girls in poor parts of the city may also find it more difficult to negotiate safer sex. They face specific health threats because of their age and sex – in sub-Saharan Africa, for example, HIV prevalence is significantly higher for young women aged 15 to 24 than young men. In Zambia, 15.2 per cent of urban young women aged 15 to 24 are affected, compared with 3.7 per cent of urban young men.[103] It is also significantly higher in slums than in non-slums and in most countries with data it appears to be higher in urban than rural areas.[104] As one report notes: "In slums, risky sexual behaviour among women and girls, or trading sex for food or cash, is a widespread strategy to make ends meet."[105]

## HORIZON JEUNES (YOUTH HORIZONS) IN CAMEROON

Horizon Jeunes is a reproductive health programme which targets urban youth aged 12 to 22 both in and out of school. It aims to delay the age of sexual initiation and reduce risk-taking behaviour among those who do have sex. It does so by using campaign messages developed by the young people themselves, which are then disseminated at live events, on radio, in printed material and by peer educators. It distributes condoms and contraceptives, trains healthcare providers in making services youth-friendly; involves parents and community leaders, including local health and education officials, and advertises in the mass media as part of a

**HIV Prevalence Rates**

|  | Urban | | Rural | |
|---|---|---|---|---|
|  | Male | Female | Male | Female |
| Cameroon | 1.4 | 5.7 | 1.5 | 3.5 |
| Ethiopia | 0.3 | 3.3 | 0.2 | 0.6 |
| Kenya | 2.6 | 7.6 | 0.3 | 5.3 |
| Lesotho | 4.6 | 21.3 | 6.2 | 13.9 |
| Liberia | 0.9 | 2.5 | 0.3 | 0.9 |
| Zambia | 3.7 | 15.2 | 2.6 | 8.2 |
| Zimbabwe | 4.4 | 11.2 | 4.1 | 10.9 |
| Cambodia | 0 | 0.4 | 0.1 | 0.3 |
| India | 0.1 | 0.2 | 0.1 | 0.1 |
| Vietnam | 1.3 | 0 | 0.6 | 0 |
| Dominican Rep | 0.1 | 0.4 | 0.3 | 0.5 |
| Haiti | 0.8 | 1.9 | 0.3 | 1 |

Source: Country Demographic and health surveys

nationwide social marketing programme. It also encourages providers to serve unmarried young women, often denied services by reproductive health providers.

An evaluation of the programme[106] showed that it had positive effects on both young women and young men. The proportion of females who ever used condoms rose from 58 per cent to 76 per cent in the treatment group, compared with a decline from 53 per cent to 50 per cent in the control group in another town. The evaluation also found that young people had delayed initiation of sexual intercourse; that those who did have sex had reduced the number of partners. Both young men and young women increased their knowledge about condom use and other contraceptives – the proportion of young women who knew about condoms rose from 39 to 74 per cent and of oral contraceptives from 23 to 60 per cent. The programme also raised awareness amongst young men of the risks of STIs and HIV, and amongst young women of their own responsibility to use protection during sex.

But while living in the city means that in theory health clinics and doctors are closer and more available, this does not necessarily mean that all adolescent girls have better access to healthcare. Services may be too expensive, or clinics not seen as friendly to young women or offering them the care and support that they need to protect themselves and their health. Migrants in slums may have better health services than they had in their

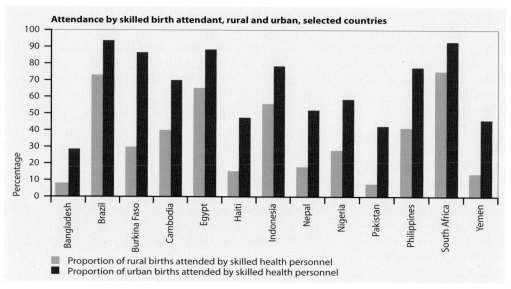

**Attendance by skilled birth attendant, rural and urban, selected countries**

Countries (left to right): Bangladesh, Brazil, Burkina Faso, Cambodia, Egypt, Haiti, Indonesia, Nepal, Nigeria, Pakistan, Philippines, South Africa, Yemen

Y-axis: Percentage (0–100)

■ Proportion of rural births attended by skilled health personnel
■ Proportion of urban births attended by skilled health personnel

villages, but they may not be able to afford them. Adolescent girls are less likely than most to have the extra cash for healthcare.[107]

Their low status may also mean that they are attended to last. One study of urban populations in Bangladesh looked at access to healthcare within poor households. They found that because women and girls had lower status than men and boys in the family, their health needs were neglected, sometimes fatally. For example, during a cholera epidemic, three times more women died than men simply because they were taken to hospital too late in order to avoid paying hospital fees.[108] In many countries, the mothers of girls with disabilities find that there are more programmes to help integrate them into normal life than there are in villages.

UN-Habitat notes that: "Youth and, by extension, children born to families in highly deprived areas like slums have far less access to health services, such as immunisation and, in some cases, antenatal and delivery care. For instance, in countries where a high proportion of poor youth and children are without immunisation, national coverage can still be as high as 40 per cent, because immunisation is much more widespread among the richest. In some countries, access to antenatal and delivery care is very unequal among slum and non-slum areas, but generally speaking the divide emerges most clearly in post-neonatal mortality rates. However, regardless of parents' economic status, urban children are still much better

off overall than their rural counterparts."[109]

This is clear when an adolescent girl in a city has a baby. She is more likely to be attended by a skilled birth attendant in a city than in a village.

## Taking advantage of urban life – access to education

*"Education is definitely more important for girls than for boys. If girls don't have the opportunities that education gives them then they are not qualified for a good life."*
Sabah, mother of three daughters, Alexandria, Egypt[110]

The Millennium Development Goals, in recognising the importance of girls' education, acknowledge that access to education has been shown to be the one thing that will protect a young woman in future life, giving her the possibility of work, self-confidence and knowledge. We know that education has a significant impact on girls' futures. According to the World Bank, an extra year of schooling can increase a girl's potential wages by 10 to 20 per cent.[111] Girls who attend secondary school may make $2,000 more per year than girls who only attend primary school.[112] As Maria Eitel, President of the Nike Foundation – which has a major programme supporting adolescent girls – notes: "Multiply that by 1.6 million out-of-school girls in Kenya and there's a potential $3.2 billion increase in national income."[113] In addition, if a girl is educated, she is more likely to be healthy and her children are more likely to go to school. A study in Bangladesh by the London School of Hygiene and Tropical Medicine found that for women with eight or more years of education, maternal mortality was three times lower and abortion-related mortality was eleven times lower than in women with no education.

## LEARN WITHOUT FEAR[114]

Learn Without Fear is Plan International's global campaign against violence in school. Fear of bullying and sexual harassment is one of the reasons why girls drop out of school.

*"Our teachers should be there to teach us and not to touch us."*

Girl, 15, Uganda

Each year, 150 million girls and 73 million boys across the world are subjected to sexual violence and between 20 and 65 per cent of schoolchildren report being verbally or physically bullied. The Learn Without Fear campaign was set up in 2008 to address the fact that cruel and humiliating forms of physical punishment, gender-based violence and bullying are a daily reality for millions of children. At present, 89 countries have not yet prohibited corporal punishment in schools. Girls in cities may have more access to education but access itself is never enough, as the campaign clearly demonstrates.

*"If they hit me, I learn to hit."*

Girl, 12, Spain

Plan researchers made a number of findings that are directly related to girls:
- In Africa, some male teachers offer good grades in exchange for sexual intercourse. Such abuse is commonly seen as an inevitable part of school life.
- In Asia, boys are more likely to use physical intimidation and violence, while girls tend towards verbal and social bullying. Reports note a rise in sexual abuse via the internet.
- In Latin America, violence against girls in school tends to remain a silent crime because of the stigma attached to the early loss of virginity. Students who get pregnant are expelled from schools.

School violence reflects violence in society as a whole, and therefore an appropriate response needs to be gender-balanced, holistic, participatory and measurable. Accordingly, in the first year of Learn Without Fear we have been able to track the following changes:
- Due to improved laws in Ecuador, Nicaragua and the Philippines more than 27 million school students have better legal protection from violence
- In Bolivia, Nepal, Pakistan, the Philippines and Tanzania, campaigners are leading efforts to pass bills on school violence-related issues
- The governments of 30 countries have invited Plan to work with them to stop school violence
- In total, 286,216 children have been involved in Learn Without Fear campaign initiatives
- 8,289 teachers across 26 countries have been trained on 'positive discipline'
- 11,813 public servants have undergone training on school violence-related issues.

This initial success demonstrates that a concerted effort by schools, parents, pupils and law enforcement agencies could largely eliminate fear as a reason for school drop-out.

*"There would be a lot less violence in schools if there were a stronger sense of community in the classrooms."*

Girl, 15, Germany

| Female school drop-out rate due to pregnancy and early marriage, slums and non-slums, selected countries[115] | | |
|---|---|---|
| | Slum % | Non-slum % |
| Philippines | 21 | 13 |
| Kyrgyzstan | 32 | 20 |
| Indonesia | 24 | 33 |
| Peru | 22 | 17 |
| Dominican Republic | 35 | 29 |
| Colombia | 20 | 16 |
| Bolivia | 28 | 20 |
| Zambia | 19 | 23 |
| Uganda | 14 | 14 |
| Nigeria | 27 | 16 |
| Mozambique | 39 | 14 |

There are big differences between rich and poor areas when it comes to education in cities. UN-Habitat notes that globally: "While children from the wealthiest 20 per cent of households have already achieved universal primary school attendance in most countries, those from the poorest 20 per cent have not."[116] It continues: "The urban advantage of better access to education remains a myth for the majority of slum dwellers. Even if schooling is available, slum families sacrifice the education of their children, particularly girls, so that they can meet the costs of food, rent and transport. Often, there simply are not enough schools within easy reach of slum settlements."[117]

Slums vary as much as any other areas of the city, and are sometimes categorised according to what are known as 'shelter deprivations' – lack of access to improved water, lack of access to sanitation, non-durable housing, insufficient living area, and security of tenure.[118] Research has shown that the more of these a girl suffers, the more likely she is to grow up illiterate. For example, in Benin, the literacy rate varied from 43 per cent to only six per cent according to whether a woman suffered one, two or three or more such deprivations.

In slum areas, many girls never start school, or drop out before finishing secondary school. This may be because of teenage pregnancy which, although it may

be lower than in rural areas, is higher than in non-slum areas (see table on page 51).[119]

## Participation and governance

*"No one is born a good citizen; no nation is born a democracy. Rather, both are processes that continue to evolve over a lifetime. Young people must be included from birth. A society that cuts off from its youth severs its lifeline."*

Kofi Annan, former United Nations Secretary-General[120]

*"When it comes to 'youth making a difference in communities' I think the value of youth has been underestimated everywhere. Youth are excellent in delivering grassroots-level development projects at minimal budgets and very effectively. Due to the fact that they are involved at the grassroots level, they can easily implement a project without the bureaucracy of organisations... they often have a lower cost base too."*

Shasheen, 20, Australia[121]

It is not easy for adolescent girls to take part in discussions about how their cities should be run. World Bank research revealed that young women between the ages of 18 and 29 were less likely to discuss politics with their friends than young men. The overall

*Children at a "Learning to Protect Ourselves" summer camp in the Dominican Republic.*

figures were 59 per cent of young women and 70 per cent of young men.[122] Among urban slum dwellers in Rio de Janeiro, girls scored significantly lower than boys on every dimension of citizenship, "including political participation, membership in community or civic organisations (excluding churches), seeking out government agencies, and having official legal documents".[123]

UN-Habitat recognised that participation was still an issue for many girls in cities. Lucia Kiwala, the Chief of the Gender Mainstreaming Unit at UN-Habitat, explained: "We found that girls were not participating as much as boys in our One Stop Youth Centres which provide a meeting place for young people to come together to access information and resources. So we started up Girls' Clubs to encourage girls to attend."[124] Girls and young women need time, information, knowledge and confidence to help them participate in city life, and there also needs to be a willingness on the part of governments and municipalities to involve adolescent girls. Some countries are beginning to recognise the importance of involving youth in such debates. The World Bank notes that: "Many countries promote advisory youth assemblies, councils, or parliaments. Some, such as those in Slovenia and Zimbabwe, bring together local youth representatives at the national level. Regional

*Habiba's father tried to kill her when he found out that she was disabled. If she lived in a village she would probably just stay at home. Now, though she lives in a poor area of Cairo, she attends a local community centre where she enjoys the company of other children.*

Habiba

NIKKI VAN DER GAAG

structures include the European Youth Forum, the Latin American Youth Forum, and the African Youth Parliament. Assemblies also operate in many locales, including the Youth Council of Catalunya and the Youth Parliament of Ryazan, Russia."

In the municipality of Barra Mansa, in Rio de Janeiro, Brazil, children aged nine to 15 help set expenditure priorities. In the Philippines, the councils are open to youths aged 15 to 21.[125] In Ceará, Brazil, young people were also involved in budget setting and in training other youth. The council says that as a result of their efforts, an additional $750,000 was allocated to children and young people in 2005.[126]

These initiatives are to be welcomed but they need to make the necessary efforts to ensure that the 'youth' consulted are girls as well as boys. Girls are, after all, experts on their own experiences – they know when they do not feel safe in the city.[127]

## 4. No safe place? Preventing violence against adolescent girls in the city

*"Safety and security don't just happen: they are the result of collective consensus and public investment. We owe our children – the most vulnerable citizens in any society – a life free from violence and fear."*
Nelson Mandela[128]

*"It's not beautiful in our area. There are many snatchers [people who snatch bags and valuables and make a run for it] and people shooting guns."*
Lean Joy, 17, Manila, Philippines[129]

As we have seen in the previous section, cities offer many opportunities for adolescent girls that they could not find in rural settings. But living in a city may also mean that girls face a number of risks and dangers, some of which are the same as those they might face in a rural area, and some of which are different. Violence, for example, is not confined to the city any more than it is just in the home or just on the street. This section looks at the risks adolescent girls in the city face, in particular in relation to violence. It showcases examples of good practice and outlines

## "NOT EVEN WITH THE PETAL OF A ROSE" – BOGOTÁ CITY CAMPAIGN AGAINST VIOLENCE AGAINST WOMEN AND GIRLS

*"She was a little girl of 13 years old and her mother left her father and got involved with a man who haunted the girl. He offered her bad proposals. He wanted to sexually abuse her and offered her money to let him touch her."*

*"This doll is crying because her husband hit her and now she has a black eye."*

*"As you can see, she doesn't have a face; she only shows parts of her body, because that is all anyone looks at... men talk to her breasts rather than her face."*

These young women were describing the rag dolls, both beautiful and terrible, that they had made as part of a project supported by Plan International and Casa Ensamble, a local arts organisation, to combat violence against women and girls in the city of Bogotá, Colombia. Gabriela Bucher, Plan's director in Colombia, said: "People connected strongly with these dolls, which were direct reminders of all that most of us do not want to see."

The project was supported by the mayor and the municipality as part of Bogotá's initiative to become a 'safe city'. Levels of violence against women and girls in Colombia are high. Every day 92 women are killed, and 100 more are beaten, by their partners. And the story for girls is no better. Every hour, 24 girls are born: 12 of these will be poor, four will live in extreme poverty, six are likely to be victims of sexual abuse, five will get pregnant before reaching the age of 19 and only eight will complete their studies.

The project made 350 dolls in all, some made by displaced women and girls, some by well-known artists. It was called "Not even with the petal of a rose" after a traditional saying about violence against women. It helped many girls and women come to terms with what they, and others, had suffered.

Along with the making and exhibiting of the dolls, the project provided training to strengthen the capacity of different groups to protect women and girls against violence. It also produced posters, banners, songs, stickers and campaigns on radio and television to raise awareness among civil society about violence against women and girls, and to promote commitment to change. A petition with 15,000 signatures was collected. Each individual who signed made a promise not to be violent. Finally, there was an institutional strengthening component: institutions responsible for the protection and care of girls and women (hospitals, family, police and others) will be supported to improve the attention provided to victims of abuse.

"For some of us," said one young woman, "our healer was the doll. Singing, dancing and dramatising our stories became our healer... and there comes a time when the wound closes and the scar doesn't hurt or bleed any more. When we take a look at it, it just reminds us that we had an accident but it doesn't hurt any more."

*Rag dolls from the "Not even with the petal of a rose" campaign.*

how cities can be made safe places of opportunity for all adolescent girls.

Violence against women and girls[130] is a global phenomenon that has no respect for class, age, income, religion, culture or place of residence. Sexual violence, and the threat of such violence, haunts many adolescent girls as they go about their daily lives in the city, whether in school, on public transport, or in the street.

Globally, six out of every ten women experience physical and/or sexual violence in their lifetime.[131] The United Nations Report on Violence Against Children identifies four main forms of violence – physical, psychological, sexual and neglect. Some kinds of violence are more common in rural areas, such as forced marriage and harmful traditional practices. Others are more common in cities and towns, such as sexual harassment in public places, forced commercial sex and trafficking.

- A World Health Organisation study in a number of countries found that in Bangladesh twice as many young women over 15 in urban (as opposed to rural) areas had experienced physical or sexual violence by someone other than their partner.[132]
- In Brazil 24.5 per cent of female respondents in the city and 15.9 per cent in the provinces reported violence.[133]
- Another study in Cape Town, South Africa showed that 72 per cent of young women who were pregnant and 60 per cent of those who had never been pregnant had reported experiencing coerced sex.[134]
- A similar study in Lima, Peru, found 41 per cent of girls and young women between the ages of 10 and 24 had experienced coerced sex.[135]

- In Ghana, adolescents in urban areas were significantly more likely to have experienced coerced sex than those in rural areas.[136]
- A study of human rights violations in Dhaka, Bangladesh, found that adolescent girls were the most vulnerable group when it came to sexual harassment and rape. The research was based on 3,000 incidents of human rights violations in 61 districts from 2006 to 2009. It found that rape was the most frequent crime (31 per cent of incidents) followed by murder (25 per cent), acid throwing (15 per cent), suicide (12 per cent), physical torture (eight per cent) and attempt to rape (seven per cent). Half the rape victims were aged below 15 and 59 per cent of the girls under 15 had been victims of attempted rape.[137]

In slums, levels of violence against girls and women are higher than in other parts of the city. The combination of poverty, unemployment, inadequate wages, social exclusion and racism can lead to frustration among men and boys and vulnerability for women and girls, particularly if they are on the street.[138] "I like being a girl, but I want to know my rights," said a girl who is a secondary school student in Kibera, a huge slum area in Nairobi, Kenya. She said that she felt she could hardly step out of her home at night without being assaulted.[139]

One study in the cities of Bangladesh found that girls under 15 were the most likely to be raped, while girls and young women between 15 and 25 were most likely to be the victims of acid attacks and physical torture.[140] It found no difference according to economic status – among the rape perpetrators, 35 per cent were rich,

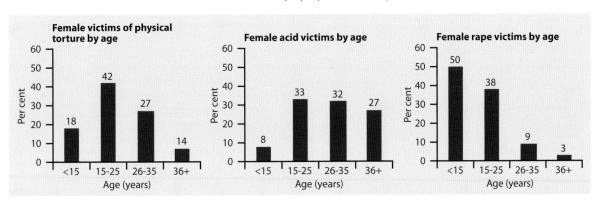

*The Old Fadama slum area.*

JUSTIN MORESCO / IRIN

36 per cent middle class and 28 per cent poor – which backs up the assertion that violence against women cuts across all social boundaries.

In slum areas, adolescent girls can be in danger while undertaking the most mundane of tasks, as Anna Tibaijuka, Executive Director of UN-Habitat, points out: "Girls in slums have to choose between defecating in a plastic bag or risking rape should they dare venture outside to a dirty public toilet at night."[141]

Focus groups with women and girls for an action research project on Women's Rights and Access to Water and Sanitation in the Resettlement Colonies of New Delhi found that:[142]

- Sexual harassment is rampant when girls go out in the open for defecation. Men disguise themselves as women and hide themselves in the fields. The situation is worse during winters when men wrap themselves up in shawls and it becomes extremely difficult to differentiate between men and women. There have been instances when girls were abducted from the fields and men were caught for sexually harassing them. After 11pm, girls are usually forbidden from going to the fields unless they are accompanied by elders.
- There was one story where a teenage girl was abducted in the morning while she had gone in the fields for defecation. Three days later, her dead body was found in a nearby

area. Since then the women are very cautious with their young girls and do not allow them to use the open fields or usually accompany them to the fields.

A report on Azni Nagar, a slum area in Mumbai, India, noted: "There are three pay-and-use or public toilet facilities available, where residents must pay 1 rupee for each use. Most of the residents find this too expensive, however, and they use a nearby open area instead. As the area is also rife with prostitution, women, and especially young girls, find it very difficult to go to the bathroom at night without being harassed, and they felt it to be entirely insecure for them. Some reported attempts of rape and sexual assault as they made the precarious journey."[143]

### KAYAYEI GIRLS IN THE SLUMS OF ACCRA, GHANA[144]

Young women and adolescent girls who live in and around the Old Fadama slum in Accra, Ghana, work as Kayayei: temporary migrants residing in a city to earn money as porters and return home either for marriage or other labour. These girls often pool together with other Kayayei to group-rent a room in a slum. However, the slums are very congested and the rental rates are often exorbitant. Consequently, violence and insecurity are often pervasive for girls and young women in this slum:

"Inability to raise rent money is one of the main reasons why some women, especially the young girls, are forced to sleep outside. When this happens, women and girls risk their personal security and their property. Many reported that Kayayei women and girls were routinely raped, sexually assaulted, or robbed when they slept outside. Rape and sexual assault were major concerns for Kayayei women and girls, and attacks did not only happen at night. Too often, women and girls reported having to suffer silently when this happened to them."[145]

Being raped brings more than emotional damage to Kayayei women and girls; they are also placed at an increased risk of HIV transmission and unwanted pregnancy. Those with unwanted pregnancies are then placed at further risk through unsafe and illegal 'backstreet' abortions.

It is not only at night time that Kayayei girls are vulnerable to violence and abuse: "In the community and during the course of their work, Kayayei women and girls also risk open attack by thieves who threaten them at knifepoint and take their money. This happens especially very early in the morning as the Kayayei women set out to work."[146]

The women in Old Fadama said they were afraid to report cases for fear of provoking the government into evicting them. Even in those cases where rape was reported, the police had little interest in pursuing these cases and holding perpetrators accountable.

Violence against adolescent girls in cities is not confined to poor areas of a city or to poor countries. It occurs in the developed as well as the developing world. Emma was 13 when she was introduced to an older man by the boys she was friends with in Yorkshire, England. He made friends with her and then raped her and forced her into commercial sex work.

"I never thought of myself as a prostitute," she reflects, her down-to-earth voice strangely disengaged as she describes her own suffering, "because, in my child's view of the world, prostitutes walked the streets, wore short skirts and high heels and I wasn't doing any of that. It is only now that I can see that, much as I wanted to believe Tarik had feelings for me, he didn't have any at all, except to make money out of me."[147]

Studies have also shown that socially isolated girls (with family being a key aspect of connectedness) are six times more likely to have been forced to have sex than socially connected girls.[148] This leaves girls in street situations who are socially isolated much more vulnerable to HIV transmission than boys. But Emma is keen to dispel the myth that these things only happen to girls from dysfunctional families:
*"Yes, there probably are a lot of girls who get involved because they come from broken homes, or are in care, but when you look at the whole situation, as I have, there are plenty who don't. The gangs know that if*

*they take a girl from a nice family, she will probably be more naïve, not as streetwise as kids who have been in care. And because you are naïve, you are more trusting, easier to impress. They like that. It makes you easier to control. They'll have anybody – doctors' children, lawyers' children – anybody."*

Today, Emma is 20 and is planning to become a lawyer. She has written a book about her experiences. She also works with Crop – the Coalition for the Removal of Pimping – in Leeds, which was set up by the families of those affected by the sexual exploitation of youngsters. Emma gives talks to parents facing the same horror that hers once did, and she is pushing for more police resources to be directed to tackling gangs like the one that groomed her.[149]

Girls like Emma who have been sexually exploited are at high risk of HIV and sexually transmitted diseases, particularly if they are involved in commercial sexual exploitation or sex for money. They are less likely than older women to be able to negotiate safer sex and are often threatened with violence. In South Africa, it is estimated that for those under the age of 15, cases of sexual abuse are beginning to overtake mother-to-child transmission as the main reason for HIV prevalence.[150]

*Kayayei girls at work in the city.*

JANE HAHN

*Nighttime streets, Codo, Brazil.*

LEO DRUMOND

## GIRLS AND GANGS IN RIO[151]

In the context of lack of job and education opportunities and social marginalisation in many cities, organised youth gangs may offer a means to make money, gain social status and provide a sense of belonging. 'Gangs' cover a wide range of social groupings, and while some get involved in petty crime or drug dealing, others are primarily social networks which come together to give a feeling of protection for young people who themselves feel under threat.[152]

In Latin American cities, it is often young black men who attract the majority of media and policy attention. However, studies in Rio de Janeiro, Brazil, have highlighted the various roles that young women and girls play in these structures, as well as the multiple effects on their lives. The impact of gang violence on girls and young women is not restricted by age but forms part of a continuum, in terms of their relationships and the consequences of violence, which evolves over time. Gang members are known for having young girlfriends – with girls as young as 13 involved in sexual relations – with the risk of teenage pregnancy and sexually transmitted diseases that this entails. Involvement tends to last until their mid- to late-twenties, when both men and women, if they have survived, leave the gang, or 'mature out'.[153] This may come about as a result of having children.

While boys and young men make up the majority of the militarised structures within the gangs, some young women rise up the ranks to take leadership roles. Others may play roles in the drugs trade and the violence that is integral to its functioning. Increasingly, girls and young women are being imprisoned for drug-related offences – rising in Rio de Janeiro State from 32.6 per cent of female convictions in 1988 to 56 per cent in 2000, with 31 per cent involved in violent crimes.[154]

Most women who get involved in gangs are confined to supportive roles. They are less likely to carry arms, and their activities may never be acknowledged as gang work at all. The younger they are the more likely it is that they are to be found carrying out low status tasks. Nevertheless, activities such as storing and carrying arms, passing messages and smuggling goods into prisons and across gang territories all play a key contributory role in the continuation of violence and criminality, as well as constituting a risk for the young women involved. Moreover, in their relationships with gang members, young women, and frequently adolescent girls, may either perpetuate or reduce levels of violence, as they strive to protect or implicate others; violence that they themselves are not immune to. For example, young women may incite the punishment of rivals, as well as suffer punishment for the acts of boyfriends and brothers.[155]

Women who live in gang-controlled areas cannot access formal routes to justice, as contact with the police is forbidden: "If something serious happened in my family, a really serious fight, we couldn't go to the police to report it, because when we came back here, we would die," says Marilia, aged 13. And although the threat of gang punishment may have the potential to protect victims of violence in the home, in reality it is just as likely to silence the victim further, as 16 year-old Rosária states: "The traffickers come straight away when they hear about something. Perhaps I wouldn't tell anyone because I can't make a complaint to the police and I would be scared that the traffickers would kill the person that had done me wrong. They killed one guy who raped girls."[156]

| Adolescent fears and experience of crime, by sex (%), Addis Ababa, Ethiopia[157] | Boys | Girls |
|---|---|---|
| **Feelings of well-being and comfort in the neighbourhood** | | |
| You don't feel comfortable walking in your neighbourhood after dark | 50.0 | 76.6 |
| You know of girls in your neighbourhood who have been raped | 9.0 | 14.0 |
| You are scared of being beaten by someone in your neighbourhood | 15.8 | 31.8 |
| You are scared of some people in your neighbourhood | 42.0 | 62.1 |
| At times you are scared that you will be raped in your neighbourhood | 9.8 | 54.4 |
| There is a lot of crime in your neighbourhood | 51.3 | 43.9 |
| | | |
| **Experience of harassment and crime** | | |
| You have been groped by someone of the opposite sex in your neighbourhood | 4.3 | 32.2 |
| People tease you as you go about your business | 19.0 | 46.9 |
| You have been robbed in the last year | 5.8 | 7.3 |

## Fear of violence

*"The streets [in the ghetto] are not safe spaces for girls because there are bad things happening. Like, for example, rape. You can be beaten, you can be killed... So we think that Safe Spaces has created a safe environment for us."*

Girl from Safe Spaces project, Mathare, Nairobi, Kenya[158]

Violence and the fear of violence can also lead to a culture in which an adolescent girl is afraid to go out of her home – and sometimes afraid to stay in it for fear of violence at home. UN-Habitat notes that: "A causal link also exists between domestic violence and urban violence."[159] This may be partly to do with shifting male and female roles – research in the Philippines found that being poor and living in an urban area was linked to a higher likelihood of intimate-partner violence.[160] Overcrowded environments at home and in the street can also contribute to violence against girls.

Outside her home, a girl knows that there are many places which may be unsafe for her to venture – unlit streets, bus stops, public toilets. Perpetrators are more likely to be able to remain anonymous in an urban environment – and to go unpunished. Girls are hidden – and so are the crimes against them. This is why it is so difficult to find data on violence against this age group. Girls may be afraid to speak out against a stranger, brother or teacher, fearing public stigma and shame and doubting that they will find justice.

When girls perceive that their environment is threatening, they start to avoid the places that make them feel unsafe. As a result, streets, squares, parks, internet cafés and neighbourhoods are often used more by men and boys than by women and girls.[161]

This survey in Addis Ababa, Ethiopia (above), showed that girls are more afraid than boys to go out after dark; more afraid of certain people in the neighbourhood, and also afraid of being raped. They are also more likely to be teased or harassed than boys.

In the Netherlands, an online survey conducted for this report[162] of girls in cities found that while most girls and young women felt safe walking around their neighbourhood in the day, at night 40 per cent of those between the ages of 11 and 18 said they did not feel safe. This rose to 46 per cent when 19 to 22 year-olds were included. Sixty-three per cent of 17 and 18 year-olds said they did not feel safe travelling around their city at night.

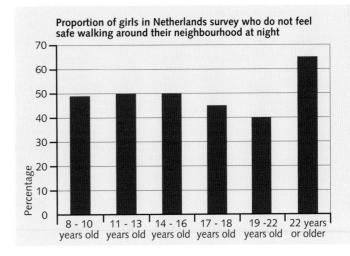

**Proportion of girls in Netherlands survey who do not feel safe walking around their neighbourhood at night**

- When asked what would make their city safer for girls, better street lighting was most important
- 35 per cent of girls between 14 and 16 said they know someone who had been assaulted – this rises to 55 per cent amongst girls who are 22 or older
- 55 per cent of 17 to 18 year-olds have witnessed violence in their neighbourhood.

These dangers and perceived dangers are not only for adolescent girls, or those who are poor, but are faced by young professional women as well, as the following testimony shows.

### NO RESPITE; LIVING ALONE IN THE CITY

*"I live alone in an apartment as a single professional young woman. Life in the city is a mix of all kinds of absurdities. Though I am secure economically and live in a decent neighbourhood, my sense of independence exposes me to multiple disadvantages, especially in the developing world where a woman is expected to live with parents or a husband. I change taxi-driver every now and then so that they do not get to know that I live alone. This is despite my desire to have a regular one to avoid the danger of bumping into strangers everyday. Though I am not very social, I make sure people visit my house to send a signal to the silent observer outside that I have people and am not alone. I am forced to lie to some people, saying I am 'engaged' or 'my marriage is fixed'… The negative preconceived notion of an independent young woman who lives alone cuts along all economic, social and professional circles and you do not get respite anywhere."*

Selam, young woman living in Khartoum, Sudan[163]

If an adolescent girl is raped or assaulted, there are psychological as well as physical consequences. One report notes that violence against girls undermined their development "by making it difficult for them to remain in school, destroying their confidence in adults and in peers, and putting them at risk of unwanted pregnancy and sexually transmitted infections, including HIV".[164] Many girls may blame themselves. Studies in cities in Peru and South Africa found that both girls and boys thought the victim of a sexual assault was to blame for what had happened to her.[165] Interestingly, in urban areas they are less likely to feel that they are at fault if they are assaulted – in a study by the World Health Organisation, more than 75 per cent of women living in urban areas in Brazil, Japan, Namibia, and Serbia and Montenegro said that no reason justified violence; while in provincial areas of Bangladesh, Ethiopia, Peru and Samoa, this dropped to only 25 per cent.[166]

### SOU DA PAZ – I AM OF PEACE[167]

Founded in 2000, Sou da Paz (I am of Peace) seeks to address violence in Brazil through a range of community programmes in São Paulo and through national and international advocacy, policy work, media and public awareness raising. However, one of its signature programmes, Polos de Paz, which was designed to create public recreation spaces in blighted urban areas, was almost exclusively reaching males only. Through research with 86 young people, Sou da Paz uncovered a variety of factors inhibiting young women from participating in activities in parks and playgrounds – notably domestic chores, caring for siblings and parental worries about the girls' safety and reputation.

In response, Sou da Paz has implemented a variety of innovative strategies to bring gender to the forefront of its work and to create an environment where young women use community spaces, enjoy leisure time, learn new skills, build self-confidence, and enjoy time with peers. Such strategies include using graffiti and hiphop to discuss gender issues with youth, and promoting soccer teams for girls. To create more enabling environments, Sou da Paz is also training stakeholders such as police, school personnel and municipal officials in charge of recreation.

## Getting around the city safely: transport

If adolescent girls are to prosper in the city, they need to be and to feel safe. This means having adequate street lighting so that they do not have to walk down dark alleys if they go out at night, and ensuring that public transport is safe and that they will be free from sexual harassment. If buses are infrequent, or taxi-drivers are known to assault young women, then they cannot travel safely to work or to school.

In many cities, neither lighting nor safe transport is available. One study in Western Joubert Park in inner-city Johannesburg, South Africa, asked boys and girls what the issues were for them in terms of keeping safe. Both groups recognised that transport was key. Girls wanted the council to: "Prevent/control child harassment in taxis"; for the "bus service to be faster; more routes and stops"; and suggested having "bigger, safer taxis for long-distance travel"[168]

Safe public transport is an essential part of ensuring that cities are safe places for adolescent girls. In some cities, local councils have instituted women-only buses or compartments on trains. In Cairo, the first two cars of each train of the Cairo Metro are reserved for women.[169] In Mumbai, two compartments on every train are earmarked as 'women-only'. Chitra Iyer, from Plan, says: "This is a blessing for women during rush hour as at least the obvious issue of sexual harassment stops. However, in non-peak hours, these compartments are often empty or thinly populated. Often men who are drunk or street vendors climb in and threaten the women or harass them. There have been cases of knife-wielding drug addicts getting into these compartments late at night and taking money, cell phones and jewellery from the few women in them. The poor security at railway platforms and the lack of security within the compartments themselves are the cause for this harassment. Thus, a woman or young girl must make a choice: risk travelling in the women's compartment where there are not enough of us, and risk an attack by a thief or a drunk; travel in the regular compartment and risk getting molested, touched or otherwise leered at; or finally, don't travel late at all."

In response to this problem, the female head of the Rail Ministry, Mamata Bannerjee, announced that in the 2010 budget there would be provision for female security officers on the trains. "It is a very good proposal," said Ananya Chatterjee-Chakrabarty, a filmmaker and professor of film studies and journalism. "Women have long felt insecure... With the increased threat of terrorism and crime on trains, women will feel reassured if the security personnel are women."[170]

A survey in urban Tanzania (see page 62) found that problems with transport were a major factor preventing girls from going to school.

In this chapter, we have outlined the global context of urbanisation and youth in relation to adolescent girls. We have looked at the push and pull factors in terms of why girls move to the city. We have looked at the many benefits of city life for adolescent girls, but also shown that cities are often unsafe places, particularly for those girls who live in poor areas. City life could be so much better for girls and young women. Planning with girls in mind and including them in the process, decent housing, safe transport and girl-friendly spaces and places would all help. As we will see very clearly in the next chapter, where we look at a specific group of girls who are the most marginalised in cities – those who live on the street – the situation is urgent.

*Looking out over the city in Santiago, Chile.*

GIULIANE BERTAGLIA CORREIA, AGED 15, BRAZIL / www.shootnations.org

## "I DON'T LIKE BEING HIT" – A SURVEY OF THE PROBLEMS GIRLS IN TANZANIA FACE IN GETTING TO SECONDARY SCHOOL SAFELY

*"I have been harassed by a bus driver. I quarrelled with the driver to get on the bus and he grabbed my breast. I cried out from pain because he pinched my breast so hard."*

This secondary school girl was one of 659 surveyed by the Academy for Educational Development (AED) as part of a study on gender-based violence against female students in the Dar es Salaam region of Tanzania.

Tanzania has made great efforts in recent years to increase the number of female students attending secondary school and to improve their performance. The number of government secondary schools almost doubled between 2005 and 2007 and girls' enrolment increased by more than 50 per cent in just one year from 2006 to 2007.

However, despite this, girls' attendance, performance and retention is low compared with boys' – for example, only 68.9 per cent of girls passed Form II national exams compared with 83.3 per cent of boys; and the retention rate from Form I to Form IV was 64 per cent for girls and 78 per cent for boys.

There are multiple reasons for this: girls have to do chores at home that leave them little time for study; society and families think it is more important to educate a boy; girls become pregnant or are forced into marriage at an early age; girls experience gender-based violence; and problems with transport to and from school.

*Another hazard of the city streets: walking through piles of rubbish.*

In 2008, the Academy of Educational Development (AED) decided to undertake a study of the issues related to gender-based violence and transport in the Dar es Salaam area. Staff knew that there were problems about the cost and demand for buses because many students had to travel a long way to get to a secondary school and students pay lower fares than adults. AED presumed that, as in other situations, this gap between supply and demand could be more problematic for girls.

The study came up with some startling findings:

- Fifty-nine per cent of girls said they missed school because they didn't have bus money. At least 18 per cent said they had missed five days or more a month.
- A significant number of girls reported that it takes two or more hours to get to school and the same amount of time to return home. More than 20 per cent of the girls reported waking up before 5am to get to school. Sixty-eight per cent of students reported needing to use two or more buses.
- Almost half reported that they were sometimes unable to attend school because bus drivers refused them entry.
- More than two-thirds said they had been abused or mistreated by a bus driver. This included physical and verbal harassment and assault. Forty-seven per cent reported being physically harassed – either hit and/or pushed. One girl described this abuse: "One day I boarded a bus and the bus conductor pushed me down out of the seat. I fell out of the bus and was really hurt." Others described being hit or having encountered other forms of physical abuse. "I have been mistreated plenty of times. I have been pushed and pulled so that I can't get on to a bus which has stopped, and I have been hit by drivers and called names. It hurts my feelings and I don't like being hit."
- If the bus driver refuses them entry, 75 per cent of the girls try alternative means of getting school, ranging from walking to asking for assistance to hitch-hiking. This is often dangerous. Twenty-two per cent of girls reported that drivers had attempted to force them to accept rides to school, but most said they had been able to escape. "Once, a driver forced me to get into his car. He wanted to have sex with me but I refused and jumped from his car. He tried to follow me, but I ran so he left and I went back to the main road to wait for the next bus to come."

This study shows that gender-based violence is a crucial issue for girls going to secondary school. It revealed just how determined they are to go to school, many of them getting up early and travelling long distances each day. But there can be no doubt from this survey that the challenges they face have an impact on their attendance, and likely their performance as well. The study recommends that "NGOs and governments... consider the issue of transportation to and from school when developing and implementing mechanisms to improve girls' education."[171]

# Hidden in plain view: adolescent girls on the streets

*"I can say that for girls it's very, very bad to be on the streets, because someone can just come and sleep with you by force. If he is older than you, you can't just say anything. I have a boyfriend. He was born in 1990 and I was born in 1991. His name is Freedom. I also have a son who is nine months old. Because I was living on the streets I couldn't stay with my son. And one of the ladies from the church, she takes care of my son until I have a better place to stay and then I will take my son back. I ask God that my son doesn't know that his mother is like this on the streets."*

Precious, 18, Durban, South Africa

## Summary

Our urban story continues with a focus on adolescent street girls, who are one of the most vulnerable groups in any city. Although there are generally fewer street girls than boys, and they are less visible, they are most at risk of abuse, exploitation and sexual assault, and least able to protect themselves. The general public treats them with contempt. Those who are meant to protect them, such as the police, offer them violence instead. Girls like Trina, who sleeps in a corridor between shops and lives in constant fear of violence. Girls like Precious, who has a baby but knows she cannot look after him on the streets and has to face the daily pain of being apart from him. Or Tanya, who says: "It is better to die of AIDS than of hunger." As cities grow, so do the numbers of street

girls like Trina and Precious and Tanya. That they should have to live like this is an outrage that should not be tolerated in the 21st century. There is an urgent need for those responsible for cities to protect these girls and improve their lives – and to give them the basic rights that all children are entitled to.

## 1. Defining disadvantage

*"If you see a girl on the street, looking dirty, don't think badly of them – because they could be a member of your family."*

Laura, 16, Nicaragua[1]

*"The government don't do anything for children on the street, they don't even think about them, when they see those children they do not even make a case for them. They should take them by the hand and say: I am going to support you, I am going to help you, you are not alone. But no – they look at them as they would anything else, like any other rubbish."*

Jessica, 17, Nicaragua[2]

In a city where many people are poor, it is sometimes difficult to differentiate between a slum and a non-slum area, between a girl who is poor and a girl who is so poor that she is on the streets. Adolescence is a time of transition and many girls will move in and out of extreme poverty or homelessness as they grow into adults. As we will see in the section on street girls, many live with family some of the time and spend the rest of the time on the streets: some are working and some are not.

So who is a marginalised girl? The United Nations Department of Economic and Social Affairs has 11 categories of what it calls 'disadvantaged youth'[3] These are:

1   Those without adequate access to education and health services;
2   Adolescents who have dropped out of school;
3   Pregnant adolescents, whether married or not;
4   Married adolescents;
5   Young single parents;
6   Young people who are HIV-positive, or at particular risk of HIV/AIDS;
7   Young refugees or displaced persons;
8   Racial, linguistic and ethnic minorities;
9   Homeless youth;
10 Young people with disabilities;
11 Girls and young women in any of these groups that are affected by gender inequalities.

What is interesting about this list is how many of the categories are either exclusively adolescent girls, or else largely girls. It is girls who are most likely to have dropped out of school and married. They may then become pregnant and have a child. The list recognises implicitly that gender and disadvantage go together when it comes to adolescent youth and that these disadvantages, once established, are likely to continue into adulthood.

UN-Habitat, in its 2010 report on the state of urban youth, notes that young people considered to be 'at risk' in urban settings include: all those girls and boys whose living or health conditions, circumstances or behaviour patterns place them at risk of falling victim to, or being involved in, crime. They include, but are not limited to, youth already at odds with the law, those living in urban slums, street children, youth gangs, school drop-outs, unemployed youth, substance-abusing youth, those who are sexually exploited, war-affected children, and those affected by the AIDS pandemic, including orphans.

This section of our report looks at the issues faced by one of the most disadvantaged and marginalised groups in the city: adolescent girls on the street. According to the UN Committee on the Rights of the Child, "[s]treet children are among the most vulnerable victims of the most extreme forms of violence… Such violence too often takes place at the hands of agents of the State, or at least with their encouragement or tolerance."[4]

### MY NAME IS TRINA[5]
*"My name is Trina and I am 17 years old and I live on the streets of Kitwe in Zambia. I stopped attending school in 2007. I have a girl of two and a half. My mother takes care of her now. We came from a rural area in 2009.*

*Both my parents live on the street. It is not easy because my mother and father are blind. I sell brushes on the streets. I make at least K20,000 to K50,000 a day ($4 to $10) depending on the business of the day and the willingness of the customers to buy our brushes. Competition is high, as all the street girls and the blind women sell the same commodities. I like talking to customers while I sell my brushes.*

*I sleep between shop corridors with the blind beggars for safety. I belong to a choir because I enjoy singing. My best and closest friend is Charles. We are planning to get married in future and he is very nice to me. If I am in trouble, I can ask Charles to help me.*

*I never feel safe [on the streets], I feel very uncomfortable because there is a lot of violence… and a lot of crime in our area. Violence is rampant on the streets and in every corner there are people ready to harm us. Thank God, we survive every single day. I have been beaten in the past by strangers, the street boys punched me. I am not happy living here – there is no privacy, everything is an open space.*

*I am intelligent but sometimes I feel very bad about myself because I stopped school at an early age, and although I can read my own language I struggle to read English, which makes me feel worthless. I hope that one day, given the chance, I can go back to school."*

## 2. Hidden in plain view – adolescent street girls

*"Being poor is in itself a health hazard; worse, however, is being urban and poor. Much worse is being poor, urban, and a child. But worst of all is being a street child in an urban environment."*

Ximena de la Barra, senior urban advisor, UNICEF[6]

The success of the film 'Slumdog Millionaire' highlighted the plight of children living on the street. Like Lalita, the young heroine, it is often street girls who are the most vulnerable of all. As the film showed clearly, adolescent street girls like Lalita face sexual harassment and abuse and often have to rely on street boys or older men to protect them. They can find no refuge with the authorities or the police, who are as likely to abuse them as protect them, sometimes locking them up because they are girls on the street rather than because they have committed a crime.

Overall numbers of street children are almost impossible to estimate, partly because many do not live on the street all the time. Often they live some of the time on the street and some with families or relatives. UNICEF believes that there are at least 100 million street children globally, although many other studies have pointed out that no one really knows the numbers. An estimated 18 million of these live in India, which has the largest numbers of street children of any country in the world.[7] And numbers appear to be increasing – for example, in Jakarta, Indonesia, there were 98,113 street children in 2004 but this had risen to 114,889 by 2006.[8] Another study noted: "A recent head-count of street children in Accra shows a consistent increase."[9]

Street and homeless girls are not just in the developing world. In the US, according to the National Coalition for the Homeless (NCH), an estimated 1.2 million children are homeless on any given night.[10] In the UK, around 100,000 young people under the age of 16 run away from home or care each year.[11]

### STREET CHILDREN[12]

The term 'street children' can mean many different things. UNICEF's definition includes three different categories:

1 Children 'of' the street (street-living children), who sleep in public spaces, without their families;
2 Children 'on' the street (street-working children), who work on the streets during the day and return to their family home to sleep;
3 'Street-family children' who live with their family on the street.[13]

*Slum conditions in Dhaka, Bangladesh.*

Many girls on the streets live with their families; many girls caught up in commercial sex work are key breadwinners: "If I die doing sex work, then I die for my family," said a young Zimbabwean sex worker, aged 15, working in the coastal resort of Beira in Mozambique.[14] She charges 50 meticas an hour: approximately $1. She tries to send home approximately $20 a week.

### "IT IS BETTER TO KEEP QUIET"[15]

*"My name's Sala, I'm 14 years old and I moved to Accra two years ago. As soon as I moved to the city I fell into a group of other schoolchildren who introduced me to sex work. I spend most of my days with these friends. These children are my only friends here in Accra. We work together and help each other make contacts and find clients. Most nights I spend with clients, but I usually spend two nights a week with my friends. I really admire our group leader; I feel I can always go to her if I needed help or advice.*

*Even though I have my friends, I don't feel very safe during the day. There are gangs in our area who often fight and at times the leaders harass us girls. I've also had to experience violence myself. I've gotten into a fight with another street girl over a client and at times have had clients punch me. Even things like using the public toilet are scary as you can be attacked there. I know I could go to the police if needed but there are times when it is better to keep quiet; like when a pimp demands sex, it is easier to submit than to face violence. Plus, sometimes the police are just as violent as the gangs; once when I was arrested a police officer hit me on the head with the butt of his gun.*

*I've never been able to go to school and because of this I don't feel as smart as those around me. I would like to be able to learn dressmaking and earn a decent living. Even though it is difficult on the street, I still look forward to a better future."*

It is generally assumed that there are more boys on the street than girls. The UK's Consortium for Street Children notes that up to 30 per cent of street children are likely to be girls, depending on the country.[16] But it is also possible that street girls are not counted because they are hidden from sight. Many may be working in brothels. Some disguise themselves as boys "to protect themselves from sexual harassment and abuse by other street children, employers, welfare workers and the police. Others tend to appear on the streets only at night."[17]

## 3. "Call me by my own name" – attitudes towards girls on the street

*"You have no one to take care of you. Nobody in the society respects you or wants to see you... People don't care whether you die, whether you live."*

Street girl in Kenya[18]

In addition to all the other problems they face, children on the street are often viewed with fear and suspicion, sometimes to such an extent that their lives are at risk – often from those who are supposed to protect them. As one street child in Bangladesh said: "Everyone calls us 'toakis' (scavengers) or beggars. Hardly anyone calls us by our own names."[19]

Research for this report (see page 83) in the Philippines by Justice for Girls found that "adolescent street girls are called 'buntog', a Cebuano term for the quail. It is a derogatory term equated to mean girl sex workers, girls with loose morals/ promiscuous, or girls allegedly engaging in 'free sex or sex for fun'."

The research also notes that "sexist slurs and curse words are used to verbally abuse girls by family members, peers and the police. Comments such as 'your mother is a prostitute' or simply calling a girl a 'prostitute' demonstrate that 'promiscuity' is viewed as a serious social transgression. Attitudes about appropriate behaviour by girls translate into the view that 'bad' girls are undeserving of protection from the community or police. 'Normal' girls, for them [referring to police], normal and proper girls will not be staying out late. They will be at home by 6pm. But if you are alone with your friends they have the wrong notion."

This can have an effect on girls' behaviour. One girl who ended up working on the streets said: "I realised that to survive I had to become cold and hard and turned in on myself. I had to be tougher and meaner than anyone else, or befriend someone who was meaner."[20] Laura, a street girl from Nicaragua, said: "It's a bit like a horse – if you keep hitting it, after a while it won't take it any more and kicks back."[21]

The other consequence of this widespread public view – which is often also shared by the police and the authorities, as we shall see in the next section – is that it makes it harder to protect street children, and in particular girls.

Cynthia Steele, Chief Executive of Empower, which works with young people in many different countries, says: "Street youth are often caught in cleansing campaigns by police who have government instructions to have them off the street, often especially in capital cities, where governments want to show a different face to tourists and delegations from other countries. Our grantees have told us of such campaigns in Mexico City, St Petersburg and Hanoi, and I am sure they have happened elsewhere. This makes it hard for those trying to work with street children because they are always on the move."[22]

Because girls on the street are regarded by many people as sex workers, and because they have no one to protect them, they are in danger of sexual exploitation and rape. Their futures are also bleak – many are rejected by their families, whose abuse may have been the cause of the girl leaving home in the first place, and they have little possibility of marriage or any kind of stable life. They are likely to become involved in drugs to stem the pain of living on the street. They have no documentation, and so no right to education or healthcare or a vote; and no place to store money safely, so there is no incentive to save. The following feature on street girls in Egypt illustrates just how difficult it is to work with these girls, and how vulnerable they are to mistreatment and abuse.

*Children eating a snack on a bridge over a Dhaka slum.*

# Trust is a dangerous thing
## – girls living on the streets in Egypt

What strikes you first about the little group of girls perched around the table making baskets is how neatly they are dressed. Asmaa, aged 13, is excited about starting school and being reunited with her mother. She is wearing a rainbow-coloured cardigan that reflects her new optimism. Shaimaa, aged 15, has a bright green long-sleeved T-shirt with sparkles on the front and a neat headscarf. Iman, aged 11, has a ponytail and a funky red top. The girls pass a sleeping toddler in pink from shoulder to shoulder as they talk, until at last she is carried out of the room, still sleeping.

The girls are in Alexandria, in one of only two daytime drop-in centres for street girls in Egypt; the other is in Cairo. There are a few other centres, but many demand a virginity test as a condition of acceptance, and others mix street children with much older women.

The four organisations involved in the centre have long been lobbying for a place where girls can also stay the night, away from the many dangers of sleeping in the street. They may yet succeed. But the difficulties are immense. There would be papers to fill in, non-existent identity papers to show, and the moral disapproval of officialdom to encounter.

So for now the girls leave the drop-in centre at night with a little bag of soap and a toothbrush to fend for themselves and each other as best they can before they return in the morning.

"The girls come in the morning and have a shower and some breakfast," says Heba, a social worker at the centre. "They learn to read, they make many different kinds of craft, they have counselling and health check-ups." In one corner on a shelf is what looks like a very large pair of dentures, complete with pink gums. Across it lies an

outsize green toothbrush. Many need even to learn basic things like how to brush their teeth.

The girls at the Alexandria centre are just a handful of the children living on the street in Egypt. No one really knows how many, though the government estimates that there are around 1.5 million between the ages of six and 17. Counting is difficult, not just because the children are not in one place and afraid of the authorities, but also because police simply sweep the streets of children when they know a count is happening. But there are apparently about three times more boys than girls.

The majority of the 90 girls that the centre deals with come from poor families who have coped badly with migration to the city. Family breakdown and violence, drugs and abusive step-parents have finally forced the girls to leave home.

"It takes them much longer to leave than the boys," says Sandra Azmy, responsible for Plan's street children projects in Egypt. "They know that once they leave, they can never go back. As unaccompanied girls, they are considered to be fallen women."

"Yes, and 90 per cent of them would probably be killed if they went back," agrees Hany Maurice Obaid, director of the centre, which is run by Caritas with Plan and two local NGOs. Boys can be forgiven. Girls are cast out forever.

The girls in the centre today are making baskets. They feel that girls have a much harder time on the street than boys. Shaimaa says: "Boys can come and go as they please, smoke cigarettes [she laughs and so do the others], go outside the home. Boys are at liberty to do what they want." Ghada notes that it is more dangerous for girls to go out at night and the girls all nod and point out that girls get harassed more and are in danger of sexual abuse. They also agree, however, that boys are more likely to get hit by other boys or by the police.

In Egypt, street girls are generally considered to be sex workers, socially beyond the pale, and even a security threat.

"They send police vehicles to gather children the way they send vehicles to collect dogs from the street," says Azza Kuraym, the leading expert on juvenile justice and street children at the government-funded National Centre for Social and Criminal Research in Egypt.[23]

These attitudes have made the task of those working with such girls exceptionally difficult. "We knew from the start that there would be lots of problems," says Hany Obaid. "Just reaching the girls takes a lot of time and effort – working daily on the street, handing out leaflets about the centre, building trust among those whose experience has taught them that trusting adults is a dangerous thing because they have been betrayed by adults so many times in their short lives."

This is why advocacy is also part of the centre's remit. There is also a mobile unit which travels the city, offering services that the girls cannot get elsewhere because they are not registered. "It is more difficult and more depressing to work with the girls than the boys," says Mr Obaid. "Many have babies, although they are only children themselves." He tells how in desperation some of the girls may sell their babies, or rent them out to beggars who make more money.

The centre also has threats from the police and authorities that don't see why 'criminals' – though these girls have often done nothing criminal at all – should have a nice time drawing and painting.

When I ask the girls what they would do for girls like them if they were the president of Egypt, Shaimaa says: "I would take all the street girls and put them in a very nice place where they can do whatever they want (not in prison) and go where they want." Iman says: "I would give money to the poor." And then adds vehemently: "And I would burn all the police officers because they are harming people." When we protest politely, she says: "All except one who was nice and gave me food at the police station. But I would burn all the others." Her black eyes burn too. Samar, aged 14, in white, has still not said a word but nods agreement.

Ghada, Iman's sister, dressed all in black with only her round face peeping out, says: "The police pick us up because they don't want us on the street, but we go back there anyway in the end. When they take you, some are good and some are bad and hit us and insult us."

The girls agree that they are taken in not because they have done anything, but simply because the police think they are a nuisance; or people view them as sex workers just because they live on the street. Ghada suddenly blurts out a story about a woman in a detention centre who made them take off all their clothes and lie on the floor and then lashed them with a whip.

I ask them about their own wishes for the future. Ghada says: "I used to want to go to school and become a doctor." And now? "Now I don't know." Her face falls. "I hope I can go home and pray and be a good person." Asmaa, who is the only one of the group currently in school, says: "I want to become a lawyer so that I can defend other people like me."

Iman suddenly says: "All I wish for is that my parents stop making me beg on the streets everyday." She then bursts into tears and is led out of the room, an arm around her shoulders. I find out later that Iman's parents make her stay on the street come what may. She has to bring back a minimum amount or she is not allowed home. Once she had a bad cut on her leg but had to stay outside until she had the money. It took all night. One of Iman and Ghada's sisters was abducted and raped. The centre social worker had problems getting her treated at all. No one was interested in a street girl. No wonder Iman wants to burn the police.

It is time to say goodbye. But as I leave, Iman has dried her tears and runs shyly in to hang a crocheted scarf around my neck. She made it herself. And it is the exact green of my cardigan.

Nikki van der Gaag

## 4. Why do adolescent girls leave home for the street?

*"My name is Malaika and I am 15 years old. Now let me tell you my story. My life on the streets began when my mother died in 1997. My grandmother took me in after my mother's death, but again disaster struck when she also passed on in 2000. I remained with my aunt, who didn't send me to school and did not care about my well-being. That's when my friend introduced me to street life, which I found to be better than being at home where I was not loved."*
From 'Testimonies from Zambia: Streetchild'

There are many reasons why adolescent girls live on the street. As we have seen, some still spend part of their time with their families. The reasons why girls leave bear some similarity with the reasons that rural girls leave for the city and why girls generally say they run away from home – divorce, abuse at home, abandonment, poverty. When poverty compels families to send their girls on to the street, particularly in conservative cultures, this is often the last resort, and the girls are often forced into high-risk behaviours because they have no other option. Don McPhee from Plan Sudan notes that: "The presence of such girls readily available in societies with suppressed sexual expressions puts these girls at high risk, often completely beyond their control and comprehension."[24]

One survey in the Philippines showed that problems at home, particularly violence, were the main reason that street children had left:[25]

- because they are physically abused by their parents or older siblings (21%)
- because they do not like their own homes (21%)
- because they were abandoned by their parents or do not know where they are (15%)
- because their parents were separated or because of their step-parent (6%)
- because they have to earn money (3%)
- because their basic needs were not met or poor conditions at home (2%)

These reasons are not so different in the rich world – the UK's Childline takes calls

G.M.B. AKASH / PANOS PICTURES

*Village girls in Bangladesh.*

from children who feel they need help and cannot get it at home. The majority of callers (65 per cent) are girls between the ages of 12 and 15. The main reasons they give for running away are conflict in the family, including abuse; and problems such as pregnancy, getting into trouble and emotional health issues. Seventy-four per cent of girls calling about running away were between 12 and 15 years old.[26]

### RUKSHANA'S STORY[27]

Rukshana's life is full of movement. She zips through Mumbai's suburbs working wherever she can. At 15, she is her 11 year-old sister Deepa's sole carer.

*"First thing when we wake up, we wrap up all our bedding and hide it in a tree. It's a 10-minute walk from the bridge where we sleep, over the railway tracks near Mahim station. Then I take my sister Deepa to the toilets near the station. We wash our faces, brush our teeth and then go to Uncle's tea stall at Platform 1. After that we go to Bandra for breakfast, and then start work.*

*We go to the shelter outside Dadar station [Mahim, Bandra and Dadar – and the names that follow below – are all areas in Mumbai or suburbs], take our goods from the locker and go into the local trains to sell them. I sell trinkets, clips, cookery and henna pattern books in the trains. Before we had the locker we used to keep all our stuff under our heads and sleep. Even when you sleep, you have to be alert. If you are deep in sleep, not only will someone take your goods, they can also pick you up and take you. It happened to one girl I know. A gang of boys picked her up and took her to Dadar Tilak bridge and did bad things to her. She had to have stitches. The boys were taken to the police station. She cried for many days. Everyone said to her: 'You are disgraced!' She thought: 'Whatever I do I am shamed, so why should I live like this?' That's why she chose to go into wrong work as a sex worker.*

*At one o'clock, we go for lunch at Bandra Platform 7, Hotel Bismillah [a café; eating places are often called 'hotels' in India]. It's my favourite place. The boy I was supposed to marry worked there. That's why I go there. He left long back, but still I go. Now he works with a caterer. Sometimes he comes to meet me. He cries and says: 'If only we had gotten married.' My mother used to love him a lot. But I didn't marry him. I was forced to marry someone else.*

*After lunch, we rest for an hour. Then we are in the trains till 9pm. After that, it's back to a café to eat and drink tea. Then to sleep at Mahim or, if I feel like it, Virar station [Mumbai's most distant suburb]. We just put down some newspaper sheets and sleep. At Virar station it's great – no tension of boys or police. Here in Mahim, boys come and harass us."*

### Begging

Some street girls become beggars. Begging is usually believed to involve very young children, but increasingly adolescent girls are forced into poverty and resort to begging, where they often face both violence and insecurity. They may be captured by organised begging cartels who break their limbs or mutilate them in some other way in order to gain more sympathy from the public. Many beggars are in fact migrants – a study of beggars in Delhi, India, found that only five per cent originally came from the city. Almost half were migrants from Uttar Pradesh and Bihar. The survey also found that a third of all beggars suffered some sort of disability, while 30 per cent were below the age of 18.[28]

In Pakistan, The University of Karachi's Centre of Excellence for Women's Studies interviewed beggar girls from 17 districts across Karachi city, most of whom were adolescents between 12 and 17. They found that the numbers of young and adolescent girl beggars was on the rise.[29]

- 78 per cent of the girls were between one and 15 years old. Only nine per cent were between six and eight years old.
- 34 per cent said they had migrated to Karachi and had been there for at least six years.
- 17 per cent said they had sexual experience, with 15 per cent saying it was consensual and two per cent saying it was in order to get work.
- Three per cent said they had been raped, some by relatives. One girl was sent to customers by her father.

## 5. "I wish I was a boy" – sexual exploitation and abuse of adolescent girls

*"A lot of men from the general public or from nearby offices come to the river. These then solicit sex from girls… A man comes and picks whoever they want to have sex with. If I am picked, I leave my child with the other girls and take the client down to the river."*

Tanya, 14, Harare, Zimbabwe[30]

We have seen that violence affects all adolescent girls in the city, whether they are rich or poor. But living on the streets, whether they are there all the time or not, puts them particularly at risk.[31] Once on the street, girls experience staggering levels of violence, from assaults by passers-by, abuse through sex work, rape and assault

*Begging on the streets of Harare.*

by boyfriends and male street 'brothers', extreme mental and physical cruelty by pimps and drug dealers, to sexual harassment, assault and brutality by police, private security and prison guards.[32]

One study in India with more than 1,000 street girls aged between five and 18 across 13 Indian states found that 68 per cent reported they had been physically abused. Almost half the girls told the researchers that they wished they were boys.[33]

As one report noted: "Street children are generally subjected to physical abuse by family members, caregivers, police and other adults."[34] If you are an adolescent girl living on the street you are likely to need protection from a male, be that another street child or an older male – which is also potentially exploitative. Older men and 'street brothers' often claim to be 'protectors' for young women who are homeless. These men and older boys continue exploitation and violence against girls.

Zerihun Mammo, founding member of the Ethiopian Teenagers' Forum, which is dedicated to working for and with children and youth, is a boy who seeks to protect girls and young women from this fate. He talks of a particular girl whose situation "really touched my heart".[35]

"Ten years ago she came to Addis Ababa from Gondar. She started working in someone's home, and when she was 15 the man who heads the household raped her. When she got pregnant he chased her out of the house and she started living on the street. She gave birth to his child. Three months after she had his child, she was raped again. She is 16 years old and when we saw her it was only four days since she had given birth [again], and she had a one year and two months old baby. I was very sad when I saw her."

One survey by Child Hope found that 95 per cent of girls living on the streets of Ethiopia experienced sexual exploitation.[36] This 18 year old from Zimbabwe was clear about the trade-off that she had to make to keep safe. "My boyfriend… He takes care of me, caters for my daily needs like clothes and food, protects me from other street guys who might want to take me."[37] Such girls often have no option but to sell their bodies in order to eat.

International Labour Organisation statistics reveal that most sexually exploited girls on the street are aged between 11 and 17. Their first sexual experience is often rape, between the ages of 10 and 14.[38] Sexually exploited street girls are at an increased risk of becoming pregnant (9.6 per cent), being physically attacked (29.8 per cent), experiencing police abuse (21.3 per cent), receiving insults (50 per cent), and having access to drugs (42.6 per cent) and alcohol (37.2 per cent).[39] In one study of street children in Cairo, almost two-thirds of children regularly took drugs or solvents, with glue sniffing being the most common substance. The children said they took the drugs "because of peer pressure, to relieve the pressures of the street, to help them sleep, and to help them endure pain, violence, and hunger".

Adolescent girls on the street are in danger not just from adult men, but from older street boys – there are reports of girls having to undergo a sort of sexual initiation rite – and from police and those in authority. Increasing numbers of girls are giving birth on the street, leading to an increase in the number of babies, a 'second generation' of street children.

*The red light district on the outskirts of Bharatpur, India.*

ABBIE TRAYLER-SMITH / PANOS PICTURES

## "IT IS BETTER TO DIE OF AIDS THAN HUNGER."[40]

Tanya is 14. Her parents died of AIDS when she was 10 and since then she has made her living on the streets of Harare, Zimbabwe.

"Life is not easy on the streets. How can you talk to people who are hungry?"

This is Tanya's indirect way of asking for money: "I have not eaten anything since yesterday morning... and I want money to take my 'sister' to the hospital."

Her 'sister' is another street child – Joyce – who sits beside her and listens to her every word. "She has not been well for some time. She has 'njovera' [a Shona word for sexually transmitted infections (STI)]."

Joyce puts her finger on Tanya's mouth to get her to shut up. Then Joyce says accusingly: "She is also suffering from njovera... Tanya, tell the truth!" The girls accuse each other of having an STI. It finally emerges that Joyce has the infection. Tanya explains how she got it. "The streets are full of people who want to hurt and use other people, especially those of us who are younger. So you have to be ready and you must always watch out for yourself. Men pick us up here – not just common men. Joyce was picked up by a man who was driving a Pajero."

Joyce interjects: "The old business guy asked me to take a bath before he slept with me the entire night. The man did not use a condom, because he said that if he did he would only give me a few dollars."

Tanya nods to show that Joyce is telling the truth and continues: "The guys usually ask us to bathe before we have sex with them. Sometimes they give us food... with luck some money as well. We are not doing this because we enjoy it. We know the risks involved, but we are poor and hungry and there is not much else we can do.

*Some sugar daddies [older men involved in relationships with young girls, sexually abusing them for money] are our clients because they have the money to give us. I know it sounds scary, but just think of yourself in the same situation: what would you do if you were a street kid with the chance to make Z$20,000 [$3] just for having sex with someone?*

"Even if they don't use a condom, it's not like I was ever going to make much out of my life anyway. I don't see myself ever leaving these streets and having a better life, so I might as well do something that will help me to survive for the moment as tomorrow is another day.

"I'm afraid to visit the hospital for HIV tests. But if I cannot have sex with these men, eventually I'll die of hunger. It is better to die of AIDS than hunger."

As she speaks, her eyes show the telltale signs of a person who has had no decent sleep in a long time. Her eyelids look heavy and she explains that she spends most of her nights half-awake, warding off potential bullies and rapists, while the days are spent rummaging through bins and rubbish heaps in search of edible scraps.

"I have a dream," she says, "to go back to school and learn how to speak English – good English. I can already speak a little bit of English, just to beg from white people."

## 6. The role of the police in 'protecting' girls on the streets

*"We hate cops. We're not best of friends because they sometimes beat us up, accusing us of loitering and littering the city. My life is one of constant fear of being caught by the police."*

Tanya, 14, Harare, Zimbabwe[41]

Negative attitudes towards adolescent girls on the streets, as we have seen, mean that they are at risk of violence and abuse, not only from street children and adults but also from the police and those authorities which are meant to protect them.

This section of the report will look at the reasons why street girls are detained by the police. It will profile and analyse the ways that violence and police brutality function as a form of 'policing' young women's behaviour on the streets. The nature of police brutality against adolescent street-involved or homeless girls will be outlined.

Sometimes girls are detained because they have committed a crime, but more often it is because they are seen to have offended some kind of moral code by being on the street. High media coverage, especially of female youth crimes, has resulted in negative portrayals of girls in conflict with the law and the criminalisation of 'offences' for which an adult could not be charged – such as just being out on the street or having a tattoo.[42]

A UNICEF report noted: "The risks for children who are perceived as 'criminal' begin even before arrest... Sexually exploited girls, including those who report rape, are at particular risk of being criminalised and experiencing further sexual violence in detention. In many countries, children who have committed no offence are taken into police custody for 'their own protection'."[43]

The Consortium for Street Children notes that: "In some countries the criminal justice system is used to warehouse homeless children."[44] Street children are arrested "for being victims of commercial sexual exploitation, for begging, 'vagrancy' and for 'status offences' such as truancy, 'running away from home', and being 'beyond parental control'." It notes that: "In these cases, although technically in conflict with the law, children in this category are actually victims of legislation that needs urgently to be reformed."

A study in Dhaka, Bangladesh, involved researchers who were street children themselves. They found that nearly all the street children they spoke to were involved in hazardous and low-paid activities in order to ensure at least one meal a day. They reported: "As we don't have any relatives in Dhaka City, we have to live under the open sky at night, after working hard for the whole day. We never get involved in any 'bad' activities. Actually, we do not have enough time to do anything else but work. The police pick us up every now and then without any specific reason. According to our research, police caught 20 children out of 30 without having any specific case against them. These children were accused of 'sleeping on the street'. If children have no other option but to sleep on the street, is it their fault?"[45]

Girls who live or work on the street are easy targets for police violence because they are young, poor, unaware of their rights and lack the consistent protection of adults.[46] According to Human Rights Watch: "Street children [and homeless children] throughout the world are subjected to physical abuse by police or have been murdered outright,

as governments treat them as a blight to be eradicated – rather than as children to be nurtured and protected. They are tortured or beaten by police and often held for long periods in poor conditions. Girls are sometimes sexually abused, coerced into sexual acts, or raped by police."[47]

For example in Bangladesh, Amnesty International has documented how young homeless girls taken into 'safe custody' during police investigations into rape allegations are reportedly exposed to further sexual abuse at the hands of 'law enforcement' authorities.[48]

## Born as girls: violence and abuse by police

*"I have been on the streets for nine years and it was very, very hard for me because my mother passed away in 1996 and I got my stepdad because I didn't know my father at all. My stepdad used to take alcohol. My sister wanted to go away because he was drunk. My sister left to be with her friends. My stepfather once sexually abused me. That's when I ran away from my house. I told the neighbours and they just said to me I must tell the police. So I told the police. My stepfather paid the police and after that they stopped bothering him."*
Precious, 18, Durban, South Africa

So how does this violence affect adolescent girls differently from boys and young men? We have seen that there is inevitably a

*Precious*

# THE RIGHTS OF GIRLS IN CONFLICT WITH THE LAW UNDER INTERNATIONAL LAW[49]

Girls living on the street may be more likely to come into contact with the law than other groups of children. According to the UN Committee on the Rights of the Child: "It is particularly a matter of concern that girls and street children are often victims of criminalisation."

Yet there are well-elaborated international standards governing juvenile justice systems and children's rights. The UN Convention on the Rights of the Child (UNCRC) contains several provisions which relate specifically to children in conflict with the law. Article 37 protects the rights of children who are arrested and detained and prohibits torture or cruel, inhuman or degrading treatment or punishment and illegal and arbitrary detention of children. Article 40 sets out principles for a child rights-compliant juvenile justice system and rights of children who are being processed through the criminal justice system.

A number of other international instruments apply to children in conflict with the law. These include the UN Guidelines for the Prevention of Juvenile Delinquency (Riyadh Guidelines) 1990, the UN Standard Minimum Rules on the Administration of Juvenile Justice (Beijing Rules) 1985, the UN Rules for the Protection of Juveniles Deprived of their Liberty (Havana Rules) 1990, and the Vienna Guidelines for Action on Children in the Criminal Justice System 1997. While, in contrast to the UNCRC, these instruments are not binding on governments, they do evidence an international commitment to abide by their provisions; and they elaborate the obligations of governments set out in the UNCRC to create a child rights-compliant juvenile justice system, and ensure that the rights of children in conflict with the law are protected. Additional sources include the Report of the independent expert for the United Nations study on violence against children, 61st Session UN General Assembly, 2006, A/61/299; and the World Report on Violence against Children, Paulo Sérgio Pinheiro, published by the United Nations Secretary-General's Study on Violence against Children, Geneva, 2006.

The UNCRC and other international commitments require a response to children in conflict with the law which promotes a child's sense of dignity and worth, respect for human rights and the desirability of reintegrating and assuming a constructive role in society. Governments should set a minimum age for criminal responsibility, and this age should not be lower than 12 years. 'Status' offences should be abolished and behaviour such as truanting or vagrancy should be dealt with through a country's child protection system. Governments must create a separate system for children in conflict with the law, which takes account of their age and unique vulnerabilities. Alternative, or diversionary, measures for dealing with child offenders should be developed and used heavily: rather than passing children through formal criminal justice systems, they should be offered support and services to address the root causes of their offending. Imprisonment should be a last resort and used only for the shortest appropriate period of time.

Other international instruments that apply to all persons in the criminal justice system when they are arrested, tried, sentenced and detained, will also apply to children. The International Covenant on Civil and Political Rights (ICCPR) contains rights to fair trial, prohibitions on illegal and arbitrary detention, provisions on treatment in detention and a prohibition on torture and cruel, inhuman or degrading treatment or punishment. While these standards are not specifically tailored to the unique needs and conditions of children, they nonetheless provide fundamental safeguards and rights for children who are in conflict with the law.

sexual dimension to the abuse of girls and young women. There are different ways that street-involved or homeless young women are 'policed', from isolating a girl for not conforming to social norms, to using violence to keep a girl 'in line', to using the formal justice system to 'police' a girl's behaviour.[50]

The Bangaldesh study on children in conflict with the law in Dhaka showed that it is common for girls to be punished by police for activities in which they are not the criminal but the victim (sex work and rape) and also for offences labelled by the police as 'sexual deviance'. Adolescent street girls are much more affected by the police because they are often treated as commercial sex workers, regardless of the context. Police target street-involved girls as being sexually 'deviant', and make judgments and assumptions about their behaviour, although they have no evidence upon which to convict girls of committing a crime.

Pakhi, aged 15, is one such girl. She was sleeping at a railway station with her friend Jostna when the police came at midnight and asked them to go with them to the police station. "Pakhi wanted to know why. The policemen replied that they suspected them of being involved in commercial sex work. Pakhi tried to convince them that she was not involved in such activity. The policemen refused to believe them, saying that they very well knew what street girls did and forced them to go to the local police station."[51]

Other young women agree to have sex with the police in return for protection. "We make friends with the police, so that they will treat us well and watch out for us while we sleep in the park, and release us quickly if we are detained," said Nawal, aged 19, from Egypt. Ilham, a 15 year-old runaway, told Human Rights Watch that she would rather work as a housemaid despite the abuse of her employers than live on the street and be forced to sell sex in return for protection:
*"I don't want to be like the other girls, who befriend police or boys, because they might force me to do something I don't want to do. Something sexual. And then later, when I marry, I might be walking with my husband and the police officer might stop me, or the boy greet me, and then what would I say? It*

SUJAN, AGED 16, STREET CHILD PHOTOGRAPHY PROJECT, BANGLADESH

*is better to keep to yourself. I befriend girls, but only girls. And any girl who does those filthy things, I stay away from."*[52]

Magistrates often order 'deviant' girls into 'safe' custody in a police or detention centre where they are subjected to further abuse. In Pakhi's case, the magistrate sent her to Dhaka Central Jail. According to Pakhi, the magistrate did not ask any question relating to her alleged involvement with sex work. "Pakhi was in Dhaka Central Jail for two months, where she was regularly beaten by the adult women prisoners. Whenever she would cry out loudly, the other girls would say: 'Don't cry. You will not get any benefit from crying. All of us are here to expiate for our sins, as we were born as girls.'"[53]

In Nigeria too, police and security forces commit rape in many different circumstances, both on and off duty. The Director for Women's Affairs within the Ministry for Women's Affairs told Amnesty International in February 2006: "Around 60 per cent of violence against women is committed in army barracks or police stations."[54]

This is despite the fact that rape is a crime under Nigerian national law and is an internationally recognised human rights violation. Very few perpetrators are prosecuted. The Amnesty report tells what happened to two young women students, aged 17 and 18, who were abducted by two men with Nigerian Police Force badges when returning home from the market.

A girl works on the Dhaka railway line.

They were forced to go with the officers to the police detective college. They were subsequently taken to the home of one of the men, having been told that they would be safer there than in custody. They were, however, repeatedly raped: "A detective colleague came into the house, he smelled of alcohol… He shouted 'shut up' and said we should take off our clothes. He took out a gun and showed us the bullets, and pulled off his clothes. He raped me three times. Afterwards I was crying and he looked for fuel to take us back. It was around midnight we were brought to other men who raped us too as payment for the petrol."[55]

The report contains many similar testimonies by young women and states that: "Women and girls who are raped by state actors in Nigeria have little hope of obtaining justice and reparation… Prosecutions for rape are brought in only a small number of cases. Victims are sometimes pressured into withdrawing the case or parents of victims prefer financial settlement out of court to a criminal prosecution… In the few cases where a conviction is secured, judges seldom impose the maximum sentence."

In Bulgaria, Antonia, who begs in a market in the city of Varna, told of her detention by police for five days. She is eight years old. "I've been taken to the police station many times. Once I stayed for five days. There was a jar in the cell in which we could go to the bathroom. There were three other girls in the cell with me. There was only one big bed, so we all shared it. There were no blankets. While I was there, the police handcuffed me and put a hat over my head so I couldn't see anything, and started beating me with a chain."[56]

Because young women are rarely charged, tried or sentenced, their interaction with the police often remains hidden and without formal recognition. They are often detained until officials decide they may be released.

A report on Papua New Guinea by Human Rights Watch showed how homeless girls and those forced into sex work are routinely placed in detention, where they are assaulted by police. Such instances were described as "cases involving opportunistic abuses of power".[57]

# 7. "We have dreams too" – street girls' resilience

*"We have dreams too, and no dreams are too small."*

Cynthia, 15, Philippines[58]

Young women themselves use a number of strategies to cope with life on the street. They may band together with other girls, or with mixed groups of girls and boys, or older women. Catherine, aged 11, sells vegetables and fruit in Harare, the capital of Zimbabwe. Her mother left her father when he beat her up, but is not a well woman. Catherine says that her mother's friends help to look after her: "These women are like mother hens to me. I am grateful for their support. If it were not for them, my mother would have died and my sister would have been out of school. They contributed a great deal towards my mother's medication."[59]

One study notes that: "Street children are often involved in mutually supportive relationships, with solidarity and self-support amongst children's groups more prominent than violence."[60] Another report on street children in Kenya noted: "Life on the streets is not all about violence and abuse. The children develop strong friendships and a spirit of mutual support and assistance. They play, sing, watch videos, tell each other stories and sometimes go to church together, among other activities."[61] As this street child in the Philippines pointed out: "Our lives are sometimes at the top, sometimes at the bottom, but we can still surmount problems."[62]

*Struggling to earn a living in Zambia.*

MANOOCHER DEGHATI / IRIN

## SUMI AND THE STREET GIRLS OF DHAKA, BANGLADESH

Sumi is 15. She escaped from her home after her parents' separation and because of abuse inflicted by her stepmother. She fled to Dhaka city where she started living in a park. Sumi became addicted to drugs and was forced to hand over her earnings to the street gangs and the patrol police. A police officer raped her and she started having health problems.

The NGO Aparajeyo Bangladesh and its partner Child Hope[63] are working together on a five-year action-based research project with nearly 1,000 street child victims of sexual abuse and exploitation like Sumi. The project's main focus is to reduce the incidence of sex work, raise awareness of safer sexual practices, improve living and health conditions, and promote greater community tolerance and understanding.

Most importantly, the project creates a protective environment for children, providing emotional and material sources needed to achieve their potential and to empower them to take decisions about their future. A drop-in centre encourages children's attendance and assures a friendly environment through recognition of dignity, tolerance and acknowledgement of the rights of children. Preventive and curative healthcare services and medicines are provided. Medical aid is made available for all the children attending the centre and health workers and doctors attend to the patients. After the first year of the project, more than 70 per cent of the children who attended the centre felt that their health condition was better than at the time of enrolment. An important part of the project is centred on counselling and group motivation to face the psychological problems and trauma derived from the abuse and exploitation that children suffer. The project's main success lies in the fact that it prioritises children's participation, so that they actively influence their own and other children's lives. For example, the Children's Development Bank, which is part of the project, is a savings and loan scheme run by children that encourages children and young people to save for their future; and offers credit to children old enough to use it, for example, to start up a new business. It also teaches skills in maths, bookkeeping and accounting. A children's committee even approves the loans. Peer support involves older children doing outreach to encourage children involved in sexual exploitation to seek help from the project. They often win the trust of other children more easily than the adult social workers.

When she first came to the project, Sumi often cried because she believed that her life was spoilt due to the actions of her stepmother. She started studying and gradually began to believe that she could succeed in her life. She became the manager of the Children's Development Bank and gives peer support to other children. Now her dream is to be a social worker herself.

*Girls outside the stock exchange in Mumbai.*

Adolescent street girls need an internal sense of self-belief – something which is hard to retain when all those in the adult world seem to despise you. They also need to develop skills such as leadership and empathy with other street children. They need a sense of something outside themselves, be it religious or other moral codes. They need positive relationships with others, including adults, and ideally with family members. They need protective bodies, such as community or non-governmental organisations which can help them.[64] What they want from others is simple: respect. As one child from the Philippines said: "I wish that our community and government would love us and guide us and not be ashamed of us."[65]

Recognising the importance of networking and solidarity for children on the street, movements of street children have grown up in many parts of the world. In Brazil, the National Movement of Street Boys and Girls was established in 1985.[66] It has gone from strength to strength since then. Today, there are 10,000 children and adolescents involved in all the major cities. Not only have they improved their own lives, but they have taken part in political action at national, regional and local levels.

This kind of involvement of young people in making decisions about matters that concern them is becoming increasingly recognised at all levels. They are the experts on what they need and on how cities can be made better places for youth. The internet and communications technologies mean that young people can share ideas about urban life and about how best to participate in decisions made at city level.

Many of these movements are now led by children themselves. In India, street and working children have formed themselves into the Bal Mazdoor Union (BMU) or Child Workers' Union.[67] The Movement of African Working Children and Youth is a Pan-African organisation that was started in 1994 by a group of girls who were domestic workers in Dakar. It operates through local groups and has a system of democratic elections to a central council. The young people themselves created a list of 12 rights that they believe should apply to working children, many of whom work on the street.

1 The right to training to learn a trade
2 The right to stay in your home village (rather than being forced to leave your family and work in a town)
3 The right to carry out our activities in safety
4 The right to work which is limited in hours and not too heavy
5 The right to rest when sick
6 The right to respect
7 The right to be heard
8 The right to healthcare
9 The right to learn to read and write
10 The right to have time for play and leisure
11 The right to express ourselves and to organise
12 The right to have recourse to justice that is fair and unbiased if we have problems.

Fabrizio Terenzio, the coordinator of ENDA, a Senegalese NGO that supports the Movement, says: "The most important thing that the Movement has done is to create hope for the millions of children who have had little hope, because their life is a hard one in which they have only one trump card: the force of their own will."[68]

There are safe and supportive environments which help girls on the streets to rebuild their lives and find sanctuary. But some of the care and detention homes which are supposed to help girls on the streets may either not be sufficient to protect them or may even be perpetuating the abuse. In one study in India, between 35 and 40 per cent of girls reported physical abuse during the time they were in care and shelter homes which were supposed to protect them from the street. Seventy-five per cent of girls in institutions because they had been in conflict with the law reported physical abuse, compared with 67 per cent of boys.

Many experts believe that except in extreme cases, a 'welfare' approach to protecting girls on the street is not effective. One report noted that the proliferation of drop-in centres that provide food and shelter in many cities has led to street children 'shopping around' for the best deal, and fails to help them consider their situation on the streets and what the alternatives might be. It notes that it is better to train girls and young women to protect themselves, and provide them with non-formal learning opportunities.[69]

Projects with adolescent street girls need above all to listen to what the girls themselves have to say, and to use existing legislation to ensure that protection means they are protected rather than abused yet again. We owe this and more to girls like Trina, Precious and Tanya. We have seen their strength, energy and resilience in the face of adversity. There is no excuse not to match this with our own, and to ensure that during the next decade of the 21st century no girls will have to live on the streets of our cities.

## THE *HOGAR DE QUERUBINES* (CHERUB HOME)[70, 71]

In December 2003, Casa Alianza Honduras opened a hostel called the 'Cherub Home' to look after 60 girls who had fallen victim to commercial sexual exploitation. It now looks after an additional 20 to 25 girls each year. At the centre, the girls receive food, clothing, schooling and training in vocational skills in addition to spiritual, psychological and emotional support. "We aim to give them back the rights that have been taken away from them. We give them the childhood, love and assistance they should have had with their families," says Bessy Valle, the director.

Andrea is one of the girls supported by the Cherub Home. Now 14, she left her home to escape six years of physical abuse by her stepfather. "I had no sense of what it was like to be a child. I had had enough." Andrea, the eldest of five girls and three boys in her family, fended for herself for a month until an uncle tracked her down. He threatened that if she didn't go with him, he would tell her stepfather and she would be returned. He offered to help and take care of her. "I thought he would help me. He told me so. I was naïve to think he would. I would have been better to stay and continue being beaten."

It took 15 days for Andrea's uncle to drive them to Chiapas, Mexico. When they arrived, he took her to a church and asked the local priest to bless her. When the blessing was over, they stepped out of the church and her uncle tried to shove her into a taxi. He was selling her for 20,000 pesos (about $1,800) to a 50 year-old man who wanted to live with her permanently and to exploit her sexually. "I refused and did not get in the taxi. I ran back to the hostel where we were staying. My uncle was so mad, he beat me and raped me."

Andrea has been living at the Cherub Home for nearly a year. She was able to tell the authorities what happened and they arrested her uncle.

*"He said I lied. He said I had agreed. I was scared. He threatened to kill me when he gets out of jail. But being in this home, I feel safe. They have oriented me. I have dreams and I hope I can continue to move forward. I hope to God that nothing has happened to my sisters."*

At risk on the nighttime streets of Dhaka, Bangladesh.

MANOOCHER DEGHATI / IRIN

# The forgotten few
## – adolescent girls' experiences of detention and rehabilitation in two cities in the Philippines

The presence of girls in public space in cities may raise suspicion, and enhances the likelihood that they will be criminalised and exposed to dehumanising conditions in jails for their protection, or institutionalised in rehabilitation centres.

This research was commissioned by Plan for this report. It was carried out by Justice for Girls International in the Philippine cities of Manila and Cebu.[72] It shows how many marginalised girls in the Philippines are at risk because of their age and sex. Because of their sex, they are cornered at the intersection of two interconnected forces: the power of the state, and patriarchy. Because of their age, those who come into contact with the juvenile justice system are vulnerable to institutional abuse and violence.

Many girls are criminalised for offences that are directly connected to their efforts to survive and cope in highly dangerous, volatile and turbulent living environments. Much like their male counterparts, they are frequently criminalised for offences related to poverty, including stealing and substance abuse. In the context of pervasive male violence, girls' coping strategies place them at greater risk of being criminalised for status offences, survival theft, and accusations of crime by an employer. In some cases they also engage in violence themselves in an effort to pre-empt or protect themselves from the ever-present threat of violence in their communities. In many cases they are also criminalised for their own protection, frequently for offences such as curfew violations, which are directly connected to gender expectations and the paternalistic sentiment that views girls as needing protection.

### THE FACTS
- Estimates indicate that girls comprise less than 20 per cent of children arrested by police in the Philippines and less than 10 per cent of those held in detention.[73]
- At least 20 per cent of girls in detention had been victims of child abuse, and a third had been sexually abused.[74] Fathers, brothers and other male relatives were predominantly cited as the perpetrators.[75]
- Girls account for more than two-thirds of child-abuse survivors and 98 per cent of sexual abuse cases of the children handled by the Department of Social Welfare and Development (DSWD).[76]
- Three of the 17 girls we spoke with disclosed that they were victims of sexual violence, with almost all reporting they knew of girls in their communities who had been victims.
- Five of the 17 girls reported running away to escape violence at home.

### Stealing to survive
Many girls we spoke to came from families of five to nine children, often living in one-room dwellings where they sleep, eat and socialise as a family. In some cases, multiple generations of the same family live in overcrowded dwellings with as many as 14 people living under the same roof. Living in these conditions poses serious risks to girls' mental and physical well-being, putting them at increased risk of violence, both in and outside the home; often requiring that they find work in dangerous and exploitive conditions to help support their families.

Many girls in this situation do not make a monetary income. Rather, their labour is exploited in dangerous, labour-intensive jobs simply in exchange for food. For example, 13 year-old 'Lisa' has a job working at weekends cleaning the public toilet in exchange for food to feed herself. Other girls reported doing similar forms of child labour, including selling items in local malls for up to 12 hours per day for food and no pay. 'Kyla' worked as a sales clerk for only one week because "they don't feed us so we had to bring our own food".

Q. *How long would you work?*
A. *8am to 7.30pm.*
Q. *For how much?*
A. *100 pesos [$4.30] per day. But I had to spend seven pesos to travel by Jeepney because it was too far to walk. It was too dangerous to walk late at night.*

Others receive pennies per day working in toxic environments scavenging, selling goods, working as food vendors or tricycle drivers. 'Nicole-May' recounts her experience grilling chestnuts as a street vendor. "I got sick from the smoke, there was so much heat and so much smoke."

Girls may find themselves in a position where petty theft provides the only option to find money for food and subsistence. The most common crime committed by children is theft. 'Hannah' was in a rehabilitation centre for almost five years for snatching money from a woman in a shopping mall so she could pay for transport to get home. Most commonly, girls are arrested for stealing things like cell phones and other items to help their families or feed themselves.

'Ana Maria' stole "because that was the time her father did not have a job and the income of her mother as a laundry woman was not enough. Her mother actually knew that she had stolen something because she gave her part of the proceeds. Her mother just told her not to say anything."

Many girls also end up in the illicit street economy, coerced and trafficked by adults into commercial sexual exploitation, selling drugs or acting as accomplices. Parents and family members are complicit in getting the girls to steal. One girl reported that her neighbours got her involved in selling drugs, an offer she could not turn down in the face of hunger and family pressure.

Q. *What did you sell?*
A. *Shabu. A white powder smoked through a metal container.*
Q. *Where did you get it?*
A. *The neighbours... friends of the family.*

## Daily violence in the lives of girls in trouble with the law

Girls constantly navigate the threat of male violence and child abuse in every corner of their communities, with home frequently representing the frontline rather than a source of refuge. The threat of violence puts them at much greater risk of becoming criminalised as they try to survive, later serving as the justification for depriving them of their liberty in order to 'protect' them.

Statistics in the Philippines demonstrate that girls in trouble with the law have experienced very high rates of male violence and child abuse in their homes, with one study reporting that at least 20 per cent of girls in detention had been victims of child abuse. Every child in this study had witnessed and experienced violence from multiple sources in their homes and communities. Many girls reported witnessing their fathers abuse their mothers or siblings and engage in extreme forms of violence.

*"When Sara's father gets drunk he quarrels with her mother. He got a gun and attempted to shoot her mother. She just cried."*

'Sara', via interpreter

Girls described physical abuse at the hands of their fathers, brothers, cousins and grandparents.

*"The sins of my siblings are all on me. My brother kicks me and hits me on the back of my head."*

'Nicole-May'

Additionally, girls reported regular beatings from parents and siblings.

*"If [I]commit a mistake, father spanks [me]. He hits [me] with a belt."*

'Sara'

*"Grandma hits me, when I don't bring anything home from begging."*

'Marialene'

Sexual abuse by male family members is common, with girls more vulnerable to child sexual abuse than boys.

Girls also run away from home to escape violence. In one study, children reported 73 per cent of the time that child abuse by a family member was the reason they left home.[77]

MIKKEL OSTERGAARD / PANOS PICTURES

*Homeless young woman living on a beach in Manila.*

been in jail for months awaiting trial for the death of her abusive male partner:
*"I couldn't speak...he threw me and pushed me against the wall face first and punched me in the neck... I grabbed the first thing I could, a knife..."*

## Policing gender and regulating morality

One reason girls are under-represented among street children is largely connected to family expectations that they remain in the home to help with domestic chores and family care.[78] This was evident among the girls we interviewed, who frequently helped their mothers by cleaning, caring for siblings and other domestic work. Girls' morality is heavily regulated both formally and informally. At home, girls may be punished violently by male family members for violating curfew, leaving the house or for perceptions that they are 'flirting'. Speaking of her friends, 'Kyla' says "their fathers scold them and physically abuse them because their fathers see them flirting". She continues, referring to the way girls are treated in the streets, "sometimes when girls pass by they are called flirts or prostitutes". The father of 'Nicole-May' physically assaults her when she tries to leave her house.

Stereotypes are also used in the community and social groups to police girls' sexuality. Sexist slurs and curse words are used to verbally abuse girls by family members, peers and the police.

## Police violence

Girls report that they are intimidated by the police and all children report extreme violence used by the police, especially towards boys. But police engage in punching, whipping, slapping, and cuffing children of either sex and putting them in cells with adult offenders, thus deliberately exposing them to violence and humiliation.[79]

*"The police hit [me] on the back of the head and told [me] I was a liar... They held a gun at [my] hand. They threatened to shoot [my] hand because I am a liar."*
'Mischa'

Girls know that police officers and other officials sexually exploit girls and women as both sex traffickers and clients.

Public space is just as violent for girls running away from home. Girls who flee violence at home may be swept up by recruiters and trafficked to urban areas to become domestic workers or turned out to be abused in the commercial sex trade. The commercial sex trade is violent by definition, and violence by employers in domestic settings is common.

Some girls also cope by engaging in violence themselves, in an effort to prevent violence perpetrated against them, almost a form of pre-emptive self-defence. Angelica says she fights because the other girls provoke her: "They say like 'who are you?' 'Are you strong?'... And that provokes [me]..."

Q. *"What was the fight over?"*
A. *"I was a transfer. I was new. They were kind of sizing [me] up and... so [I] offered that we have a one-on-one fight because I was afraid they would hurt me... They were bullying [me]... they slapped [me], pulled my hair and four girls brought me to a place... so [I] offered to fight with the leader of the group... The neck of the other girl was broken."*

Finally, some girls are criminalised for violence they commit in direct self-defence of male violence perpetrated against them. 'Nyca' has

Q. *What do you think of the police? Do you like them?*
A. *No, because the police are womanisers.*
Q. *Can you give me an example?*
A. *They get girls from the bars, sometimes they get them pregnant and then they live with them. They keep them on the side.*

'Kyla'

The girls experienced police violence simply by bearing witness to the brutality enacted on other children and adults upon arrest.

'Angel' was so afraid of the police that she refused to talk about them in the interview. Crying and putting her head in her hands, she continued to express concern that if she said anything about them the police might retaliate by apprehending her brother.

## Discipline and punishment – diversion and jail

In response to international pressure there has been a strong push in the Philippines to minimise the criminalisation and incarceration of children. Major strides were made when the progressive Juvenile Justice and Welfare Act was enacted in 2006. This legislation raised the age of criminal liability from nine to 15 years old, and called for the release of all children incarcerated for crimes they committed before then. However, there has been much resistance to this law and a bill is now pending which would lower the age of criminal liability once more.

## Jails and police cells

Despite the new legislation, which explicitly states that "children shall not be locked up in a detention cell", children are still being placed into jails with adults, in squalid overcrowded conditions with inadequate basic necessities, where they risk violence and environmental hazards. As of May 2008 only 208 of 1,076 of jails reported they had separate cells for minors.[80]

Arrested for minor infractions, children are hauled into police stations or tiny *barangay* jail cells. With no universal standards or oversight, conditions depend upon the resources, politics and integrity of the community. Isolated and vulnerable, most girls are picked up for curfew violations,

theft or substance abuse violations. They are usually held overnight and released in the morning. Some are detained but never charged.[81]

Girls have been deprived of basic necessities, forced to sleep on the floor while adult women sleep on cardboard cartons. As the most vulnerable, they are bullied and threatened with violence from other inmates. Not allowed to eat until the women are finished, they often go hungry, surviving on the leftovers the women provide.

Q. *Did you have food?*
A. *Just the leftovers of the older women. Leftover fried rice and dried fish.*
Q. *Did you get enough to make you feel full?*
A. *I had no choice because I only eat what is given to me.*
Q. *Did you get full?*
A. *No.*

Girls are vulnerable to sexual violence from other inmates as well as police officers. 'Nikalena' was sexually assaulted. Explicitly connected to gender, sexual violence is used as a tactic of humiliation and degradation on both boys and girls. In one report, a child was quoted as stating: "boys become girls inside police detention cells".[82]

## Youth detention centres and pre-trial custody

While the law states that children who are to be detained can be held in youth detention facilities, these may be comparable to or worse than the adult jails. Children are frequently taken to these centres by the police or DSWD social workers after they have spent some time in police or *barangay* jails.

Here, children may spend months in pre-trial detention, as the authorities determine how they are to be processed. Some children are released to their families, while others are moved to other youth facilities and rehabilitation centres. All of the girls we spoke to who were held in these centres were detained awaiting trial.

'Nyca' did not see a judge for over a month after she was incarcerated. She has been in custody for approximately nine months and her trial is still ongoing.

*Philippine street life.*

NIKKI VAN DER GAAG

run by the DSWD. The policy assumes that children who violate the law are "children in need of special protection". It is aimed at recognising the social and economic disadvantage of most children who are criminalised. Informed by principles of restorative justice, the Juvenile Justice and Welfare Act views rehabilitation centres as a more humane and safer way of detaining children who are deemed unfit for diversion programmes. Progressive on paper, this policy should mean that no children will set foot inside prison walls. However, as demonstrated by the children's experiences above, there are many hurdles to overcome before this dream is realised.

The young women in rehabilitation were being held for a range of minor offences. One girl, however, was awaiting trial for defending herself against an abusive husband which ended in his death. The girls' sentences varied, two have an ongoing trial, while three had been on suspended sentence in the rehabilitation centre for four and five years respectively, with no clear idea of when they will be released. This, according to the social workers, is due to the conditions of the discharge, which are based on the situation of a girl's family. The availability of family care and support need to be established before the girls are released.

One girl in custody for theft of a cell phone reveals her vague understanding of the factors that could play into her sentence:

Q. *Do you know when you will leave here?*
A. *Don't know.*
Q. *Have they told you what you need to do in order to leave?*
A. *I still have to attend the hearings. If my behaviour has improved.*
Q. *What do you need to show your behaviour has improved?*
A. *Be nice. Ignore the accusations and bad words from other residents.*

The girls we spoke to did not have a clear idea of when they would be able to return home. Eighteen year-old 'Marialene' has been living in the rehabilitation centre since she was 12 years old and now has doubts over her ability to leave the institution.

The young women express an inability to establish healthy and warm relationships

## Rehabilitation centres

Girls held in rehabilitation centres fall into three categories: Children in Conflict with the Law (CICL), 'Sexually Abused' (SA) by families and communities, and 'Sexually Exploited'(SE) in the sex trade. They are segregated into respective dorms based on commonality of experience for, as the social workers explain, more appropriate intervention planning and development.

Yet the distinction between the three categories is blurred, and the usefulness of distinguishing between them unclear. There is strong evidence that young CICL girls have experienced an array of violence or sexual violence, and have been subsequently criminalised for survival strategies. What is the difference between a child who is caught stealing to feed herself after running away from an abusive parent, and a child who runs away from home and is apprehended in another context and referred to the DSWD? *At the end of the day they are all abused.*[83]

We had conversations with seven girls, currently in rehabilitation centres, who were defined as Children in Conflict with the Law (CICL). Under the new legislation, children who are sentenced to spend time in custody are to be held in rehabilitation centres under a suspended sentence. These rehabilitation centres are with the other girls in the centre. While they report having friends, they characterise these friendships as precarious and superficial. Many girls express concern that they can't trust the others.

*"I only have a few close friends because the others are telling me they want to be friends, but behind my back they are saying bad things."*

'Jendy'

*"There is no one here I can tell my problems to. There is one girl I am close to but I don't feel she is sincere. There is no unity... We don't share problems."*

'Marialene'

Programmes and 'therapy' at the centres involve a number of psycho-social interventions. They focus on trauma associated with sexual violence, through cognitive behavioural therapy, gestalt and reality behaviour therapy. More prominent, however, are the programmes and institutional focus on 'character development'.

The facilities feature a range of activities to prepare the girls for their release, including education programmes, 'character development', social programming and spiritual development. The girls are woken at 4am and engage in a variety of daily activities that consist of a mixture of chores, 'productivity' programming and educational programmes, and sometimes recreation. Productivity classes consist of baking, cosmetology, sewing, computer activities, daily prayer and weekly bible study. They also hold special activities, including film showings, television nights and other recreational events. While some institutions offer regular sports, some only offer sports recreation programmes for one month, with little to no opportunity for vigorous outdoor activities to be structured into the programme for the rest of the year. Although the programmes and education do offer prospects for future employment, there is an obvious focus in the rehabilitation curriculum on feminising the girls and reincarnating their virtuousness.

If the aim of recent changes in legislation in the Philippines is to 'protect' children, girls included, and improve their rights under the law, we must be clear about the definition of 'protection'. 'Protection' (or to be protected/safe) must be conceptualised as a positive state, where it means living free from violence and coercion and with adequate access to basic necessities of life, healthy environments and healthy relationships. It means giving girls equal access to education and meaningful opportunities to achieve their goals. It means ensuring that they have control over their bodies and reproductive health. Addressing criminalisation and institutionalisation of girls, and all the subsequent abuses and violations of their rights that come with it, must begin by a genuine commitment by all parties to tackle the underlying causes of poverty and discrimination.

*Begging in the busy streets of Manila.*

MIKKEL OSTERGAARD / PANOS PICTURES

- Ensure the United Nations Special Representative on Violence against Children has a specific mandate on street girls in their regular country visits, reports and research.
- Include an explicit focus on adolescent girls within the 2011 Human Rights Council discussion day, which is on street children.
- Systematic, sex-disaggregated data should be collected and form the basis for appropriate anti-violence campaigns for girls.

Municipalities should:
- Take concrete action to prevent and punish urban violence against women and girls. This will require **gender-sensitive social policies in crime prevention and community safety**.
- **Enforce a 'zero tolerance' policy** on the use of violence by police against girls who are homeless, girls in slums, and especially street girls. Increase the number of female police officers, especially in units working in poor and slum urban neighbourhoods. Provide appropriate gender and child rights training for police, law enforcement and the judiciary who deal with street girls. Police and local government units should be empowered with the skills, commitment and mandate to address the needs of marginalised girls.
- **Stop criminalising girls' survival strategies** on the streets. Ensure that all children in conflict with the law, including girls, are only detained as a last resort.
- **Provide safe residential spaces, outreach programmes, legal services and helplines for street girls,** where they can receive information, support, counselling and training. Street girls should know their rights, and know which structures they can turn to for help.

## MUNICIPAL POLICIES AND TRAINING FOR SAFE CITIES

### The Safe Delhi for Women Initiative in India.[90]
The project is supported by UNIFEM and implemented in collaboration with the Department of Women and Child Development of the Delhi government, the non-governmental organisation JAGORI and UN-Habitat. At the launch in November 2009, it was noted that: "Violence against women and girls in public places is widespread in Delhi and usually tolerated as a feature of city life. When women complain, they are often ignored or blamed for the abuse – accused of acting provocatively or being inappropriately dressed. The Safe Delhi initiative works towards creating a city that is safe and accessible to women, by mobilising local authorities and community duty bearers and implementing practical measures: for example, in urban planning, policing and transportation. UNIFEM and UN-Habitat have joined efforts on a new global Safe Cities Free of Violence against Women and Girls programme that will support similar initiatives in several cities around the world.

### Police training in Pakistan
In March 2010, Plan Pakistan launched a three-year project of police training and capacity building in Islamabad.

The project, Police Capacity Building on Democracy and Human Rights, is funded by the European Commission and will train 5,000 police personnel from the Islamabad Capital Territory Police and representatives from the Ministry of Social Welfare & Special Education and the National Child Protection Centre in child rights, gender-based violence and human rights tools and their applications,

*Child rights training in Islamabad.*

especially the use of nonviolent methods, police ethics and democracy.

Inspector General of Police Syed Kaleem Imam said: "We look forward to a new face of Islamabad Police and hope that we are able to set an example for the rest of the country... There is a dire need to create awareness about the rights of children, and to root out those reasons which push them to get involved in criminal activities." [91]

The project will help the Islamabad police force, children, families living in Islamabad and the law enforcement agencies, to be aware of and to apply demonstrably international human and child rights standards in their day-to-day work.

### 3 All girls should have the right to secure and decent housing

Not having stable or decent housing can push girls to work on the street or to exchange sex for somewhere to live. For millions of girls, urban housing insecurity lies at the heart of their vulnerability and exposure to violence and exploitation. Girls in slums face unique challenges related to lack of privacy and exposure to violence. And women and girls suffer disproportionately from forced evictions, and find themselves displaced to the periphery of the city. The right to secure and decent housing must be safeguarded for the most vulnerable girls in the city, especially girls who live in slums, girls who live and work on the streets, and girls who are forcibly evicted. Therefore:

BENNO NEELEMAN

National governments and donors should:
- Develop a **national strategy on children's housing rights** which reflects the needs and priorities of adolescent girls. This should be consistent with the standards outlined in the Convention on the Rights of the Child.
- Incorporate a girl-friendly perspective into national policies on housing and urban development, in consultation with girls themselves.

Municipal authorities should:
- Immediately **halt the practice of forced evictions** and ensure secure housing tenure to girls, boys and their families.
- Establish a **dedicated budget stream** to ensure those threatened by eviction are afforded alternative decent housing.

### 4 All girls should have the right to move safely in the city

The threat of gender-based violence and urban crime mean that girls' perceptions of their personal safety can restrict their ability to move freely throughout a city. Lack of urban lighting, water and sanitation services, and safe transportation leaves adolescent girls more vulnerable to gender-based violence. Because adolescent girls often have less access to economic resources, they are more likely to depend on public transport. As shown in Chapter 2, adolescent girls' feelings of insecurity are due to their experiences of sexual harassment and violence while waiting for, using, and walking to and from public transportation. In order for adolescent girls to maximise the opportunities of living in an urban centre, they must be safe, and *feel* safe, in cities. Adolescent girls should be able to use public spaces, go to school and participate in urban life without fear. Therefore:

Municipalities should:
- Ensure that **public transportation is safe, efficient, reliable, and flexible** to girls' needs, and accommodates their daily travel patterns.
- Commission a **strategy with broad-based transportation solutions** that address the safety needs and concerns of adolescent girls.

*Living in a slum in Cairo, Egypt.*

- Provide **training to transport staff** to raise awareness on the barriers girls face when using public transportation, and on the scale and severity of sexual harassment and violence.
- Guarantee that there is **adequate street lighting** to make streets safer for all, including adolescent girls.

Civil society organisations should:
- Launch **public education strategies** to raise awareness of the prevalence of sexual harassment in urban public transportation spaces as an issue of concern for everybody, not just girls and women. This should include information on safety strategies for girls and women when using public transportation.

## SAFE TRANSPORT IN CITIES
A safe city for girls is a city which has secure transportation, not only on public transit systems, but also on footpaths, pedestrian streets, sidewalks and bicycle lanes. Here are some ways that municipalities can design safe public transportation:
- Bus routes that cater to girls' schedules;
- 'Request stop' bus programmes that allow girls to get off buses closer to their destinations late at night and early in the morning;
- Designated waiting areas for bus or subway services, which are well-lit and monitored, so that girls can wait comfortably and safely;
- Subways designed in ways that prioritise the prevention of violence;
- Women and girl-only buses and subway cars in cities where overcrowding has led to sexual, physical or verbal harassment or abuse;
- Affordable public transit;
- Well-lit and clearly visible pathways so that girls can be safe when they walk to and from public transit.[92]

The Adopt-a-Light programme in Nairobi, Kenya, steers commercial advertising revenues into community development. It is inspired by the need to achieve safer cities through the provision of adequate street lighting. Various private companies were asked to 'adopt a streetlight' and in return, the business utilises the streetlight

STAN THEKAEKARA

as a place for advertising. The project was initiated through relations with South African organisations that have been working successfully in partnership with the local councils in nearly all the major cities in South Africa for over six years.[93]

*Public transport in Bangalore, India.*

### 5 All girls should have the right to affordable and accessible services in the city

Urban environments often mean poor girls have inadequate sanitation facilities, unsafe water supplies, and insufficient health services or support. Cities must ensure all public services are not only available but accessible to girls who require them. This means cities must become places where girls' needs are taken into account in municipal service provision, and where every girl has access to decent, affordable, safe, equitable and girl-friendly services. Therefore:

Municipal authorities should:
- Ensure that adolescent girls have **equal access to all urban public services**, including girls who live in slums and street girls.
- Ensure that **slum-upgrading projects** are developed with the needs of adolescent girls in mind: water, sanitation, energy and road infrastructure in urban slums must be built in a way that addresses the unique barriers girls face in accessing services.
- Target municipal budgets to equip and staff **girl-friendly health clinics** in urban slum areas.
- **Conduct systematic reviews** of basic service needs for adolescent girls.

**6 All girls should have the right to age-appropriate and decent work in a healthy urban environment**

This means that no girl would be so poor that she would have to trade her body to survive on the street. Too often, adolescent girls are drawn to the city in search of employment, but become subject to insecure and hazardous labour in the informal economy or on the street. Cities must become places where girls' economic rights and futures are guaranteed, and where girls can use their skills and access these economic opportunities in order to emerge into young adulthood as successful economic citizens. Therefore:

Governments should:
- Ensure girls have **access to quality education** that prepares them to take advantage of future economic opportunities offered by cities. Adolescent girls need business know-how, life skills and technology-based education tied to real market opportunities.

Municipalities should:
- Strengthen opportunities for decent employment in the city. Design and enforce quotas to increase adolescent girls' participation in urban work placement programmes and municipal IT training courses.
- **Monitor guidelines for police and municipal representatives** to ensure they do not discourage petty trading or street vending – frequently the only way girls can support themselves.

The business sector should:
- Encourage **community engagement and outreach** –skilled female staff could routinely visit schools and youth centres to provide positive role models for girls.
- **Expand access to financial instruments for credit and savings**, including microfinance, and to business support services for adolescent girls. Mobile banking units in slum areas should have a specific remit to reach adolescent girls and young women.

DINA TORRANS

**7 All girls should have the right to safe spaces in the city**

*Safe spaces: a youth centre in Udaipur, India.*

Adolescent girls can face obstacles to building friendships and developing safe social networks. Even in cities, girls often have less time, and face restrictions on their ability to engage in social interactions, recreation and organised sports. This is partly because cities lack safe spaces where adolescent girls can go and be together with peers. Safe spaces build self-esteem and leadership skills, and provide important opportunities for girls to exchange information, make friends and learn about critical issues affecting their lives. Girls have a right to laugh, play and make friends in an urban environment. Planning and designing public spaces is an important part of creating cities that are safe for adolescent girls. And a city that is safe for girls is also safe for everyone.

Municipalities should:
- Ensure that **every municipality has dedicated girl-only spaces**. This can include working with community organisations and identifying targeted

budgets for adolescent girls' sports and recreation opportunities in urban centres.

- **Adopt and enforce guidelines for urban planning professionals** to ensure girls' safety is fully integrated in all municipal planning processes.

Urban planners should:

- Design cities in ways that reflect adolescent girls' actual safety concerns, as well as their perceived sense of dangers. To do so, urban planners must **pay constant attention to the ways that adolescent girls use public spaces in cities** – which spaces they are left out of, when and why. Planning professionals should identify all public spaces that are unsafe or risky for adolescent girls.[94]

Civil society organisations should:

- **Integrate girls-only spaces in urban programmes** where adolescent girls can gain confidence, build self-esteem and mobilise together.
- Develop public education campaigns to **engage more adolescent girls in sports and recreation opportunities.**

### KEEPING GIRLS SAFE IN CITIES

Safe Spaces is a very young organisation, founded in early 2008 by Peninah Nthenya Musyimi. Now aged 32, she was the first girl from Nairobi's Mathare slum to graduate from university, which she attended through a basketball scholarship. Safe Spaces is dedicated to creating safe spaces for adolescent and teenage girls in the Mathare slum and to empower them to create a legacy of female-driven development, community leaders and role models for girls in the slums. The aim is also to provide a safe space for young females to voice and discuss their issues.

Gender–Sensitive Public Toilets is a new initiative which began in Nigeria during 2008, the International Year of Sanitation. In north-east Nigeria, many girls and women are constrained by cultural and social norms which restrict them from participating in public activities. Consequently, girls and women do not make use of public facilities that lack privacy. In response, urban planners designed public toilets for girls and women in schools, health facilities, car-parks, markets and other public places. As a result, gender-sensitive public toilets in cities are meeting the cultural needs and societal obligations of Nigerian girls and women.

### 8 All girls should have the right to participate in making cities safer, more inclusive and more accessible

Cities should support girls' active and meaningful involvement in all parts of urban design and management, including public transportation. Girls are experts of their own experiences in cities and they are able to identify what can make cities safer for themselves, and everyone. It is more cost-effective to design urban spaces and services together with women and girls, than to change the infrastructure once it has been put into place. Encouraging girls' participation and contribution to municipal decision-making processes will not only ensure cities are more inclusive and better able to provide services for girls, they will also help foster a new generation of active citizens and future municipal leaders.

Governments should:

- **Listen to adolescent girls, and include their perspectives in municipal policy and planning.** For example, the Growing Up in Cities programme supports children in low-income urban neighbourhoods all over the world to assess their local environments and to work with local officials to improve them.[95]
- **Learn from and adapt good practice** to ensure that both girls and boys meaningfully participate in city design and management. For example, the Child Friendly Cities Movement is a network of city governments committed to involving children in the process of making cities better places for all children.[96]

Municipal authorities should:

- **Conduct an audit of women and girls' safety in cities** to identify the places where adolescent girls feel they are the most vulnerable to violence.
- **Create city youth advisory councils** with equal numbers of girls and boys and allow

them to meaningfully contribute in local council meetings. Youth advisory councils must be inclusive of the diversity of girls in cities, including girls who live in slums and street girls.

- **Collect statistical evidence regarding the experiences of adolescent girls in cities.** This means using 'girls' as a specific lens of analysis, instead of focusing generally on 'youth'.

Civil society organisations should:
- **Provide leadership and life skills training** to build the capacity and confidence of adolescent girls so that they can take an active role in city life.
- Establish the production of an annual **'State of the City's Children Report' which ensures a monitoring and data-collection system on the state of children and their rights.** All data should be disaggregated by age and sex.[97]

### WOMEN'S SAFETY AUDITS
The Women's Safety Audit is a tool that enables a critical evaluation of the urban environment. The Women's Safety Audit tool was first developed in Canada and has been adapted in many cities all over the world.[98] Safety audits help to identify urban security issues and local solutions, together with municipal governments. Adolescent girls, including girls who live in slums and street girls, should be included as key participants in urban safety audits. The results of Women's Safety Audits have included changes to the physical environments of cities to become safer for women and girls; local programmes and policies which better promote girls' and women's safety; increased partnerships between women, girls and their local government, and increased public awareness of gender-based safety issues in cities.[99]

All children and young people should benefit from the opportunities and possibilities available in cities. Adolescent girls should not be disadvantaged because of their age and gender but be able to benefit fully from city life, in ways that are accessible, affordable, safe, adapted to their needs and equitable for all.

PLAN

*Working on their manifesto at the Street Child World Cup.*

# THE STREET GIRLS' MANIFESTO

This report has shown that adolescent girls are the best source of information on their needs. All too often their voices are not heard in crucial decisions about how our cities are planned, designed and governed. The following manifesto comes from street girls and former street girls from seven different countries, who had gathered together in March 2010, in Durban, South Africa, to compete in the first ever Street Child World Cup.

*"We, the girls living and [who] have lived on the streets and those of us in shelters from seven countries [The UK, Tanzania, South Africa, the Philippines, Ukraine, Brazil, and Nicaragua] met during the Deloitte Street World Cup Conference event which took place on 20-22 March 2010, in Durban, South Africa."*

The campaign aimed to raise awareness of the rights of street children and ensure that their voices were heard in the media. A conference was held to gather the opinions and thoughts of the street children themselves.

## WE THE STREET GIRLS HAVE THE FOLLOWING RIGHTS AND WE WANT THEM RESPECTED:

- *The Right to live in a shelter and home*
- *The Right to have a family*
- *The Right to be safe*
- *The Right to be protected from sexual abuse*
- *The Right to go to school and get free education*
- *The Right to good health and access to free health services*
- *The Right to be heard*
- *The Right to belong*
- *The Right to be treated with respect and decency*
- *The Right to be treated as equal to boys*
- *The Right to be allowed to grow normally*

## WE IDENTIFIED THE FOLLOWING WAYS TO BE SAFE IN OUR COMMUNITIES:

- *Step-parents should love all children*
- *Community leaders should punish people who abuse children*
- *Adults should know about child rights*
- *There should be good lighting on the streets*
- *Street children should be treated with decency and respect*

## WE IDENTIFIED THE FOLLOWING FACTORS THAT MAKE US SAFE AT NATIONAL LEVEL:

- *Training for police to keep children safe*
- *Tough laws on child abuse*
- *Good relations between government and children*
- *Put money into support workers who can pay detailed attention to children*
- *Governments should build homeless shelters for street girls to feel safe in*
- *Give us access to education – there should be better security in schools*
- *There should be more social projects*
- *Get rid of corruption*

## WE DECLARED THAT THE FOLLOWING ACTIONS AT A REGIONAL AND GLOBAL LEVEL WILL MOTIVATE OUR GOVERNMENTS TO PROTECT STREET CHILDREN:

- *The whole world should recognise and protect street children*
- *All countries should have good child laws*
- *Girls should be allowed to speak and be heard*
- *There should be awareness campaigns about street children*
- *There should be more awareness of the problem of violence.*

# Adolescent girls and communications technologies – opportunity or exploitation?

## 1 Introduction

*"I'm interested in technology, multimedia – the business. I love entertainment, music, I'm meeting new people. [In school] I was exposed to media, the web, the internet... I loved it, that's where I could connect with my friends."*

Tibusiso Msibi, student, 18, Swaziland[1]

## Summary

In this chapter, we look at one of the most dynamic and fast-changing arenas of the 21st century – communication technology – and how it affects adolescent girls in particular. We will show how online patterns of behaviour and who has access to technologies are a reflection of the way that society operates offline. We examine how attitudes towards the empowerment – and the abuse – of adolescent girls reveal themselves through technology, as they do in other areas of their lives. Using case studies, girls' voices, expert opinion and original research, we highlight the positive and negative consequences of communications technologies – and in particular mobile phones and the internet – for adolescent girls all over the world. We show how information and communications technologies (ICTs) have exposed adolescent girls and young women to new ideas and ways of thinking that open up huge possibilities for learning, networking, campaigning and personal development. We then explain the darker side of these technologies: how cyberspace is an arena where sexual predators can operate with impunity. The internet creates new intimacies that seem safe, magnifying the power of the peer group and inviting in the stranger. Adolescent girls and young women are prime targets for new methods of abuse, including trafficking, via the internet, mobile phones and other communications technologies. They are also sometimes the perpetrators themselves. And this danger is expanding exponentially as ever more sophisticated new technologies arrive on the scene. Greater knowledge about ICT-related sexual exploitation and violence against girls is needed, and more emphasis on prevention and stronger international standards is critical. Girls need to be empowered to use the new communications technologies safely, on their own terms and in ways which promote their development and build their future.

### DEFINING ICTS

Information and communication technologies (ICTs) can include the whole range of technologies used for communication, from the telephone and radio to the latest social networking technologies. The World Bank definition is: "the hardware, software, networks, and media used to collect, store, process, transmit, and present information in the form of voice, data, text, and images."[2] This technology is changing all the time. In recent years or even months, there has been increasing convergence of computer-based, multimedia and communications technologies – for example, the ability of mobile phones to be used much like a computer. In this report we will be mainly looking at computers and mobile phones, which, as we will see, are the technologies most used by adolescent girls around the world.

## 2 The digital revolution and the digital divide

*"Mobile phones and wireless internet… will prove to be the most transformative technology of economic development of our time."*

Jeffrey Sachs, Director of the Earth Institute at Columbia University, US[3]

*"The so-called digital divide is actually several gaps in one. There is a technological divide – great gaps in infrastructure. There is a content divide. There is a gender divide,*

*with women and girls enjoying less access to information technology than do men and boys. This can be true of rich and poor countries alike."*

Kofi Annan, former Secretary-General of the United Nations[4]

During the past decade, communications technologies have revolutionised our world. They have changed the way billions of people work, communicate, network, and spend their leisure time. Increased internet and mobile phone use has been linked to rises in GDP – for example, a World Bank report notes that 10 per cent more broadband use means an extra 1.3 per cent on GDP.[5] Young people in particular are spending more and more time using these technologies to communicate with their peers, both in the next town or village and worldwide. The spread of such technologies globally has been phenomenal. There are now more mobile phones than clean toilets.[6]

But both internet and mobile phone use vary enormously from country to country. Millions of people are still missing out on the technological revolution and all the benefits this brings.

| Mobile subscribers per 100 inhabitants[7] | | |
|---|---|---|
| | 2002 | 2007 |
| Africa | 4 | 28 |
| Americas | 30 | 72 |
| Asia | 12 | 38 |
| Europe | 51 | 111 |
| Oceania | 49 | 79 |
| World total | 19 | 50 |

| Internet users, per 100 inhabitants[8] | | |
|---|---|---|
| | 2002 | 2007 |
| Africa | 1 | 5 |
| Americas | 28 | 43 |
| Asia | 6 | 14 |
| Europe | 26 | 44 |
| Oceania | 44 | 53 |
| World total | 11 | 21 |

The adoption of these technologies has varied hugely, not only from continent to continent and country to country but between rural and urban areas, from the richest to the poorest sector of the population, between young and old and between the sexes. This is often known as the 'digital divide'. The developed world continues to have more access to these technologies than the developing world, often by a long way (see tables below), although overall figures mask the digital divide that also exists within countries. Wendy Lazarus, of the Children's Partnership in the US, notes: "One in five children live in poverty today in the US. And low-income children are only half as likely to have a computer at home."[9] In Indonesia, among 15 to 24 year olds, 29 per cent of the richest sector of the population use the internet, but only five per cent in the poorest sector.[10]

All over the world, women generally have less access to communications technologies than men, and less training in how to use them. In most countries, women have less access than men to the internet and to mobile phones. In Asia, women make up 22 per cent of all internet users, in Latin America it is 38 per cent, but in the Middle East it is only six per cent.[11] As the statistics in the table below show, in almost all cases, men outnumber women when it comes to internet use.

Children on the computer in China.

occupation, education levels and whether they live in a rural or an urban area. An additional $100 of monthly income increases the likelihood of mobile phone ownership by 13 per cent. And 80 per cent of women in richer households own a phone compared to 40 per cent in poor households. When age, income, occupation and education are taken into account, urban women are 23 per cent more likely to own a mobile phone than their rural counterparts.

So what about adolescent girls? We know that they are more likely to be using these technologies than their mothers and grandmothers. In the Cherie Blair Foundation survey, girls and young women between 14 and 27 had the highest rates of mobile phone ownership among women, and where they didn't own a phone, were prepared to borrow one from someone who did.

**Percentage of internet users by sex, selected countries, 2008[12]**

|  | Women | Men |
|---|---|---|
| Iceland | 90 | 93 |
| Belgium | 70 | 75 |
| Japan | 70 | 82 |
| Hong Kong, China | 63 | 70 |
| Latvia | 62 | 65 |
| Brazil | 31 | 34 |
| Turkey | 25 | 45 |
| Thailand | 18 | 17 |
| Egypt | 10 | 5 |
| Nicaragua | 10 | 9 |

Research by the Cherie Blair Foundation showed that there are similar disparities among women and men when it comes to mobile phone ownership – women are 37 per cent less likely than men to own a mobile phone if they live in South Asia, 24 per cent in the Middle East and 23 per cent in Africa.[13]

The Foundation's research, in low and middle-income countries, outlines five factors that influence women's mobile phone ownership – household income, age,

**Ownership and usage of mobile phones by age, women in low- and middle-income countries[14]**

| Age | Own% | Borrow% | Yet to make use% |
|---|---|---|---|
| 14 – 20 | 61 | 29 | 10 |
| 21 – 27 | 65 | 27 | 8 |
| 28 – 36 | 65 | 20 | 15 |
| 37 – 49 | 60 | 20 | 20 |
| 50 – 74 | 50 | 25 | 25 |

Adolescent girls and young women themselves are keen to use technology. A recent survey in Kenya predicts that the largest growth in ICT take-up in the coming years will be among young women between the ages of 18 and 35. Interestingly, the

## "WE NEED A COMPUTER MORE THAN HOT FOOD"

Nikki van der Gaag finds out that technology is seen as a priority in urban Egypt, and how it also helps keep girls safe.

"We badly needed a new oven, but when I talked to my children, they said that we could manage, and that we needed a computer more than hot food!"

Mrs Faysa smiles wryly. Aliya, her daughter, says that her brother is better on the computer than she is, but that she is learning fast. Even in poor areas of the city like this one, young women recognise the importance of information and communications technologies. They usually have mobile phones and can find access to computers, perhaps in the house of a friend or a relative. Although a woman is 26 per cent less likely to own a phone than a man in Egypt, this gap seems to be closing for the younger generation.[16]

Internet penetration in Egypt rose from seven to 14 per cent between 2006 and 2008, by which time 40 per cent of the population had a mobile phone.[17] Recent figures put mobile phone penetration at 55 per cent.[18]

"They used to be very expensive," says Azza Shalaby, Plan's Gender Adviser in Egypt. "I remember that my father gave me one as a wedding present. But now they are very cheap, and even poor people see them as a necessity."

Rana says she has used the internet to share experiences and even to create a magazine with other young people in her home town of Alexandria and also worldwide. Many young people say they have a Facebook and email account. Rana's friend Noura, aged 15, won a computer in a school competition and says: "Most of our friends have computers and mobiles."

These are girls whose parents came from the village to the town in search of a better life and whose mothers were illiterate. Now their mothers, encouraged by their daughters, are learning to read and write and recognising the power of education and the importance of technology. Leila, Noura's mother, who has two other girls, says: "I am joining literacy classes so that I can read and write like my daughters. I never went to school, so I hope that my daughters will have a high level of education. Education is important for girls so that they can understand the world. My daughters will be better than me because I was not educated, and I suffer from not being able to read and write."

She is delighted that Noura now has a computer in the house and immensely proud of her daughter for winning a prize. This would not have been possible back in the village, as another mother points out: "In the village I couldn't even work. Women in rural areas still suffer a lot from discrimination, though this is beginning to change. There is more freedom for girls and women in the city now because of technology and more awareness."

For girls like Noura, technology remains a route to discovering new ways of looking at the world. "I couldn't live without my mobile or my computer now," she says.

*Noura and her friends take advantage of the ICT opportunities in urban Egypt.*

communications technologies that are growing the fastest – social networking sites, the use of the internet on mobile phones – are generally those used most by young people.[15] Women and girls recognise that being connected online is as important as being connected offline. Fatma Alloo, Founder of the Tanzania Media Women's Association, commented as long ago as 1998: "We must recognise that information technology is here to stay. What we have to decide is whether we... play the game and turn it to our advantage or lose out completely."[19] But in some countries, girls still lag behind their brothers when it comes to accessing and using communications technologies – as we will see later in the report. In Indonesia, for example, girls and young women aged 15 to 24 were half as likely to use the internet as boys the same age.[20]

This digital divide will have serious consequences for those girls and women who are left out. Even in the rich world, not being part of an online social network can mean missing out not only on what is happening in your peer group, but on opportunities for taking part in a wide range of activities. Clover Reshad, aged 12, who lives in the UK, notes: "There are a few girls at school who don't use Bebo and Facebook but it's not because they don't want to – it's because their parents won't let them. I feel sorry for them."[21] Being left out online is being left out of something that has become central, indeed, essential, to many adolescent girls' lives.

The next section will show why it is crucially important that we invest in young women in all parts of the world so that they access these technologies – for education, for work, for networking and to build the skills, knowledge and expertise that they need to participate fully in the 21st century. They have the capability and the appetite; the adults who run the world at the moment need to provide the mechanisms and the money.

## 3 Giving us freedom – why communications technologies are important for adolescent girls

*"Fortunately for us, the internet gives us freedom since it takes us out to other people, places and other realities. No one controls where we go with the internet. It is for us a way of escaping from our closed society. It is vital to us, it gives us liberty."*
Young woman in Mauritania[22]

As many technologies become cheaper and easier to access, even in the most remote rural areas, it is crucial that adolescent girls and young women, as well as young men, are able to benefit from their use. This means not only having access to the technologies, but the skills and expertise to be able to use them to full effect – and to know how to keep themselves safe when doing so.

Overall, access to technologies can help towards the achievement of the Millennium Development Goals (MDGs), counter gender inequality and build adolescent girls' assets. There are seven specific reasons why these technologies are important to adolescent girls:

1  To keep in touch with others, which reduces their isolation in countries where this is an issue;
2  In order to further their education and acquire new skills;
3  In order to take an active part in their communities and countries;
4  In order to have the skills to find work;
5  To build specific skills and knowledge on subjects they might otherwise not know about, such as HIV and AIDS;

6 Because evidence has shown that learning to use these technologies can build self-esteem;

7 Last but definitely not least, in order to keep safe.

## Keeping in touch

First, as a means of keeping in touch with friends and family and reducing the isolation that many young women feel if their parents do not allow them to socialise. For example, a number of mobile phone projects have enabled young women to keep contact with the outside world after they are married, when normally this would confine them to the house.[23] This young woman from Mauritania noted: "The internet is a safe partner with whom we can communicate discreetly, a partner that can provide us with the information we need to adapt to this modern world. Such information cannot be given to us by our mothers, who cannot break the rules of our traditional society."

Some 70 per cent of girls in the Mauritanian study put emphasis on the fact that the internet provides freedom to them as women, since they no longer need to limit themselves to the controlled information given by their society and families. They can verify information, they can surf and read newspapers, access media channels that are not provided in their countries or that may be forbidden in their own country.[24] Young women like Roza Al-Yazji, who lives in Syria and has a speech disorder and learning disabilities. Via the Salamieh Telecentre, she learned to design brochures, make presentations and access the internet to chat with her friends. Now she says: "I am no longer imprisoned behind the bars of my isolation. Salamieh Telecentre is my second home, it has became a part of my life. I am disabled, but I am not disqualified."[25]

**GIRL TWEETS**[26]
Girls are increasingly using new media outlets such as Twitter to communicate, share and engage with others. Girls are not only tweeting at their peers, they are interacting with decision-makers

and taking part in global discussions on girls' rights. Organisations such as girlsandwomen.com, a coalition of private and third sector organisations that came together to amplify girls' voices in the run-up to the G20 meeting in July 2010, used Twitter to recruit girl supporters. Twitter was used as a platform for allowing girls from all over the world to participate in this high-level meeting and to take part in discussions without the need to be physically present at the G20.

Twitter is also being used by international organisations that support girls. Practitioners can 'tweet' about their work in 'real time', allowing a glimpse into development work. In a time when most communications between organisations and individuals are mediated by other media, an 'unedited' view from the grassroots can build more support and galvanise action as successfully as organised marketing strategies. Twitter allows experts from the field to weigh in on development aspects, developing relationships and sharing knowledge with each other to enhance the body of knowledge and shape opinions; and also engaging with institutions, foundations and corporations which are interested in the technical elements of development work and therefore find mass-produced materials inadequate.

## Furthering their education

Second, young women need access to information and communication technologies (ICTs) and to the skills needed to use them in order to learn and develop. This includes access at school, which is why a number of projects focus on girls' access to computers and the internet and on teaching them the skills they need to use technology in the wider world. A range of school networking projects which promote access to ICTs in schools have sprung up over the past three years in Afghanistan, Botswana, Egypt, Ghana, India, Mozambique, Namibia, Pakistan, Senegal, South Africa, Uganda, Zambia and Zimbabwe, although not all have a gender perspective. Recognising this fact, SchoolNet Uganda has targeted girls-only schools to install computer labs.[27]

## NOKIA – LEARNING AND HEALING THROUGH DIGITAL STORYTELLING[28]

In many African countries, young girls face the threat of violence and sexual abuse, including pressure to engage in unsafe sexual behaviour. They must make difficult choices or deal with the consequences of abuse on their own.

The Sara Communication Initiative (SCI) is a programme of the Pearson Foundation's Digital Arts Alliance and was developed with UNICEF's assistance. Through SCI, more than 200 adolescent girls in Tanzania, Zambia, South Africa, and Namibia have used Nokia mobile phones and laptops with film-making software to create short films about their own experiences and thoughts around topics such as sexual harassment, HIV/AIDS, early marriage, genital cutting and girls' domestic workload. Videos made by girl participants in the Sara Communication Initiative have been shown to peers and educators across Africa, as part of preventative and rehabilitative efforts to address the abuse of girls. 'Sara' is also the name of the teenage girl who is the main character in the stories, which are found on the radio, on video, online and in print.

"I wish I could be just like [Sara]," says Kefiloe, a girl resident of the Kids' Haven Orphanage. "Sara's got this confidence in her, she's got this power and for me, it's like whoa, she's a very good role model for me."

A class in Tanzania taking part in the Sara Initiative.

PEARSON FOUNDATION

## Becoming an active citizen

Third, adolescent girls need access to ICTs to be able to play a part in their communities, their government and at an international level. For girls and young women who may not be able physically to take part in political or even community activities, ICTs offer a unique opportunity to communicate with others, to campaign, to denounce human rights abuses and violence, to champion girls' rights and to access information that they might not otherwise come across. In Egypt, Plan's child media programme, Esma3oona (Hear Us Out), is a weekly programme on terrestrial state TV in which children and young people discuss issues such as child abuse, gender equality, street children and education. Young people, and this must include girls, use their new skills to show officials what needs changing in their communities.

"People now take us seriously after they've seen the show. Also, the officials were able to see the problems in our community and how it is affecting us, so it encourages them to take action," says Amar, one of the participants.[29]

"Since they have a camera and a computer, they can use it to go out and shoot a garbage or sewage problem in the area, come back, do the editing and then send the tape to local authorities," explains Mohamed Kamal, Plan's media coordinator.[30]

### TAKE BACK THE TECH![31]

Take back the Tech! is an international campaign which uses technology to raise awareness and take action on violence against women. In 2009, there were campaigns and actions in 24 countries – from audiocast in Malaysia, chat relay in Brazil, protest march in Second Life, song-writing in Pakistan, calendars in Argentina, tweets in Mexico, posters in cybercafés in the Congo, or a mural on the streets of Soweto in South Africa. Using both online and offline media, and in more than 12 languages, campaigners used technology to get their messages across – violence against women is not acceptable. In Pakistan, Jehan Ara appeared on web-TV's In the Line of

Wire webcast, where she said: "Some have stories to share, some have experienced online violence themselves or their friends… as regular users of technology. They needed to do something about it. Bloggers started blogging. We made videos of why the issues were important in Urdu and English, to spread the word."

## Finding work

Fourth, ICTs have financial value for adolescent girls and young women. If they don't acquire the skills of modern technology they will be disadvantaged in the workplace. In the Cherie Blair Foundation survey, 41 per cent of women reported having increased income and professional opportunities through owning a mobile phone.[32] "By being better connected, women feel safer, find employment, start businesses, access banks, learn about market prices and altogether benefit socially and economically," said Cherie Blair.[33]

"In today's world, computers are the tools we use for work, to learn, to communicate and to find out about the world… In terms of employment opportunities, with new jobs, 95 per cent are going to require some kind of technology," says Wendy Lazarus of The Children's Partnership in the US.[34]

## Accessing information

Fifth, adolescent girls have accessed technologies for advice on HIV infection and prevention and protection, pre- and post-natal care, and sexual and reproductive health rights information. One study of the gender impact of computers in African schools found that young women used the internet frequently to access information normally kept from them by society about sexuality, puberty and HIV.[35]

### LEARNING ABOUT LIVING

Learning About Living is a project in Nigeria using computers and mobile phones to teach Nigerian teenagers about sexuality and HIV prevention. The programme includes an interactive e-learning tool with cartoons and sexual health tips based on the national Family Life HIV/AIDS Education (FLHE)

curriculum. It is aimed to teach sexual health and prevent HIV and gender-based violence, and now has an innovative mobile component. The MyQuestion service, launched in late 2007, is a free question and answer service that teenagers can contact by free 3-in-1 text message, by email, and a toll-free voice number.

Because it is an anonymous and electronic service, it removes the stigma and judgment that teenagers fear when asking for information. Uju Ofomata, project manager of Learning About Living, says: "Anyone who wants proof as to the need of this project should come and take a look at the questions we got in. In two months flat, we got over 10,000 questions coming in from young people, very real questions dealing with their everyday lives. It is obvious from the questions that we received how very much young people want this information… At the end of the day, their lives may be saved."

MyQuestion's text message option, though available only on the MTN network, is free.

Learning About Living also includes a competition service called MyAnswer that educates young people about AIDS, HIV and sexual health by giving them a chance to win prizes.[36]

## Building self-esteem

Sixth, studies have shown that when young women do master technologies, this can have a huge impact on their self-esteem. WorldLinks is a programme that provides internet connectivity and training to secondary school students and teachers around the world. An evaluation of the gender impacts of WorldLinks in Ghana, Senegal, Mauritania and Uganda found that 95 per cent of girls said that participating in the programme had increased their confidence and self-esteem. These girls in Achimota College, Ghana, said:
*"Our self-esteem has really improved because of the programme. Now we can rub shoulders with boys that want to step*

on our toes. Our self-esteem has increased and we walk with our chests out! Anytime we are confronted with questions, we feel confident answering, even with older people we come boldly!"

Girls in Martin Luther King School in Senegal said:

"We are no longer dependent on boys. We feel capable of solving our problems with great autonomy without help from our fathers, brothers or relatives."[37]

This may well be because the young women live in countries where gender biases mean they have fewer opportunities than young men, and accessing the internet gives them exposure to the outside world that they would not otherwise have.

## Keeping safe

And finally, girls and women say that technology, and mobile phones in particular, makes them feel safe. One study found that when people first buy mobile phones, the first reason they give is safety.[38] In the Cherie Blair Foundation study, nine out of

TARIQ AND STAN THEKAEKARA

ten women reported feeling safer because of their mobile phone.[39] The report notes that this cut across age, location and social status. Although we will also show in this report how communications technologies can expose adolescent girls to risk, it is important to remember that keeping connected is also a way of preventing violence and abuse.

*Checking her messages in Bangalore, India.*

**GIRLS AND INTERNATIONAL STANDARDS ON EQUAL ACCESS TO INFORMATION/MEDIA[40]**

It is possible to look at the right to equal access to information as a two-part right. First, there is the right to access to information, which is enshrined in international human rights law under Article 19 of the International Covenant on Civil and Political Rights (ICCPR) and Articles 13 and 17 of the Convention on the Rights of the Child (UNCRC). Secondly, there is the right of girls to have equal access to information and media, by virtue of the non-discrimination provisions of various international instruments, including the ICCPR and UNCRC, and in other international instruments, such as the Convention on the Elimination of Discrimination Against Women (CEDAW).[41]

International standard-setting documents work alongside international instruments to protect and promote the right to equal access to information and media, in recognition of the challenges women and girls face in realising their rights.

The Beijing Platform for Action, which was developed during the Fourth World Conference on Women in 1995, sought to accelerate the removal of "all the obstacles to women's active participation in all spheres of public and private life through a full and equal share in economic, social, cultural and political decision-making".[42] Section J of the Platform for Action focuses specifically on "women and the media" and requires states to "increase the participation and access of women to expression and decision-making in and through the media and new technologies of communication".[43]

In the five-year review of the Beijing Platform for Action, the secretary general's office reported that: "Poverty, the lack of access and opportunities, illiteracy, lack of computer literacy and language barriers, prevent some women from using the information and communication technologies, including the internet."[44]

In the 15-year review, conducted in 2010, the office re-emphasised the importance of access to and control over ICTs for women and girls.[45] The World Summits on the Information Society in Geneva in 2003 and in Tunis in 2005 also reiterated these concerns regarding women's access to ICTs. The outcome documents for these summits recognise the 'gender divide' in access to ICTs, expressing a commitment to overcoming this divide.[46]

But in general, the international instruments did not anticipate the role that technology would play and the pace of change, and therefore do not set out concrete steps or activities that countries should undertake in order to ensure equality of access to ICTs and the media.

The report cites a project in India, run by Idea Cellular, one of India's five biggest mobile operators with over 50 million subscribers. The company asked women what they were concerned about in their use of mobile phones, and they said that they were worried about not being able to call a member of their family if they ran out of credit. Idea Cellular came up with the idea of a 'Women's card' which not only has "information tips on beauty and fashion, health, fitness, cookery, career and private counselling on women matters" but also has the possibility of inputting a three-digit code which sends a 'Please Call Immediately' SMS to three people in case of an emergency.[47] The Cherie Blair Foundation report notes that: "Use of the SMS alert was extensive, and both female and male subscribers appreciated the sense of security provided by the feature."

## 4 Breaking the silence: girls, the super-communicators?

*"I was not computer literate when I started using the internet on my mobile phone so it was quite an eye-opener. Now I want to learn everything. My uncle bought a computer two months ago and his wife has been teaching me some basics."*

Patience, a young refugee from Zimbabwe living in South Africa[48]

*"Girls are creative, they are more into history, English and art – it's the boys who are more into the techie things."*

Clover, 12, UK[49]

This section will show that adolescent girls are competing with boys for the most use of communications technologies such as

the mobile phone and the internet, but that often they are using them for different reasons and different purposes.

In the developing world, many adolescent girls, especially if they come from poor areas, are likely to access the internet via a mobile phone rather than a computer. There are a number of reasons for this:

- Unlike computers, mobiles do not need a regular power supply, and street girls and slum dwellers often do not have electricity.
- Mobiles can be easily stored and hidden from prying eyes – sometimes they are the only source of 'privacy' a girl enjoys when she lives in a small one-room house with many family members, in slums where there are no quiet spaces, or in communities where they are never allowed time to themselves.
- Mobiles have a low entry and maintenance cost – talk time is available in low pre-paid denominations, so they can budget for it. Cheap China-made handsets are available in many countries.
- Mobiles help girls multi-task – they are an all-in-one communication device, FM radio, camera and calculator.
- However, the majority of mobile phones in developing countries are entry-level phones (not smartphones) and don't have internet access. Even as technology advances make entry-level handsets internet compatible, poorer sectors of society cannot afford internet data fees, though this is likely to change in the medium term.[50]

## How adolescent girls and boys use technologies differently

*"I use the computer a lot. At least a couple of days a week to help with my homework, and I keep an eye on [the social networking sites] Bebo and Facebook every day to see who's on it. I'll check shops to see if I can buy things I want cheaper online or to make sure they have something in my size. I MSN [instant message] my friends. The computer also makes it easy to stay in touch with my dad because he lives in Los Angeles."*

Clover, 12, UK[51]

Evidence shows that girls and boys use technologies in different ways. While most of the research to date is in the North, the overall conclusions are that adolescent girls are most interested in communication, while boys focus on the technology itself. It would be interesting to see more studies that focus on adolescent girls' use of these technologies in the South as well.

The Pew Internet project in the US found four main differences between girls and boys.[52] First, that while boys were more interested in exploring the technology for its own sake, girls were interested in what it could do. Second, girls tended to talk about technology as end-users while boys used more technical terms. Third, only boys were interested in putting computers and other hardware together; and fourth, boys and girls had different perceptions about the appearance of technology, boys being attracted to functionality and girls to appearance.

Other studies have also noted differences in the way girls and boys approach technologies. Canadian research with middle school students noted that: "Whereas boys were keen on technology used for entertainment and fun, girls preferred using technology for communication. In general, boys were interested in playing video games on different computing platforms."[53]

Girls in the study noted that:

*"In sixth grade, I think girls are a lot better at technology than boys, because the boys just want the gory stuff – most of the boys do that – they'd rather be outside playing sports or attacking people with fake swords."*

*"Girls are really good at cell phones, like I know a lot of guys, who can't do [it]. I mean, they have cell phones... they know how to call people, and that's about it."*

Boys said that girls: "don't waste their time trying to figure out – 'oh, how does this work, how does that work, how does this get through there'. They just go, 'Oh, that's there, that's there – that's fine'."

In her study of adolescent girls' personal websites in the US, Michele Polak finds "a virtual space that is surfed, occupied, created, criticised, and well-managed by tech-savvy girls".[54] Calling themselves 'gURLs' she says, these websites are where girls can "find a sense of self, creating not only a girl-space for their own voices, but a space for other girls to interact, argue,

discuss, brag and vent about anything with no limitation on topics tied to any traditional feminine narrative. With the anonymity the internet provides, a diversity of themes are up for discussion." She points out the many innovative and creative ways in which girls use these sites and the major focus on community.

Other studies also showed that in general girls were more interested in the aspects of technology that were about communication:

- A study in Norway found that boys were more likely to use the internet for gaming, e-commerce and videos. In contrast, girls use the internet for chatting and email. The authors classify female usage as predominantly 'relational', while male usage is described as 'technical' and 'instrumental'.[55]
- In Canada, one study found that young women generally use the internet to socialise with friends (68 per cent) while young men used it for gaming (68 per cent).[56]
- Research by Nielsen Online in the UK showed that young women aged 18 to 24 accounted for 17 per cent of all users of social sites, compared to 12 per cent for young men of a similar age.[57]
- One study in Brazil found that between the ages of 10 and 17, girls were more likely than boys to have used the internet and were also more likely to own a mobile phone.[58]
- In the US, the study by Pew Internet found that 35 per cent of girls, compared with 20 per cent of boys, have blogs; 32 per cent of girls have their own websites, against 22 per cent of boys.[59]

*Engrossed in their mobile phones in South Korea.*

## 5 Barriers – what is keeping adolescent girls from accessing communications technologies?

With the importance of communications technologies for adolescent girls established, and with adolescent girls keen, willing and able to use these technologies, this section examines the barriers that are preventing equal access with boys.

The first barrier is the fact that women, and by extension adolescent girls who are on their way to becoming women, are still viewed as second-class citizens in many societies. The second barrier exists in school, where boys both outnumber girls and tend to dominate access to computers. The third barrier is psychological. Because they don't have equal access at school, girls may be less confident than boys when it comes to going into IT jobs, because they don't feel they have the same skills and knowledge as the young men competing for the jobs. Finally, there is the issue of language – in order to use these technologies, English is usually a requirement, and for girls with only basic literacy in their own language, this is a major barrier.

Without the knowledge, language, skills and confidence to use communications technologies, adolescent girls are not only missing out on a crucial part of youth culture and networking: they are being deprived of the very skills that are needed for work and life in the coming decades of the 21st century.

### Access to technology – power and control

*"I can immediately call the wholesale market to inquire about prices and place direct orders. I am now recognised as*

Adolescent girls' access to technology is limited by the societies, communities and families in which they live. In a patriarchal society, it is men who control technology, whether this is 'new', such as computers and mobile phones; or 'old', such as radios and televisions. As one report notes: "At home, husbands might regulate the family radio, mobile phone or television, controlling when and how other family members use them."[62]

Being in charge of tools and technical skills has always conferred power on the user; power that is men's not women's. The fact that technology is seen as high status and women as low status may mean that men and boys are given access where girls and women are denied it. Another paper notes: "What the research shows us is that patriarchal habits persist in the family, school and mass media. Boys are educated to explore and conquer the world; girls, despite the advances experienced by democratic societies, are still educated to care for others."[63] This also means that families may have different expectations of their sons and daughters, which also extends to whether they need mobiles or the internet.

*Worldwide the web is used to campaign for equality.*

ROGER ALLEN / DAILY MIRROR

## SMS FOR LITERACY – MOBILES BOOST YOUNG WOMEN'S LITERACY IN PAKISTAN[64]

A partnership project in Pakistan demonstrated the positive impact of mobile phones on girls' lives and is working to overcome community resistance to female ownership.

Pakistani mobile operator Mobilink has learned a great deal about attitudes regarding women and mobile phones, especially as penetration rates soared in Pakistan in recent times. In addition to creating a product tailored specifically for the women's market, Mobilink has sought to demonstrate the power of mobile phones to improve literacy rates for adolescent girls in rural areas where reading materials are often scarce. Yet there is often resistance to girls having the independence that mobile phones symbolise.

For four months in 2009, Mobilink partnered with UNESCO and a local non-governmental organisation (NGO), Bunyad, on a pilot project in a rural area of southern Punjab province. The project involved 250 females aged 15 to 24 who had recently completed a basic literacy programme. Each of the girls was provided with a low-cost mobile phone and prepaid connection. Teachers were trained by Bunyad to teach students how to read and write using mobile phones. The company set up a system for the NGO to send out SMS messages in an effort to maintain and improve participants' literacy, which often lapses because of inadequate access to interesting reading material. Crucially, the low-cost phones were enabled to send and receive messages in Urdu, the local language, rather than in English. The girls received up to six

messages a day on a variety of topics including religion, health and nutrition, and were expected to practise reading and writing down the messages and responding to their teachers via SMS. Monthly assessments of participants' learning gains were conducted to assess impact.

Programme organisers encountered considerable resistance on the part of parents and community leaders to the idea of allowing girls to have mobile phones, largely due to the conservative social norms of the area. This resistance began to soften, however, once people began to see the nature of the messages the girls were receiving and the benefits the programme conferred. Exams taken by the girls participating in the programme showed striking early gains in literacy, with the number of girls receiving the lowest scores dropping nearly 80 per cent.

Participants and their families are even taking advantage of other features of the phones, including the calculator. While 56 per cent of learners and their families initially maintained negative feelings towards the programme, 87 per cent were satisfied with its results by the end. Users can pay $6 to buy their phones at the end of the programme. There are plans to expand the programme further.

Its success demonstrates how mobile phones can be used to increase the reach and effectiveness of basic education programmes. It also illustrates the fact that suspicion of mobile phones can be overcome by showing parents and leaders how mobiles can be used to transmit culturally sensitive information whilst increasing girls' sense of security.

*A group of young women taking part in the programme.*

*Sending a text in Pakistan.*

In addition, girls' domestic roles, even at a young age, mean they have less free time than boys to explore and experiment with new technologies. And they are less likely than their brothers to have the financial resources to pay for, say, a mobile phone and its running costs, or access to the web in an internet café – which is why we have seen that in many countries they have to borrow phones from friends and relatives. Boys are also more likely to be allowed to use internet cafés because parents are concerned about their daughters going out on their own. For example, in Ghana, only 6.6 per cent of females use internet cafés compared with 16.5 per cent of male youth.[65]

### ASHWAQ – THE SAUDI 'INTERNET ADDICT'[66]

Ashwaq's father had heard the scary stories about men using the internet to seduce young, impressionable girls. So when his three daughters asked permission to go online, the answer was an emphatic 'no'.

But the girls persisted and he eventually relented – a bit. They could each spend half an hour a day browsing the web.

With time, however, rationing fell by the wayside and although Dad is still not happy about it, his daughters now use the internet pretty much when they want, said Ashwaq, 23. And for this self-described 'internet addict', that has been all to the good.

Ashwaq, who asked that her surname not be used so she could speak frankly, said that web access has given her "a window to the outside world," brought her "a lot of cyber-friends," and "changed my personality".

A few years ago, she was so anti-social that she would not have returned a reporter's phone call, she said. And because of what she's learned online, including about religion, she's become more open-minded.

"When you grow up in a place with strict rules, you become intolerant of things outside Saudi Arabia," said the optometrist-in-training. "I've changed in that way."

The internet has expanded most people's horizons. But for Saudi women it has been a critical boon, providing a virtual leap over the many restrictions they face and connecting them, as never before, to the outside world.

Most Saudi women cannot work, travel or attend school without permission from their husbands or fathers. They are forbidden to drive. Women generally do not participate in sports and the few public libraries that exist are open for women only a few hours a week. Socialising takes place mostly within extended families because of the country's strict gender segregation.

Women whose families do not allow them to attend university can take online courses at home. And women starting a business or mobilising their sisters around a cause have found the internet a vital tool.

For some Saudi clerics, this internet socialising is another depravity from the West that is "corrupting young people". As one preacher put it: "Facebook is the door to lust."

Many Saudi women remain very cautious online. Ashwaq's Facebook page, for example, has a photo of items on her desk, including a Post-It pad with a note saying: "I'm a tired optometrist."

University student Juhaina Aljehni said that she goes online every morning to "check out some well-known forums for the latest news or trends in Saudi".

It has also led her to this conclusion: "I found out that men have the upper hand and that a lot of women's lives revolve around men."

## School – computers are for girls too

*"The single most important factor for increasing the ability of girls and women to take advantage of IT opportunities is education."*[67]

*"Literacy now is not just learning to read and write but learning how to use a computer."*

Rana 16, Alexandria, Egypt[68]

A sticker on a computer in an African school states: "IT is HOT for Girls." A boys-only class scratched out the 'H' and replaced it with an 'N': "IT is NOT for girls."[69] This prejudice against girls and computers in school is also true in many countries in the developing world. Anuranjita Tewary, Director of the Girls in Tech Mentorship Program, based in Silicon Valley, California, US, says: "I have noticed that at high school, boys will be the ones setting up the computer etc, while girls sit on the sidelines."[70] One report notes that: "In the classroom, the expectations of teachers are also distinct. Scientific education is considered more necessary for boys and this creates barriers for girls: in class they are asked less, they are given less time to answer and are interrupted more."[71] One girl in Ghana notes that: "Some of the boys want us to think that as girls we do not need to know about computers. But we know it really IS about knowing computers."[72]

**DOWNLOAD** If girls do not have equal access to computers at school, it is difficult for them to become part of the digital world. IT requires not just a familiarity and know-how with computers, mobile phones and other technologies; it is also about being able to think creatively. These technologies are interactive and creative and young people in particular have shown that they are keen to make their own videos, write blogs and upload their music.

A review of the WorldLinks programme in Senegal, Mauritania, Uganda and Ghana which provides internet connectivity and training to secondary school students and teachers, found that boys used computers more often than girls. As this young woman pointed out:

*"Once the bell rings and it is time for computer classes, boys run quickly to fill up the computer room. They reach the computer room before us and take up the machines. We do not have a lot of chances to access the computers under such circumstances. Usually by the time boys decide to get up it is already time for the computer class to end. Something needs to be done by the school to stop the boys from dominating the computer rooms.'*[73]

In order to give girls the opportunity to learn about ICTs and to overcome any reservations about using them, a number of programmes run 'technology camps' aimed specifically at girls and young women.

## CISCO NETWORKING ACADEMY[74]

*"Because situating women in good jobs produces a wealth of social and economic benefits, Networking Academy is committed to promoting ICT gender equality. We have recently become the first private sector member of The United Nations Girls' Education Initiative, reaffirming our resolve to play an active role in the collective effort to promote girls' education and gender equality around the world."*
Coks Stoffer, General Manager, Cisco Netherlands

Cisco Networking Academy is a global public-private education initiative equipping students with ICT skills and knowledge so they can access jobs in the internet economy. Cisco's academies are currently training more than 900,000 students in 165 countries across the globe. In developing countries 26 per cent of these are women. Cisco firmly believes that no country or region can fully participate in the global economy without a well-educated ICT workforce, and ICT skills are necessary for individuals to engage in the global economy.

In addition, Cisco are promoting a diverse and inclusive workforce, which benefits Cisco financially by enabling the company to do a better job of anticipating global market demand, generating innovative ideas, and responding to a wide range of customers. Networking Academy promotes diversity within Cisco and throughout the ICT workforce by concentrating on bringing ICT education to less-developed regions and proactively

*Young women attend a Cisco Networking Academy.*

PLAN

ERIC MILLER / PANOS PICTURES

*A call-centre worker in South Africa.*

seeking to enrol female students. For instance, 31 per cent of students graduating from the Networking Academy courses in Africa are women. The majority of female survey respondents said they have more confidence and their career opportunities are better as a result of the programme.

In March 2010 Cisco became the first private-sector member of the UN Girls' Education Initiative (UNGEI) Global Advisory Committee, further cementing its commitment to gender equality.

## Computing: jobs for the boys?

*"I definitely wanted to do it, because way back in high school, I really liked computer studies, but when I was in high school, I could not go to a computer class because I could not afford to pay for a computer course. But when I cleared high school, I got friends and told them about what I wanted to do and they gave me a scholarship. I studied IT for free... I was therefore among the people who got the opportunity to study IT."'*

Young female web designer in Kenya[75]

Despite the fact that they are familiar with the technologies and keen to use computers, in general young women are not studying IT at university or finding work in the computer industries. This may partly be to do with attitudes. Sarah Blow is a 26 year-

old software engineer in the UK who has a website, Girly Geekdom. She says: "Even though both my parents worked in IT, I was told to look at marketing and law by my school careers adviser." But she is hopeful for the future: "The message is slowly getting across to girls that the industry isn't all about that clapped-out stereotype of geeky guys with glasses."[76] An Australian study found that social conditioning about technologies meant that girls perceived ICT careers and studies in a negative light:

• It would be a boring job
• ICT attracts nerds
• You have to be good at maths
• It is too technical.[77]

While data is limited, in Australia, women make up only 20 per cent of ICT employees and 25 per cent of ICT university students and numbers are declining from year to year.[78] This is true in other countries. In the US, the percentage of female computer science undergraduates at major research universities has dropped from 37 per cent in 1985 to 14 per cent in 2006.[79] In the UK in 2005-6, there were 75,360 male students studying computing at university compared to 23,370 women.[80] "An IT industry dominated by men is only using half the available talent and creativity. We know girls are turned off by IT as a career option because it is not something they connect with. Technology appears to be marketed by men for men. It's time we started switching bright and talented girls on to science and technology," said the UK's Patricia Hewitt when she was Trade and Industry Secretary.[81]

## Basic education and training

These comments are underlined by another research report which notes that: "Women in developing countries do not receive the basic education and training needed to be ready technology adopters and are often seen only as 'users' or 'receivers' of technology, rather than as innovators involved in technology design and development.

"The more sophisticated the technologies, the less likely women are to be involved. As one commentator points out: 'At work, men may determine that operating ... a computer is not something women should be allowed to learn. Even technology programmes that target women can be co-opted by men once their utility and profitability are established – so women who do gain access to a technology do not see the economic benefits associated with it.'"[82]

"The majority of people behind the web, who programme sites and create the new technologies, tend to be men," says Bryony Matthewman, 24, a British artist and graphic designer who is better known to her millions of fans as Paperlilies. She is one of the top 50 most popular contributors to YouTube.[83]

## The generation gap

Surprisingly, the difference between the proportion of men and women working in computing jobs is wider among the younger than the older generation. In 2006, some 3.5 per cent of men in Europe aged below 40 were employed in computing compared to less than one per cent of women.[84]

"Girls in my generation are not really encouraged to go into IT. A lot of girls get into the sector via vocational colleges, and it can be intimidating being the only girl in a group of boys," said Dawn Breen, who works for a software company in the UK.[85]

However, once they are computer literate, young women in countries in Latin America, East and Central Europe, South and South East Asia, and South Africa, see the computer industry as a route to independence.

- In South Africa, women hold 19 per cent of data communications and networking jobs, 18 per cent in information systems and information technology management, and 39 per cent in education, training and development.[86]
- In India, women occupy nearly 20 per cent of the professional jobs in the software industry, including at technical and

managerial levels.[87] They are also well represented in what are known as BPO (Business Process Outsourcing) industries such as call centres.

- In Malaysia, women make up 30 per cent of IT professionals.[88]
- Women constitute 20 per cent of the software industry in Brazil.[89]

True, many of these jobs may be in data processing, or in call centres, but young women see them as an opportunity to build a different life for themselves, like Guizhen Xu, from China.

### THE STORY OF GUIZHEN XU

**Guizhen Xu, 23, has not had an easy life. Her dream is to go to college. She was abandoned by her parents at a young age and helped her foster father on the land while studying hard in school. But then her father was diagnosed with senile dementia and cervical spondylosis. She had to look after him at home and spent their small savings on his treatment. When he died, she was on her own.**

**Neighbours helped her to travel to Nanjing, where she found work and saved from her meagre earnings so that she could go to college. She says: "I want to go to college because I believe that it would bring changes into my life. I also really enjoy studying."**

**Her dream was still a long way off when she heard about the Community Technology & Learning Centre Programme (CTLC), a free computer training project co-organised by Plan and Microsoft. With no previous knowledge of computer operation, she successfully completed the course. At the same time she took quite a few other training courses to satisfy her quest for knowledge. Since she could not afford college, this was the next best thing.**

**Then in June 2007, a financial aid programme for migrant workers to continue their studies was officially co-launched by the Asian Women's Fund and Nanjing Women's Federation. Guizhen Xu was too excited to sleep. In the following days she completed the application form, obtained the necessary certificates of work experience and family background, and then contacted the Nanjing Radio**

PLAN

*CTLC project in China.*

and TV University. Because of her good grades at high school, she was offered a place to study administration management. She decided to go to evening classes so that she could work during the day to support herself.

Despite the harshness of her life, Guizhen Xu always has a smile on her face. And at last she may be able to realise her dream.[90]

There are a few women who have made serious money from the internet – Martha Lane Fox, the co-founder of lastminute.com, and Natalie Massenet, who set up Net-a-Porter, have made their fortunes through the web. But they are still the exceptions – and mostly in the rich world.

### NOKIA: SCHOOL RELEVANCE THROUGH MOBILE CONNECTIVITY TO THE WORLD OF LEARNING[91]

Every day brings formal learning challenges for girls in developing countries. Does a girl try to stay in school when there are few books and only lightly trained teachers, or follow in the footsteps of her peers by dropping out? Millions of children are leaving school without having acquired basic skills. If current trends persist, there will be 56 million children out of school in 2015.

In response to this global challenge Nokia has partnered with the Pearson Foundation and others to significantly improve educational quality and student achievement in primary school level mathematics, science and life skills, through the innovative use of cell phones and digital technology. This technology provides schools with video content that supports science, maths and life skills teaching, and improves the quality of interaction between teacher and student.

"The reaction of teachers and students has been very positive," says Mr Mbogella, Chief Country Advisor for the Tanzania project. "We have conducted research involving schools with and without the video content, and the results are amazing. Students who watched the videos showed greater motivation and achieved better test results."

In addition, there are few women in positions to make decisions about information technologies in developing countries, whether nationally or on international bodies, in private companies and standard-setting organisations or in international development agencies. One study found that in ministries of developing countries, only 5.5 per cent of senior government officials are women. It noted, however, that women are the ministers of communication or telecommunication in Mali, South Africa and Colombia, and deputy ministers of communications in Angola, Belarus, the Czech Republic, Ghana, the Kyrgyz Republic and Tanzania. "These women have the potential to influence the course of information and technology development in their countries as well as regionally and globally through participation in ITU regional and world conferences."[92]

### BECOMING WHO YOU WANT: ONLINE MENTORING FOR YOUNG WOMEN IN BRAZIL[93]

Ana Célia Arcanjo, aged 22, lives with her parents in Recife, Brazil. While she was growing up, her family and friends assumed she would become a poorly paid labourer, or maybe not find work at all. Despite Brazil's recent economic boom, 40 per cent of youth in Recife are unemployed, and less than half of the city's 18 to 24 year olds are continuing their education.

However, thanks to the Academy for Educational Development (AED)'s Programa Para o Futuro, Arcanjo is now a key breadwinner in her household. She learned to set up computer networks,

*A programme participant meeting her mentor.*

ERIC RUSTEN, COURTESY OF AED

diagnose and repair technical problems, and install and configure software. Perhaps most important though, through AED's 'eMentoring' methodology, Arcanjo and 49 of her peers used email and instant messaging to conduct conversations with working professionals, who taught them marketable skills and gave them career counselling. One skill Arcanjo learned was to present ideas professionally and accept criticism graciously. "No one from our communities could teach this," because they do not have the same knowledge or experience as the mentors, she said.

Finally, it is not just the jobs in IT, science or engineering that are the issue. Increasingly, technology skills and access to technology are becoming as necessary as literacy for 21st century employment. One study in South Africa and Tanzania found that many respondents identified mobile phones as essential for contacting employers and getting contacted about job openings, particularly in remote areas and areas of high crime.[94]

## 6 The dark side of cyberspace – how technology is increasing sexual exploitation

*"An average person with a computer, modem and search engine can find violent, degrading images within minutes – a search that could have taken a lifetime, just 15 years ago."*

Donna Hughes[95]

We have seen how ICTs can be very empowering for adolescent girls, socially, politically and economically. But we also know that they can expose them to risks,

especially at a time of their lives when they are beginning to develop sexually.

We also know that the majority of children affected by sexual exploitation worldwide are girls,[96] and that one in five women report having been sexually abused before the age of 15.[97] Although, as one expert noted, "by and large, the internet is just a new medium for old kinds of bad behaviour"[98], ICTs extend the possibilities of such abuse to an altogether different arena.

Online abuse and exploitation can be roughly classified into four broad categories – producing, trading or downloading sexually abusive materials, and seducing children into sexual abuse and exploitation.[99] The UK's Child Exploitation and Online Protection Centre (CEOP) has detected "a significant shift by child-sexual offenders to the use of P2P (peer-to-peer) technology for the distribution of images, usually on a non-commercial basis. By operating within networks, offenders normalise their behaviour through membership of a hierarchical community of like-minded individuals, gaining prestige by trading and introducing newer, more exclusive images. The production of new images of child exploitation is incentivised by access to higher positions within the network hierarchy. This type of behaviour provides a gateway to further offending, where images are made to order through ongoing contact abuse with children accessible to one or more individuals in the network."[100]

In developing countries, poor girls who have no access to the internet are still potentially vulnerable – for example, their photos can be taken and posted up on the internet without their knowledge and without them having access to a computer themselves.

This section examines the factors that make adolescent girls vulnerable to exploitation via communications technologies. It looks at how ICTs have shaped and changed trafficking operations. It assesses the significance of other forms of internet-related abuse, like cyberbullying and cyber-harassment, and shows how these affect girls and young women in particular. It also profiles new research and showcases IT solutions that come from young women themselves. It shows how ICTs can be used in counter-trafficking efforts to ensure girls' security and protection. Finally, it makes recommendations about how girls can better protect themselves, and be better protected, from harm. The potential of the internet is vast; it is important that fear does not limit that potential.

## Facts on IT-Enabled Sexual Exploitation

- The Internet Watch Foundation reported a 34 per cent increase in reported internet child abuse, with 91 per cent of the victims under 12 years old.[101]
- According to a 2007 study, 55 per cent of all child abuse sites are hosted in the US, followed by 28 per cent in Russia; eight per cent in Europe and seven per cent in Asia.[102]
- In Malaysia, women's activists have cited the use of intimate images to blackmail young women into staying in a relationship.[103]
- One European study on internet use found that two in ten parents reported that their children had encountered harmful or illegal content online.[104]

- As many as 70 per cent of internet sites are invisible – they have a reference but cannot be located – including most illegal image sites. Young people downloading free DVDs, songs and games use the same software as paedophiles.[105] Peer to peer (P2P) is the most common method of sharing and accessing indecent images of children online.[106]
- Some 60 per cent of parents in Europe whose children access the internet have no rules on its use.[107]
- Of young people surveyed in Thailand, 63 per cent had stumbled on content which had shocked them.[108]
- In China, 44 per cent of children said they had been approached online by strangers.[109]

In Egypt a group of young people have formed a Youth Internet safety group (Net_ Aman) with a mandate to increase awareness about internet safety and the huge potential of ICTs. Their aim is to offer children and youth the chance to identify harmful content and decide on the best way to deal with that through a participatory approach.

### WHAT LAWS ARE THERE TO PROTECT GIRLS FROM VIOLENCE, EXPLOITATION AND ABUSE ONLINE?

"National governments are urged to devise and implement legislation and to harmonise laws to protect children from all cyber crimes, including online grooming, luring or stalking, exposure to illegal or inappropriate materials and all actions related to child pornography (including creation, dissemination, accessing, downloading, possession and incitement). National laws must mirror or surpass existing international legislation."[110]

The obligation to protect girls from violence, exploitation and online abuse is contained in several key international human rights instruments, including the UNCRC, the ICCPR, CEDAW, and the subsequent Beijing Platform for Action, the International Covenant on Economic, Social and Cultural Rights, ILO Convention 182 on the Worst Forms of Child Labour, the Optional Protocol to the Convention on the Rights of the Child on the sale of children, child prostitution and child pornography and the Protocol to Prevent, Suppress and Punish Trafficking in Persons, especially Women and Children, Supplementing the United Nations Convention against Transnational Organised Crime (2000) ('Palermo Protocol').[111] There are also a number of regional frameworks.

The Optional Protocol to the Convention on the Rights of the Child on the sale of children, child prostitution and child pornography is perhaps the most detailed.[112] It requires governments to criminalise producing, distributing, disseminating, importing, exporting, offering, selling or possessing child pornography for the purposes set forth in the protocol. In combination with the provisions in the Convention on the Rights of the Child, governments have an obligation to criminalise child abuse in all its forms, including all the methods that can be used to perpetrate such abuse.

The international and regional instruments provide a structure for the protection of children from all forms of sexual exploitation and sexual abuse with some providing detailed guidance on areas of protection.[113] Though it is difficult for the law to 'keep up' with technological changes, the international standards are clear in imposing an obligation on governments to protect girls from abuse, violence and exploitation that is associated with new developments in, and increased use of, ICTs. The challenge is for states to create the legal frameworks that are necessary to effectively ensure girls are safe in the new 'spaces' opened up to them by ICTs.[114]

The group has four major goals:

1 Research the current e-safety needs of young people in Egypt to understand better the wide range of concerns shared by youth and their families;
2 Assess the most appropriate guidelines for young people in safe use of the internet;
3 Create and design effective education and awareness resources to communicate e-safety information to young people and their parents;
4 Contribute to wider strategic programmes and assess those programmes from a youth perspective.

## Why are girls and young women particularly vulnerable?

- A 17 year-old woman allows her boyfriend to film them having sex. When they break up acrimoniously, he puts the material on the web. She is terrified from then on that her family, her teachers or future employers might see it.
- A 15 year-old girl is contacted via instant messaging by a much older man. He flatters her and persuades her to meet him. When she does, he sexually assaults her. She does not dare tell her parents or the police.
- The female owner of an internet-based modelling agency in Lugansk, Ukraine, recruited 14 to 17 year-old girls under the pretext of modelling contracts but the victims were trafficked to the United Arab Emirates and the Seychelles and forced into commercial sexual exploitation.[115]

Adolescent girls are vulnerable to online abuse for the same reasons they are vulnerable to offline abuse. Physically, puberty is when girls begin to be seen as sexually 'available', although adolescents, regardless of age, cannot consent to sexual exploitation. In this sense, age of consent is irrelevant. This has been argued by the UN Special Rapporteur on the sale of children, their commercial sexual exploitation and child pornography. Offenders seek to legitimise their behaviour by stating that adolescents should naturally engage in sexual behaviour as they are 'sexually available'.[116] Psychologically, many adolescent girls are not equipped with the skills and knowledge they need to protect themselves; for

example, they may give out information they wouldn't share in another setting.[117] The speed of change, and the fact that young people are accessing websites of which their parents have little knowledge, means that they have little protection from abuse. Once an image is on the web, it is virtually impossible to recall it, meaning that images taken of girls will continue to affect them as they grow into adulthood. One study in the UK found that adolescents, particularly young girls in the 16 to 17 age group, were in serious danger of 'online seduction'.[118]

The internet is also being used for online solicitation or 'grooming' (securing a girl's trust in order to draw her into a situation where she may be harmed).[119] It enables sex offenders to engage girls on many levels, from sexual chat to enticing them into physical contact. There have been many cases where predators contact girls for both online and then physical meetings, during which girls are emotionally and sexually abused.[120] Adolescent girls are particularly vulnerable to this type of online solicitation.[121] One of the biggest challenges is making direct connections between images of girls on the internet and actual cases of trafficking; in other words, perpetrators are often marketing images, rather than real people.[122]

And it is often the most vulnerable girls who are most at risk. For example, a study in Latvia found that the most vulnerable potential 'victims' were young women from 10 to 22 years, primarily in the southern and Russian parts of the country, where unemployment is high and prospects are poor.[123] Research in the US found that girls and boys who feel isolated, misunderstood, depressed, or lack support from family are most at risk of aggressive online solicitations and are likely to send personal information about themselves.[124]

**KEEP YOUR CHATS EXACTLY THAT!**[125]
**'Keep your chats exactly that!' is a South African advocacy campaign run by GirlsNet, a project that aims to "open up innovative opportunities of ICTs to girls and encourage girls to make use of ICTs in order to make them active participants in the Information Age".**

**'Keep your chats exactly that!' aims to keep girls safe online and to prevent**

them "becoming victims of violence or harassment when they use the internet and cell phones". It also aims to help young people use ICTs to raise awareness.

Leading up to the campaign, young women from GirlsNet conducted focus-group discussions to investigate their use of social networks, which showed that some girls said they had withdrawn from mobile social networks because of sexual harassment. They also found that young people wanted to access, use and own technologies themselves. Women'sNet Executive Director Sally Shackleton said: "Access to ICTs are mediated by gendered inclusion and exclusion. Women are still not in control of the tools they are using."[126]

## What technologies are used to abuse adolescent girls?

Technologies change with incredible speed. For example, computing power is moving increasingly from the desktop/laptop to the mobile phone, at the same time that mobiles are being used by increasing numbers of children and young people. This change could bring sexual harassment and exploitation even closer to potential victims.

The Vienna Forum on Human Trafficking identified various forms of technology which offer access to girls by traffickers and other perpetrators of abuse. These include:
• Newsgroups: sites for exchange of information can be misused to find young women to exploit and to upload and download illegal pornography.
• Web message and bulletin boards: exchange of information misused by sexual perpetrators: similar to newsgroups but can be private and password protected.
• Websites: can be misused as venues for distribution of pornography, maintained

recreationally for profit. Pornographic images are created through online stalking, where stalkers befriend girls in chat rooms and ask them to take pictures of themselves.[127] 'Page-jacking' involves misdirecting or trapping people onto pornographic websites.
• Web-based chat rooms (including live video chat) and new social media networking tools (Facebook, MySpace, Craigslist) are an especially dangerous and commonly used method for girls to come into contact with traffickers or other perpetrators of abuse.[128] No messages are archived or stored, and no log files are maintained.[129]
• File Transfer Protocol (FTP) is a way of exchanging files on the internet and used to exchange child pornography. It allows users to have direct access to another's computer hard drive to upload and download files.
• Search engines: misused by criminals to find illegal content.
• Peer-to-peer networks and file swapping programmes are used to find and download files on online networks and misused to share illegal material. Transmissions are not logged or traceable.[130]
• Mobile phones, as we will see below, are also increasingly being used to abuse and bully, especially if they also include access to the internet.

## How perpetrators are using technology to recruit and exploit girls

Exploitation and sexual abuse of young women is easy, anonymous and largely untraceable via the internet, and is thus an obvious tool for perpetrators to use.[131] Cyber crime is attractive to perpetrators because:[132]
• It is easily committed
• It is cheap for the criminal
• It is difficult to trace
• It is highly profitable and investment costs are low – though perpetrators are not always motivated for commercial gain
• The criminal can be at home, while the crime can have consequences in various countries and for numerous victims
• It can be hard to locate, as criminals operate in various countries, making it hard for national police agencies to track them down

- Victims are less likely to attract police attention, and can be controlled.[133]

Criminals are able to more easily distance themselves from the crimes they commit and IT provides a degree of anonymity that enables exploitation to carry on with impunity. It is difficult to determine the profile of perpetrators of IT-enabled abuse, since the very nature of exploitation is embedded in anonymity: "Global communications forums have increased the privacy and decreased the isolation of the men who exploit and abuse women and children."[134]

**SERBIA: AN EXAMPLE OF INCITEMENT TO PROSTITUTION OF A MINOR**[135]
This is an extract from an online chat. It was logged as part of a research project with young people in six Serbian towns by the NGO ASTRA to monitor internet abuse.
Man: *Where are you from? You're 15?*
Girl: *Yeah, you?*
Man: *29*
Girl: *Ok*
Man: *Go to school?*
Girl: *Yes, primary, 8th grade*
Man: *Have a boyfriend?*
Girl: *No*
Man: *And you'd like to?*
Girl: *Well, of course I would, but he'll come when he comes*
Man: *Your girlfriends, they have boyfriends, have sex with them?*
Girl: *Some yes, some no*
Man: *Virgin?*
Girl: *I won't tell you*
Man: *Ok, I know... you're embarrassed. You'd like to lose your virginity soon? You'd play with my banana? C'mon, talk to me, why you hesitate, say something*
Girl: *And how's that you're so rude and you're 30?*
Man: *Honey... you'll see when you grow up... you'll be crazier than now... and now tell me... you'd like to play with banana?*
Girl: *And you really feel strong when you talk with girls?*

Man: *I enjoy it, you're the sweetest in that age*
Girl: *Aren't you bored? Our peers are boring to us*
Man: *I'm not bored, I want a young girl and I'm talking with you, you'd be with me sometimes and I'd help you in a certain way... financially? Well?*
Girl: *How do you mean to help me?*
Man: *Say, you make me happy quickly and get 100 euros, only 10-15 minutes, I think it's ok offer*
Girl: *Well I'm not that kind of girl and I'm only 15*
Man: *Of course you're not, and everything will be between me and you, and you'll always have cash*
Girl: *But why? I couldn't tell it to my friend?*
Man: *You can say whoever you like. Is the offer ok?*
Girl: *No*
Man: *Tell your offer*
Girl: *I'm not offering anything*

## Trafficking via technology

*"Traffickers in [some] countries are no longer uneducated, 'paan-chewing' men, but carry cell phones, video cameras, and speak cultured English, allowing them to exploit women and children more efficiently and effectively than ever before."*[136]

The ILO estimates that 80 per cent of those who are trafficked are female and 50 per cent are under the age of 18.[137] There is still not very much information on how traffickers are using communications technologies, let alone how much adolescent girls are involved.[138] But we do know that new places and locations for trafficking have emerged, as the internet has enabled communication with clients to go to nondescript addresses not previously associated with sex tourism or the sex trade.[139] The use of new technology in trafficking is particularly prevalent at the initial exploitation stage; people seeking to 'buy' adolescent girls are able to search online through websites.[140] One consultant notes: "I have heard of East European and Balkan girls being advertised as 'coming soon' and providing contact details if you want to reserve some time with the girl. If they get sufficient demand for a girl in a particular place, off she goes. Really simple, and really hard to crack." (Brian Iselin, Syria.[141])

While technology is used for trafficking purposes, it is also being used to track traffickers. The International Organisation of Migration (IOM) has a Counter-Trafficking Module Database.[142] The private sector has also been working with governments and international bodies on this issue. For example, Microsoft's Child Exploitation Tracking System (CETS), is a "unique software tool that helps governments store, search, share and analyse evidence in child exploitation cases across police agencies, helping protect children from exploitation online, and making possible more effective identification and prosecution of offenders." As of December 2009, the Child Exploitation Tracking System has been deployed in more than 10 countries and is being used by more than 1,000 investigators worldwide.

The US and United Nations Office on Drugs and Crime's joint project, Operation Childhood, works with international partners – Thailand, Cambodia and Vietnam – to tackle child sexual abuse and trafficking on a national level through international cooperation and capacity building programmes.[143]

## Child-to-child abuse

A teenager who posted death threats on Facebook has become the first person in Britain to be jailed for bullying on a social networking site.

Keeley Houghton, 18, of Malvern, Worcestershire, was sentenced to three months in a young offenders' institution after she posted a message saying that she would kill Emily Moore. She pleaded guilty to harassment.

On 12 July 2009, Houghton updated her status on Facebook to read: "Keeley is going to murder the bitch. She is an actress. What a ***** liberty. Emily ******* Moore."

Moore, also 18, had been victimised by Houghton for four years, the court heard, and had previously suffered a physical assault as well as damage to her home.[144]

As the above story shows, not all abuse via technology is carried out by adults on children. Some is child-to-child. Emily's mother Connie said: "The internet is a sinister, silent enemy. You simply don't know how to start to tackle the problem. But faceless as a computer may be, it is every bit as threatening as a physical bully, if not more so, because the audience reading these horrible messages can be enormous."[145]

### USING THE LAW TO PROSECUTE SEXUAL EXPLOITATION, ABUSE AND VIOLENCE ONLINE

There are several notable challenges associated with using the law to prosecute those who perpetrate cyber crimes. These occur at all stages of the process, from detecting the crime in the first place to taking a case through prosecution. One immediate barrier to prosecution of sexual exploitation, abuse and violence online is the lack of domestic legislation. Despite increased awareness of the problem, many countries still do not have adequate domestic provisions that criminalise relevant acts.

Legislation must address and take into account the fact that girls are more exposed to the risk of sexual exploitation, violence and abuse through the channels of new technology. As the G8 Ministers stated in 2007, "[b]ecause producers, traders, and collectors of child pornography can be found in any country, all countries must work together to solve the problem. If such images are legal anywhere, they are more available everywhere."[146]

### Jurisdiction

Protecting children online is a global issue, so a global response is needed.[147] While the lack of national legislation is a significant problem, it can also be difficult to prosecute the perpetrators of child sexual abuse and exploitation that takes place online, due to the many different jurisdictions that are involved in the commission of an offence. For example, if an indecent photo is taken of a child, the crime 'takes place' in the jurisdiction in which the photo is taken, in the jurisdiction of the server to which the photo was uploaded, and in the multitude of locations in which the picture is downloaded and, potentially, shared and viewed. Effective prosecution of those participating at any stage of the process of producing, disseminating and viewing images of child abuse can be limited by extradition laws which sometimes require that the relevant act has been criminalised in both the location from which an individual is being extradited and in the state to which they will be extradited. International cooperation is essential for ensuring procecution of offenders who have committed online offences against children, owing to the transnational nature of these crimes.

## LEGAL RESPONSES TO YOUNG PEOPLE WHO SEXUALLY EXPLOIT OTHERS THROUGH NEW TECHNOLOGIES[148]

The main international instruments on juvenile justice provide the standards for the response to young people who sexually exploit others through ICTs. These documents are Articles 37 and 40 of the UNCRC and the UN Minimum Rules for the Administration of Juvenile Justice, with further guidance from the UN Guidelines on the Prevention of Juvenile Delinquency, the UN Rules for the Protection of Juveniles Deprived of their Liberty and the Economic and Social Council's UN Guidelines on the Administration of Juvenile Justice[149] According to these standards, responses to juvenile offending should be geared towards "promoting the child's reintegration and the child's assuming a constructive role in society".[150] Actions that respond to young people who sexually exploit others through ICTs should follow these standards.

The appropriate reaction to sexual exploitation of children through ICTs is difficult to achieve and remains a developing area of law, at an embryonic stage in many countries.[151]

States face challenges in crafting legislation that protects children from online exploitation and harm, while distinguishing between those actions that are "predatory and exploitative" from those that are conducted by children who do not share the predatory and exploitative intent.[152] In Australia, for example, the Crimes Legislation Amendment (Sexual Offences Against Children Bill) 2010, seeks to update criminal legislation to combat "contemporary offending" including child sex tourism, overseas child pornography, child sexual abuse online, postal and online offences.[153, 154] In response to concerns that this legislation could lead to the criminal punishment of children who engage in 'sexting', a parliamentary committee recommended that the Attorney General be given discretion over whether to pursue criminal charges against those under the age of 18.[156] This would, according to the Committee, "take account of sexting as a common practice among young people, in order to avoid criminalising or stigmatising young people as child sex offenders."[156]

What happened to Emily is known as 'cyberbullying', defined as "when a child, pre-teen or teen is tormented, threatened, harassed, humiliated, embarrassed or otherwise targeted by another child, pre-teen or teen, using the internet, interactive and digital technologies or mobile phones. It has to have a minor on both sides, or at least have been instigated by a minor against another minor."[157]

While bullying online is an extension of bullying offline, there are a number of differences. First, it follows you home. Offline bullying you can escape from, but if someone is bullying you online, you experience it every time you turn on your mobile phone or computer – which for many young people, is much of the time they are awake, if they are not at school. This has huge consequences in real life, as this 15 year-old girl from the UK pointed out: "It's easier to say horrible stuff about people on [the internet]. It got really horrible in Year 10. Lots of people were being bullied over [the internet]. It gets brought into school. When friends do this, it's horrible. It makes you really upset. You don't want to go into school again."[158]

Second, the consequences may be there forever. In the US, Bill Albert of the National Campaign to Prevent Teen and Unplanned Pregnancies noted that the line between public and private behaviour has become blurred. "The technology is so new that people haven't found their moral compass when using it. The problem is that even if you think you are sending a picture only to your boyfriend or girlfriend of the moment, it can go from private to global in a nano-second. And something like that can stick with you, almost like a cyber-tattoo, for the rest of your life."[159]

A Microsoft survey in Canada found that adolescents and teenagers are more likely to be cyberbullied than younger children – 51 per cent and 23 per cent respectively, and that on the whole, adolescent boys tend to be the bullies and girls tend to be the victims.[160] Focus-group discussions leading up to the campaign in South Africa 'Keep your chats exactly that!' (see page 121) found that young people had shared nude pictures of themselves with their friends. They also mentioned constant bullying, stalking and harassment while using their phones.[161] Seventy-five per cent of US teens in one survey said that they thought there should be stricter rules about online bullying.

| Percentages of student experience of bullying and cyberbullying[162] | | |
|---|---|---|
| | Male | Female |
| Bully | 40.8 | 27.8 |
| Bully victim | 53.7 | 44.4 |
| Cyberbully | 22.3 | 11.6 |
| Cyberbully victim | 25.0 | 25.6 |
| Aware of cyberbullying | 55.6 | 54.5 |

Another study found that in the US, 41 per cent of adolescent girls between the ages of 15 and 17 said they had experienced cyberbullying, compared with 29 per cent of boys the same age, and 34 per cent of girls and 22 per cent of boys aged 12 to 14.[163]

### VIRTUAL POLICE – A PIONEERING PROJECT FOR INTERNET SAFETY

Nearly a third of Finnish 15 year-old girls have been sexually abused or harassed on the internet; substantially fewer boys have received similar treatment.[164] A growing, but usually hidden, trend is violent bullying by girls of other girls. According to new Finnish research,[165] nearly half of the girls surveyed admit using such behaviour, whereas a third of the boys admit doing so. Amongst the respondents, violence inflicted by girls tends to be more widely accepted than that by boys. For example, nearly 40 per cent of girls thought it was all right to 'assault' a boyfriend. The prevalent forms of 'assault' were bullying, mocking, slapping and elbowing. Beating and kicking are equally prevalent behaviour amongst girls and boys.

A public discussion focusing on the adverse side of the internet highlighted that whereas boys are more likely to fight with their fists or through direct verbal mockery, girls are using the social media to bully and insult. All too often the abusers falsely believe that they are less liable for their actions on the web than in real life.

Young Finns seem to make little distinction between the real and the virtual world. But although they may be openly and skillfully discussing their problems on the web, they are often unable to seek help in the real world.

With the aim of making the web safer for young people, in September 2008 Sergeant Marko Forss of Helsinki Police started a police profile – 'fobba' – on IRC-Galleria,[166] the most popular social media site amongst Finnish youth. Forss went on to invent and establish the Virtual Community Policing Group. This revolutionary facility for young people received national recognition for 'Best Practice for Cooperation' in 2009.[167]

The police have created an online space which works as a virtual police station, enabling young people to report online crime in confidence.

The police profiles are open and undisguised: members of the group use their own names and photos for their web profiles. During the past year, the police profiles have received nearly 50,000 contact requests.[168] For a small country like Finland this is a huge success.

The Virtual Community Policing Group has attracted great interest and is a pioneer in global police work in social media. Its success is based upon public trust in the police.

"The aim is not to limit freedom of speech," says Senior Constable Jutta Antikainen, alias 'jutta'. The work itself is normal police work, only the environment is different. After a crime is reported, the procedure is the same. The only difference is that young people are now more likely to talk to police and report web-based crime; trust is gained faster using the internet.

*From left: Jutta Antikainen, Mikko Manninen and Marko Forss.*

FINNISH POLICE

## Sexting

Sexting is the practice of sending nude pictures via text messages, which is something that happens between young people themselves. It was brought to public attention by a case in the US in January 2009 where three teenage girls of 14 or 15 who had sent such photos of themselves, and three teenage boys of 16 or 17 who had received them, were charged with child pornography. Another US survey found that eight out of ten female 'sexters' were under 18.[169] This is not just a phenomenon that takes place in the global North, though it may be an urban one. As part of a programme to develop community-based protection systems for children and adolescents in Ecuador, Plan carried out a study in two cities and found evidence that boys were filming girls and sharing the videos via Bluetooth.[170]

According to one nationwide survey by the National Campaign to Support Teen and Unplanned Pregnancy, 20 per cent of teenagers say they take part in sexting. "This is a serious felony. They could be facing many years in prison," CBS News legal analyst Lisa Bloom said. "What are we going to do, lock up 20 per cent of America's teens?"[171] Witold Walczak, legal director for ACLU in Pennsylvania, who is fighting the case on behalf of the pupils, said: "Child porn is about the abuse and exploitation of minors by adults. That's not happening here. The kids who do this are doing potential harm to themselves. They are both the perpetrator and the victim. Why would you want to compound that with a criminal prosecution and conviction?"[172] In March 2010, the State Senate of Illinois passed a law under which under-18s who share nude photos of their peers would not be subject to criminal penalties but would face juvenile sanctions.[173]

Sexting has also occurred in the UK, New Zealand and Australia. The New South Wales state government in Australia launched an education campaign in May 2009 after receiving reports that girls as young as 13 were sexting. "I urge parents to warn their children about the consequences of sexting," said state Community Services Minister Linda Burney.[174]

## How can girls keep safe online?

There has been much debate about how girls can keep safe online, both from adult predators and from other children. Many of these are an extension of programmes and services that aim to keep girls safe offline as well. The Girls' Net project in South Africa has provided some safety tips aimed directly at girls themselves:[175, 176]

- Never give your personal details to anyone you have met online. This includes the name of your school, pictures of yourself, the place you live, anything someone could use to identify where you live.
- Do not send pictures of yourself to anyone – even if they send you one first (it might not even be a picture of them).
- If the person you are chatting to insists on information, or keeps pressing you about your details – stop chatting!
- If someone keeps trying to call or chat, or threatens you, tell someone you trust and get help.
- Report people who use abusive language, harass or abuse you to the people who run the social network you use – the perpetrator can be banned from using it.

## Online spaces for girls

Girls are savvy internet users, carving out new spaces for themselves online. The spaces created by girls are mostly aimed at 'building a community'[177], creating a supportive space where they can play with their identity and share their thoughts with other girls. This is of critical importance during adolescence as girls are "coming of age in a sexualised and media-saturated culture"[178] where body image can be a strong negative force. The online space to share and find support which might not be available in offline environments is an important support mechanism.

Spaces created for girls by social organisations such as girlsinc.org and lmk. girlscouts.org offer girls information, advice and a safe space to interact with their peers. LMK, by US-based Girl Scouts in partnership with Microsoft Windows, focuses specifically on online exploitative situations including cyberbullying and sexting and features a group of 23 teenage girls who provide online advice to girls using the site. As their website states: "These girls are stepping up to make the internet a safer place. Just like you, they have tons of opinions and stories to share, so check out their perspectives and discover how you too can improve the quality of your life online."[179]

It also provides advice to girls on how to protect themselves against online sexual predators and privacy breaches on social networking sites.

## Parental involvement – safety or surveillance?

*"Kids don't need protection; we need guidance. If you protect us you are making us weaker: we don't go through all the trial and error necessary to learn what we need to survive on our own... don't fight our battles for us; just give us assistance when we need it."*

From the Children's Call for Evidence, Byron Review, UK[180]

*"My Mum and Dad haven't got a clue, I set up the virus software and parent filter to control my brother. They should make it easier for parents to set up."*

Girl, 16, Cardiff, Wales, from the Children's Call for Evidence, Byron Review, UK[181]

It is not surprising, with all these stories and facts about exploitation and abuse of girls and young women via communications technologies, that parents are worried about their daughters' safety when using the internet. In urban areas in particular, parents may feel happier about their daughters' safety if they know they can contact, and be contacted by, them. Overall, mobile phones are used by girls more often for communication with their parents or caregivers. In a UK study, girls were found to make 50 calls or texts to parents or caregivers a week, versus 29 calls made by boys. Girls also received 67 calls/texts from caregivers versus 30 to boys. This heightened connectivity with girls is likely due to increased concerns about safety and security of girls.[182]

However, the line between freedom and control is a fine one. On the one hand, there are hugely positive aspects of ICTs that can have immense benefits for young women's lives. On the other, parental fear

about the dangers of the internet may lead them to see these technologies as negative and thus prevent their daughters from using them. This is particularly true as girls enter the transition period of adolescence, and parents try to use technology to check what their daughters are doing. For example, in some countries, brothers are monitoring their sisters' access to ICTs, and fathers and husbands may control their daughters' and wives' access to mobile phones.[183]

A number of surveys have examined how much parents are involved in discussing their children's online use. What emerged most strongly in all countries was the difference between what parents thought their children were doing and what the young people themselves perceived.

- In the UK, 81 per cent of parents are confident they know what their children are looking at online – 31 per cent of UK children disagree.
- India has the highest level of use of safety software – 55 per cent of parents have set controls on web usage.
- In Brazil parents think their children are spending 56 hours a month online. They are actually spending around 70 hours.
- In the US 86 per cent of teenage girls said they could chat in a chat room without their parents' knowledge and 30 per cent said they had been sexually harassed in a chat room; but only seven per cent told their parents immediately, because they were worried they would be banned from using chat rooms again.[184]
- In Thailand, 46 per cent of parents had not given their children any guiding rules for using the internet – 11 per cent had not even thought about it. Sixty-seven per cent of young people accessed the internet on computers with screening software. But 55 per cent of this group indicated they could get around such software.[185]

One 17 year-old girl said: "I wouldn't listen to my parents anyway, as they don't know enough."[186] Another young person noted: "Parents could be better educated in the way of computers, since kids are learning young, and can use the internet easily. If parents know the ins and outs of computers, protecting kids from adult material on the internet will be far easier."[187]

## Protecting girls online

There are a number of initiatives aimed at preventing online abuse of children. These also need a particular focus on adolescent girls.

- The Virtual Global Taskforce was created in 2003 to "better protect children from sexual exploitation wherever they are in the world".[188] It has six members: the Australian Federal Police, The National Child Exploitation Coordination Centre as part of the Royal Canadian Mounted Police, Italian Postal and Communication Police Service, the Child Exploitation and Online Protection Centre in the UK, US Immigration and Customs Enforcement and Interpol. Taskforce members work together to put in place systems to "share information and intelligence" in order to respond as quickly as possible to "cases where children are believed to be at immediate risk".[189] The Taskforce's projects include 'Operation Pin', a false child pornography website that captures the details of people trying to download child pornography from it.[190]
- The International Telecommunications Union has created the Child Online Protection Initiative. This identifies risk to children in cyberspace, develops tools to minimise such risks, creates awareness, and shares knowledge with the public.[191]
- UNIFEM'S Say No-UNiTE platform was launched in November 2009. The 'Say No' website allows activists working on gender violence issues to share ideas by posting an

'action' online. The action can be viewed and commented upon by other registered users, who can use the website to develop ideas and contacts with activists around the world. There are over 237,419 online 'actions' to date and heads of state and ministers from 69 governments have signed up to end violence against women.[192]

### PROTECTED SPACES – JAPANESE GIRLS, THE *KEITAI*, AND URBAN SPACE

The following account from Japan shows that girls are using the mobile phone to create physical space around them that deters men from approaching them.

In Japan, the *keitai* (translated as 'something you carry with you') – a mobile phone particularly used for emailing and sending photos – has been massively adopted: 70 per cent of the entire population carries one. According to one study, grade school and adolescent girls were almost twice as likely to carry a keitai. Of particular interest to producing urban space is the mobile use of the *kogyaru* – street-smart teenage girls – and *oyaji* – older men and fathers. Kenichi Fujimoto has focused on the dynamic and interplay throughout the 1990s, first with the adoption of pagers, and now with the proliferation of the keitai. He considers these "territory-generating apparatuses", wielded by savvy teen girls with a predilection toward loose socks and munching snacks on the train.

The keitai offers a tactic in Michel de Certeau's definition, a means of fighting the dominant male culture in Japanese urban space. The keitai does not even need to be used: its presence creates its own meaning. Its social and cultural constructions bombastically create kogyaru space. Fujimoto writes: "With a keitai, a girl can turn any space into her own room and personal paradise (*kekkai*), whether that be her favourite café or her own stall in a flea market. The keitai is a jamming machine that instantly creates a territory – a personal keitai space – around oneself with an invisible, minimal barricade." Even when signals aren't sent out as voice or text, carrying a 'cute' keitai is itself an effective visual anti-oyaji signal.[193]

This chapter has looked at the benefits of communications technologies for girls and how they are keen to adopt them and become aware of how they can improve their lives. They use them to communicate, to learn, to network. But we have also seen the barriers adolescent girls face in accessing these technologies, and the dangers that present themselves at the push of a button. The section on page 135 makes recommendations on keeping girls safe online and unleashing their potential.

# Brazilian adolescent girls in a digital world

For this year's 'Because I am a Girl' report, Plan commissioned original research in Brazil from the International Institute for Child Rights and Development (IICRD) through the Child Protection Partnership (CPP) Canada which worked with NECA, Obra de Berco, Secretariat of Social Inclusion of Municipality of Santo Andre, Estrela Dalva, Childhood Brasil, SaferNet, Plan Brazil. They held focus groups with 49 boys and 44 girls aged 10 to 14, developed and posted an online survey which was filled in by 400 respondents, and undertook a literature review and a review of protection practices in Brazil on girls and information and communications technologies (ICTs). They were assisted by an advisory group of adolescent girls.

The purpose of the research was to examine adolescent girls' rights and protection in Brazil within the context of ICTs. The research showed that the use of ICTs was growing very fast (see box below), particularly among 15 to 17 year olds, where between 2005 and 2008 there had been the highest percentage increase of all sectors of the population, from 33.7 to 62.9 per cent. The majority of girls in this research had mobile phones (86 per cent) and used the internet (82 per cent). Just over a quarter said they were 'always online'. For those girls who had access to a computer, they generally spent from one to seven hours a day online.

### THE FACTS ON BRAZIL AND INFORMATION AND COMMUNICATIONS TECHNOLOGIES
- More than 53% of Brazilians (86 million people) over 10 own a mobile phone, representing a growth of 54.9% (56 million) since 2005.[194]
- The number of people over 10 who logged on to the internet in the past three years has increased by 75.3% to 56 million users.
- Access to the internet has risen both for men and women in the past three years, from 21.9% to 35.8% for men, and from 20.1% to 33.9% for women.
- In 2008, 57.1% of users logged on to the internet from home, while 32.5% did so from Lan Houses (Local Area Network – internet cafés) and 31% from work computers.
- By 2009 Brazil had over 90,000 Lan houses, accounting for approximately half all internet access.
- Contacting or communicating with friends is given as the main reason for internet access – 83.2% – followed by entertainment at 68.6% and educational purposes at 65.9%. Education had dropped from first to third place since 2005.

## Online safety

Nearly all the girls and boys in the focus groups thought there was more danger online for girls than boys.

Girls said they go online at home, at a friend's or – for most of the girls living in shanty towns or favelas – at a Lan house. Many girls say that there are no risks at these places generally or that there is no risk because they are with people they can trust and who can protect them. Other girls indicate that there are risks such as theft of a cell phone, copying passwords or relationship profiles, rape, people posing as other people, kidnapping, shooting or illegal drugs.

*"Lan houses are not safe. There is drug dealing and people do whatever they feel like. There are no conversations. Users [of the Lan*

*houses] can be arrested if not duly registered – taken to a police station, where officers call up their mothers and later on the teenager is taken to Fundacao Casa [detention centre]."*

Girl, 13, São Paulo favela

*"A safe place is my brother-in-law's home. He's got a 'big piece' [38-revolver]."*

Girl, 11, São Paulo favela

When asked to identify the three dangers they or their friends face online, the girls said being hacked, people not being who they say they are, photos being spread around, false Orkut [social networking] page, viruses. Other comments included:

*"My friend met a girl and went to her and he was a guy."*

Girl, 13

*"My friend confided in a friend and showed him a picture of her naked and then he spread it to the whole club."*

Girl, 12

*"The girls open the webcam and show parts that shouldn't be displayed."*

Girl, 13

The respondents from the focus groups did not agree about whether it is safe to share information online. In one group, all participants said it was safe, while in another all participants said it was not safe. One 12 year-old girl stated: "The problem is not the information you post, but the people you accumulate: friend or stranger."

In the boys' group, boys said they believed that MSN was more dangerous than the other social network sites because it was more one-on-one. Boys believed that girls face much more risk online than boys. One 14 year-old boy explained how his friend "was online with a girl and asked her to take off her clothes when they were talking at MSN with the camera turned on. She did because he promised her a kiss. Suddenly the father of the girl arrived and took her out by pulling her by the hair."

The young people in all groups were roughly split when asked whether a friend of theirs had had a bad experience on Orkut, MSN or another relationship site. Some of the bad experiences included being contacted by someone or meeting someone who turned out to be someone else; a fake account being made on Orkut just to offend others; an account set up using someone else's personal information; a virus, hacking, gossip being spread, and theft of passwords and identity.

Virtually none of the girls had warned their friends about something bad online.

A group of teenagers in Brazil.

When there was a warning, it was about a computer virus.

## Links between online and offline behaviour

Although the girls themselves did not make the connection between online and offline behaviour, the research found that the realities and risks girls navigate online appear to be shaped by their offline environments. For example, girls from the São Paulo favela live with high levels of violence and drug trafficking, and poor quality education. They dress more provocatively than their private school counterparts, and appear to be more sexualised at an earlier age, perhaps because of the limited childhood they experience. This enables them to participate with older age groups, interpreted by our researchers as a rise in social status within their community. They appear to engage in risky behaviour with little regard for immediate consequences.

A flavour of the context in which the São Paulo favela girls live is captured by one girl who says that at school "some students end up carrying guns, using drugs, boozing and smoking cigarettes in the restrooms". Similarly, the adolescent girls from the Santo André favela had all been to the funk music club between midnight and 6am without their guardians' knowledge, where they interacted with men aged 20 and over, who in some cases were more than twice their age. In contrast, the girls from the Santo André private school live in a middle-class neighbourhood, all have computers and cell phones at home and live in an environment where "we look for work on the internet or things to help us do our homework".

The researchers noticed a marked difference between the private school and favela girls in their focus-group participation. The Santo André favela girls, for example, had difficulty understanding the scope of the issues raised in discussions. Their answers indicated that the internet is an instrument that enables them to express their libido by visiting sexually oriented sites and meeting with boys to boost their sense of value.

## Protecting girls online

While they may not appreciate the breadth of the online environment, the girls in this research appeared to have some awareness of potential online dangers. At the same time they clearly express a desire for their parents to be more involved in monitoring their behaviour, providing advice and helping them determine what is safe online and what is not. Ironically, many of the girls who did go to a parent when something bad happened online

*Online in a Brazilian internet café.*

indicated that they were reprimanded rather than helped. This was equally applicable across the focus groups. This is probably because many parents know very little about the online environments navigated by girls.

Most girls said their mother, teacher or friends advise them about online safety.

*"My mother said do not give my real name."*
                                            Girl, 13
*"My teacher said not to pass personal things and do not click on viruses."*
                                            Girl, 12
*"My friends told me to be smart, for me to be careful with the sites I visit."*
                                            Girl, 12

It appears that the greater the awareness and knowledge about ICT use, the greater the degree of security the girls feel online, but only 21 per cent said they felt safe. Fewer than half of the girls who responded to the survey indicated that their parents knew what they accessed online. However, about a third of them looked to their parents when they encountered online dangers. Only about a third of the girls knew how to report a danger or something that makes them feel bad online. Despite a majority indicating they have learned about online dangers (60 per cent), slightly fewer than half the girls still say they would go to meet someone in person that they had met online.

Surprisingly, even with significant legislative improvements to the ECA Statute of the Child and Adolescent (Law 8.069/1990) and in particular Articles 240 and 241, which expressly prohibit the production, sale or distribution of child pornography or explicit sex scenes involving children or adolescents in Brazil, no documentation, published material and/or scientific documents appear to focus on violence inflicted on adolescent girls through ICT usage.

## Recommendations

*1 Connect families and caring adults so they are a protective factor in the online lives of girls*

Adults are discovering that they are way behind young people in the use of ICTs, and young people are realising that the internet is not as safe a place as they might have thought. In a 2009 training session that CPP led with adults and young people, the question was posed to the group: "Would you post your photo and details about your life at the bus station?" Most of the young people said they would not. This provides some insight into how young people regard the online environment. They may forget that posting information online means that it cannot be retrieved and that there is the potential of it reaching a billion people, a few more than at the local bus stop where a poster is likely to fade and fall away before long. Some young people do not see the online environment for what it is. However, this reality became very poignant for the girls in the focus groups who indicated that young girls are posting or are having others post sexualised images of them online.

Widespread, targeted education initiatives that engage both girls and their families in the locations where the girls may access their virtual world would be a positive first step. Such learning opportunities could demystify some of the online world for parents, while providing key information for the girls, and open a welcoming channel of communication between girls and their parents that can be accessed without fear of rebuke.

*2 Foster child protection links between offline and online environments in communities*

In both the favela and private school context, there are opportunities to build stronger child protection practices between offline and online environments. For example, one of the Lan houses in the São Paulo favela is run by a good owner who offers a safe place to the adolescents and affordable access. This is one of the few places where the adolescents feel safe. Building on this type of Lan house, offline protective practices such as education that encourages safe online use, codes of conduct for behaviour on- and off-line, and enforcement of applicable rules and laws on- and off-line can serve to improve the opportunities and possibilities of even the most vulnerable adolescents. The Lan house may be intended to offer digital access but in the end may offer a socio-educational base in the community. Similarly, a home, school or community centre in other contexts may provide the natural nexus for protecting children on- and off-line.

### 3 Harness the potential benefits of ICT in support of adolescent girls

The research suggests that girls' current online activity is devoted primarily to socialising and entertainment. While these activities can foster girls' development, there appear to be numerous additional ways that girls might be supported in the online environment to specifically support their safe navigation of the virtual world. These might include:

Working with girls to create platforms, or strategies within existing platforms, where they can share positive or negative things they encounter online or off (for example, sharing an alias used by 'perverts' in chatrooms so other girls can avoid them, or sharing information about safely using Lan houses).

Fostering an online platform where girls can share information with security officers and the stakeholders from the Brazilian guarantee of rights system that furthers girls' protection.

Accessing online advice or therapy that may not otherwise be available to girls. This concept is in its infancy in Brazil and such therapy could also be an opportunity made available to adults.

Create ICT education opportunities for girls to navigate ICT safely taught by girls.

### 4 Engage systems at all levels to uphold, implement and enforce laws

Local, state and national actors have a role to play in ensuring the online environments and points of online access used by adolescent girls are regulated and safe. There are also several additional private and public actors in Brazil who operate as part of the system that affects girls who need to work together on prevention, protection and prosecution efforts, including internet service providers, owners of social networking sites, Lan houses and internet cafés, law enforcement, prosecutors, judges, the guardianship councils and non-governmental organisations.

With amendments to Brazil's Statute of the Child and Adolescent that criminalises possession of images of child abuse, Brazil has a strong, national legal framework to protect children online. This is supported by the UN Convention on the Rights of the Child's Optional Protocol on the Sale of Children, Child Prostitution and Child Pornography, and the Rio Pact. In addition, law at the state level exists in the State of São Paulo to register users of Lan houses, and additional legislation is being considered to block pornographic sites for users under the age of 18 years. While these laws provide a framework, there is a need for clarity about their application and enforcement so that they address the lived realities of adolescent girls in Brazil.

There appears to be an urgent need to build confidence and trust in authorities at the local level, in the communities where girls live. The vast majority of focus group participants did not readily see a role for police in helping to keep them safe online. In fact, in one of the boys' groups it was noted that police will sometimes plant drugs on the boys, arrest them and demand money for their release.

### 5 Undertake further research on girls and ICT

More research is needed that specifically targets adolescent girls and ICTs in order to understand better the realities of adolescent girls online. Such research might consider how online social norms impact her protection and development. For example:

What might be the implication of a girl's status in the virtual world where there is pressure to have a high number of 'friends' on social networking sites such as Orkut? Does this place adolescent girls at greater risk by encouraging them to accept communications and invitations from strangers?

What degree of self-protection do girls engage in as a matter of course? For example, some girls in the focus groups appear to provide fake names and ages to protect themselves while exploring online communications and relationships.

How do adolescent girls develop healthy sexuality when what is cool is determined by online sites located in an environment dominated by sexually explicit videos and pictures? For example, a focus group respondent mentioned that when going to a soap opera site, pornography sites pop up. Where do they find healthy role models?

# Unleashing girls' potential
## Recommendations on adolescent girls and ICTs

*"I feel that it's important for teens to advocate for online safety because the internet is an amazing thing! It is a useful and fun tool, and more and more kids are using it all the time... By teaching teens and their parents about dangers online, and how to deal with them, we can help teens to enjoy the internet safely and responsibly."*

Ada, 14, US[195]

*"When people share data on Orkut, they can find out where you live, may smuggle you, kidnap you."*

Girl, 12, Brazil[196]

The very nature of online culture makes it hard to control, and in many ways we lose a lot when we try to do so. But in order to protect girls and young women and to enhance the opportunities which modern technologies bring, we do need to find ways to balance this new, open and less censored space with some level of regulation.

Power relations in society determine the costs and benefits from new technologies, and so ICT programmes and policies are not gender neutral. Policymakers need to ask themselves who benefits from ICTs; who is at risk from access or no access to ICTs; who is dictating how these technologies are developed, and how they can be used to serve or defeat the larger goals of equality, justice and safety.

International and national laws and policies are trailing the rapid advancement in IT platforms. Existing conventions and national legislation need to be stepped up and more rigorously implemented. The pace of development in the ICT sector is only going to accelerate. The remaining question is – will the world work together to ensure

UK students using computers for a school linking project.

PLAN

that the violence and commercial and sexual exploitation that girls are subject to in everyday life, is not simply translated and exacerbated by the power and reach of the online world?

A balance must be struck between a child's right to privacy, and their right to protection as set out in the Convention on the Rights of the Child, especially Article 13[197], Article 16[198] and Article 17[199]. The 2008 Strasbourg resolution on children's online safety called on all states to: "Support the development of education-based approaches... to ensure children and young people around the world have access to a safe online environment respectful of their privacy."

More must be done to increase access and availability of technology throughout developing regions. As mentioned earlier in this chapter, ICTs can leapfrog the development of emerging economies and support developing countries to achieve the Millennium Development Goals. Investing in ICT infrastructure is critical: "In the 21st century, affordable, ubiquitous broadband networks will be as critical to social and economic prosperity as networks such as transport, water and power," says ITU Secretary-General Hamadoun I. Touré.[200]

We call on duty bearers at all levels to invest in creating the infrastructure needed to ensure girls and boys, in developing and emerging economies as well as in richer ones, have access to ICTs and are given the opportunity to use these technologies to their, and their countries', advantage.

We call on duty bearers at all levels including governments, the business sector and civil society to work together to do more to protect girls online and to ensure that girls have the capacity and knowledge to protect themselves and each other. While girls themselves may sometimes conform to internalised traditional gender roles, it is important for them to develop their own knowledge and perspectives in order for them to be genuinely present in these spaces. Girls may recognise the risks of their online presence but they often lack the experience, knowledge and tools to mitigate those risks. Adolescent girls must be empowered to use the internet and other communications technologies safely, on their own terms, and in ways that promote their overall development and build their future possibilities.

The call to action in this section draws on the primary and secondary research carried out for this report, and includes the experiences and opinions of adolescent girls. They are also based on the good practice which already exists, examples of which are highlighted both here and earlier in this chapter.

## CALL TO ACTION

### Increase girls' access and control over IT hardware

- Governments, the business sector and civil society should work together to invest in infrastructure. This should not be limited to hardware, but must include large-scale investments in speed broadband communication networks. Ensure computer centres are available in schools and ICT 'nuts and bolts' education is mainstreamed into national curricula so girls will be able to access and use new technologies.

- Donors and civil society need to conduct better research to identify and document the differing needs and uses of ICT users, according to both their gender and their age, to ensure adolescent girl users are 'visible' to policymakers.

- IT companies should **invest in increasing girls' access** to technologies through *community communication centres* and the adoption of low-cost open-source technologies that encourage knowledge-sharing and skills-building at the local level.

- IT companies need to go beyond just 'listening to girls' to proactively **enabling girls to be involved in developing new initiatives** for future ICT planning and policies. Consultative 'girl only' panels should be created and consultations should be held regularly to ensure girls are having their say and influencing technological developments.

- IT companies need to involve girls fully in the designing and monitoring of new technological applications with a view to the emerging risks they present, especially in mobile 'smart' phones which are readily available to adolescent girls in developed regions.

## DIGIGIRLZ: "I THOUGHT YOU HAD TO BE A GEEK TO WORK HERE"

Microsoft's DigiGirlz programmes give high-school girls in the US the opportunity to learn about careers in technology, connect with Microsoft employees, and participate in hands-on computer and technology workshops. Its DigiGirlz High Tech Camps work to dispel stereotypes of the high-tech industry. During the camp, the girls listen to executive speakers, participate in technology tours and demonstrations, network, and learn with hands-on experience in workshops. One of the girls who attended the camps said:

*"I am now much, much more interested in technology-related careers. They are so much fun."*

*"I thought you had to be a geek to work here, but this camp changed my mind,"* commented another.[201]

### Invest in maths, science and vocational education

- Governments and international donors need to increase girls' **access to quality primary and secondary education** through financial or technical assistance, scholarships, quotas and other incentives – in particular, science and mathematics **and vocational training**. Girls must be equipped with the necessary skills to prepare them for a full range of roles in information technology as users, creators, programmers, designers, and managers – and not just call-centre operators or administrators.[202]

### Increase governance, accountability and online protection

- Multilateral and donor agencies need to **allocate resources and establish benchmark criteria** for incorporating gender dimensions into new or existing IT programmes.

- Governments must **regulate the commercial use of children's online play spaces**. Thus governments would effectively stop children-orientated websites from selling ad-space to advertisements targeting children.

- Governments must **regulate the collection of personal information** of all children under 13 years of age on commercial websites. Furthermore, for youth over the age of 13, disclosed information may only be used in relation to the web content and only with the explicit consent of the teen user. Websites must ensure their consent forms are youth-friendly and presented in simple, clear language.[203]

- Governments need to set up mechanisms to **ensure that girls' needs and rights are represented in government agencies** tasked with developing and implementing ICT programmes and policies.

- Governments, donors and civil society organisations need **to make sure that girls' needs and rights are represented in monitoring and reporting mechanisms** for ICT programmes and policies.[204]

### Redesign online content and language

- Reclaim the word 'GIRL' from search engines. **Challenge internet service providers** to find ways to ensure that typing in the word 'girl' does not inevitably lead to page upon page of pornographic and violent material.
- Lack of language skills places an additional burden on girls' ability to access the internet and mobile phone programmes. IT companies and internet service providers should do more to **break down language barriers** to information through the development and roll-out of multilingual tools and databases, interfaces for non-Latin alphabets and improved automatic translation software.
- Governments and Civil Society Organisations should develop content which is both locally relevant and challenges social stereotypes. Priority needs to be given to content that is developed by girls and which helps them support their needs, aspirations and well-being, such as the **US-based Girl Scouts 'Let Me Know'**.[205]
- Governments and industry regulators must hold Internet Service Providers **accountable for defamatory and illegal content**. This includes social media sites,

and user-created content which is posted on a public profile.

- Increase democratisation of information. Civil society organisations, **UN agencies and gender activists should include girls** in formulating IT content in order to make this information truly relevant and accessible.
- Industry regulators must **hold social media website owners accountable** for monitoring user-generated information and content. Platforms which allow children and youth to contribute content and interact through the website must be required to enable full external moderation of content.

 ### SUPPORTING GIRLS: SUGGESTIONS FROM RESEARCH IN BRAZIL

The Brazil research for this report[206] suggests numerous additional ways that girls might be supported to navigate the virtual world safely. These might include:

- Working with girls to create platforms, or strategies within existing platforms, where girls can share relevant information. For example, sharing an alias used by paedophiles in chat rooms so other girls can avoid them, or sharing information about safely using internet cafés. Because they can be easily changed by offenders, these 'aliases' should be shared between girls and reported to law enforcers.
- Fostering an online platform where girls can share information with security officers.

In an online survey, the girls themselves suggested several ways that they themselves or others can help them to be safe online. These included:

*"Do not give information about yourself to people you do not know."*

Girl, 13, Santo Andre

*"My friend who I trust gives me guidance and I give advice to her."*

Girl, 13, São Paulo

*"Have a help bar."*

Girl, 15, Espirito Santo do Pinhal

*"A message highlighted in red when there is a risk of danger."*

Girl, 17, Espirito Santo do Pinhal

It is important that the content of any online education programme is accurate and includes advice on reporting crimes to law enforcement.

### Stop violence against girls and women online

- IT companies, in collaboration with governments, should conduct more research on **how perpetrators use technologies against girls** in order to introduce effective measures against them.[207]
- Governments should pass laws requiring Internet Service Providers to **report the discovery of child sexual abuse images**. Such legislation has successfully been enacted in both the United States and Australia.[208]
- Government agencies should **establish national tip-line websites** for reporting the online sexual exploitation of children and ensure appropriate follow up. These should be part of every country's arsenal of child protection tools and could align to the format of the Child Help Line that places a duty on all adults to report suspicions that a child is in need of protection.
- Social media websites should all include a **'panic button'** option[209] for children and youth to report other users who make them feel unsafe, or to report an abuse in progress.
- **Municipalities and local/community police should ensure girls can safely use internet cafés** such as the Philippine make-IT-safe campaign.[210]
- **Internet service providers** (ISPs) should **develop effective codes of conduct** including the reporting and removal of abusive websites by ISPs in conjunction with law enforcement agencies.[211] For example, the UK Code of Conduct for mobile phones, facilitated by the GSMA in Europe, whereby child safety filters are enabled by default. This can be applied in other regions too.[212]

### Implement international legislation and increase collaboration

- **Legislation must address the fact that girls are more exposed to the risk of sexual exploitation**, violence and abuse through the channels of new technology than boys.

- **Policymakers must ensure that adolescent girls are empowered to use the internet** and other communications technologies safely, on their own terms, and in ways that promote their own overall development and build their future possibilities.[213]
- **Legal instruments need to be enacted, strengthened and implemented** to protect adolescent girls from online abuse. Governments should sign up to the Council of Europe Convention, which is the first international treaty explicitly calling for approximation of legislation, cooperation between states and the criminalisation of images of child abuse. It also sets a common criminal policy for images of child abuse.
- **Increase collaboration between different actors.** Government, business and civil society sectors need to work together to tackle online protection effectively. This includes sex- and age-specific training for girls on how to protect their privacy and keep safe when online, as well as how to report abuse; and building trust between adolescent girls and authorities such as the police and judiciary through joint activities and gender-awareness training.
- Establish national and independent watchdogs and strengthen **mechanisms for consumer protection** in the ICT industry to monitor the portrayal of stereotypical and/or negative images of girls and women.
- The use of old laws and policies to **enforce actions against defamation, malicious speech**, etc need to be widened to take account of virtually limitless and cross border harm done to girls whose images are appropriated for improper use on the internet.
- The veil of anonymity on the internet needs to be pierced and **governments must tighten privacy legislation** aimed at the obligations of internet service providers.
- Laws need to be designed and enforced that encompass a total prohibition on the collection, use or disclosure of personal information of anyone under the age of 13, with or without any alleged consent. **Consent to the use of personal information on the internet must be free and informed** and therefore child and parent appropriate.

## PLAN'S CHILD PROTECTION ONLINE SAFETY RULES

1  No personal details
2  Don't send pictures
3  Don't hand out your password
4  Never arrange to meet anyone in person
5  Never hang around in a chat room if someone says or writes something that makes you uncomfortable or worried
6  Never respond to nasty, suggestive or rude emails
7  Never believe junk or spam email
8  Don't open files from people you don't know
9  Always report when you see bad language or distasteful pictures
10  Always be yourself
11  What is posted online becomes public and cannot always be removed. So, no post about friends, family and teachers.

The digital revolution is here to stay. The big question is: how do we find the balance between protection and participation and empower girls to navigate these new technological frontiers? This will be a continuing challenge as we consider adolescent girls on the cutting edge of change in the 21st century.

# Conclusion

In this report we have heard the voices of adolescent girls from all over the world, living in many different circumstances and facing many different challenges. No two girls will be the same, but, wherever they are and however they live, they have the same rights and the same call on all of us to make these rights a reality.

This is the fourth report in the 'Because I am a Girl' series. In all of them we have come across discrimination and neglect as well as resilience and determination. Whether we look at girls in war zones, girls in the global economy or girls in cities and in technology, we find the same combination of girls getting a raw deal and girls coping with all that life can throw at them. There are some who are overcome by the hardships they endure, who do not survive or thrive; but many succeed against the odds. In this report there is Precious from South Africa, who survived the streets to become a mentor for other street girls; in the 2009 report, we featured Geeta from Nepal who started her own business; and in 2008 we showed how Princess from Liberia was forced to fight in the war but is now working as a carpenter. We can learn from their experiences, from the stories they have told us and the common threads that run through girls' lives and through the report series. We have made specific recommendations to improve the opportunities of girls in the two arenas that this report has focused on, but more generally we can all contribute. We need to listen to adolescent girls' views and ensure that their voices are heard by decision-makers. We need to learn from what they have to say. We need to include them in research, in planning and in policies. We need to invest in girls' skills and ensure that they have access to information, the skills to use it and the power to protect themselves. And finally, we have shown that what many of them have achieved in the face of adversity is truly remarkable. We need to celebrate these achievements and ensure that all girls, wherever they live in the world, have the same chances in life as their brothers.

## SILENT NO MORE: CHILD RIGHTS IN EGYPT

*"My mother used to listen to my brothers and not to me. I used to be afraid and never imagined I could do what I can do now. Now they listen to me as well and treat me the same as my brothers. I am the secretary of the school parliament. I want to be a child doctor. I want to distribute all the experience and knowledge I have to other girls around the world."*

Asalaa, 12, Alexandria

*"To be honest, before I joined these meetings I thought girls were useless and couldn't do anything. Now I realise this is not true and they can do as much as boys. In fact, I went and talked to my parents about this. At first they were surprised but then they agreed with me."*

Farouq, boy aged 12, El Marg

*"Nobody can take my rights from me now. These programmes are also changing the behaviour of the families – they have stereotypes that a girl must stay at home with her husband, and at the beginning there was much resistance to girls joining the programme. This is now going away because parents are seeing the difference in their daughters. We used to be silent at home and not say what we thought. We will not be silent any more."*

Manal, 15, El Marg, Cairo

ANURAK PATHKIT

# Because We are Girls
## 'Real Choices, Real Lives' cohort study update

# Millennium Development Goals

**ERADICATE EXTREME POVERTY AND HUNGER**

**Goal 1:**
**Eradicate extreme poverty and hunger**

**IMPROVE MATERNAL HEALTH**

**Goal 5:**
**Improve maternal health**

**ACHIEVE UNIVERSAL PRIMARY EDUCATION**

**Goal 2:**
**Achieve universal primary education**

**COMBAT HIV/AIDS, MALARIA AND OTHER DISEASES**

**Goal 6:**
**Combat HIV/AIDS, malaria and other diseases**

**PROMOTE GENDER EQUALITY AND EMPOWER WOMEN**

**Goal 3:**
**Promote gender equality and empower women**

**ENSURE ENVIRONMENTAL SUSTAINABILITY**

**Goal 7:**
**Ensure environmental sustainability**

**REDUCE CHILD MORTALITY**

**Goal 4:**
**Reduce child mortality**

**A GLOBAL PARTNERSHIP FOR DEVELOPMENT**

**Goal 8:**
**Develop a Global Partnership for Development**

# Empowered and Lifted Out of Poverty? 'Real Choices, Real Lives' and the Millennium Development Goals

*"I want her to be a good person and I want her mother and her to prepare and have a career. It is the only way to overcome poverty in an honest way."*

Grandmother of Noelia,
Dominican Republic

**The 'Real Choices, Real Lives' study was set up in 2007 to follow 142 girls from birth until their 9th birthday in 2015 – the target year set by world leaders for achieving the Millennium Development Goals. The study is now in its 4th year and continues to follow 130 girls in nine different countries across the world – Brazil, El Salvador, Dominican Republic, Benin, Togo, Uganda, Cambodia, Philippines and Vietnam.**

What do the lives of the girls in the 'Real Choices, Real Lives' study tell us? Are they being equipped to overcome poverty, to have the career which Noelia's grandmother, quoted above, says is the only way forward? In September 2010, the world's leaders, politicians and decision-makers will be meeting at the United Nations to discuss progress towards meeting the Millennium Development Goals (MDGs): global poverty targets which should be achieved by 2015.

The decisions they make will directly affect the lives of the 130 girls whose families have, for the last four years, given us detailed information about their daughters' lives, and their hopes and fears for them. The reality revealed is that girls do not have the assets they need – the health, education, or skills – to thrive, and the effect of this failure will be felt by their children and their children's children. Evidence from the 'Real Choices, Real Lives' study shows how a consistent

failure of governments to invest in targeted programmes that address the challenges faced by the world's poorest girls is having a real and detrimental impact on the lives of this small group of girls from nine countries around the world.

This year's research shows that many of the families taking part in the cohort study still face a daily struggle to ensure their daughters' very survival. Over the four years of the study, five of the little girls have died. In Togo this year, Yassiminatou sadly died before she could get to a healthcare centre, while Gastine's life was only saved because she had speedy and free access to a local health worker. As we will see in the case of girls from the cohorts in Benin, Togo and Uganda in particular, the lack of adequate

*Gastine and her mother*

PLAN

healthcare and nutrition is already making its mark. The effects of poverty on under-five year olds are often irreversible.

Researchers working with our cohort study in El Salvador have expressed concerns that girls have no access to a pre-school programme and are not being adequately nourished or stimulated at home. With only five years remaining before the MDGs should be met, the reality for the girls taking part in our study – who will be between 9 and 10 years old in 2015 – is that time is running out.

This year, we examined the choices families are making. How do they feed and educate their families, what are the pressures around migration and family members working away from home? How do they make money, and what do they spend it on? We explored the attitudes of the girls' parents towards education, towards keeping their girls safe, and we talked with them about their hopes for the future. We also examined the views of the girls' teenage relatives and neighbours, and analysed these interviews alongside the earlier interviews with the girls' grandparents. The in-depth interviews across three generations revealed largely positive and progressive views on girls' education. These positive attitudes should help deliver the Millennium Development Goals, but they break down in the face of poverty – families will still choose to invest in a son's schooling ahead of a daughter's. The lack of investment in girls by their families, but crucially also by governments in key areas such as girls' education and healthcare provision, has ultimately meant that progress towards meeting the goals is off-track.

Indeed, one of the crucial targets affecting girls – to reach gender parity in primary school enrolment – should have been met by 2005. Several of the MDGs are directly at threat through lack of investment in girls, starting with MDG 1. Crucial investments are also needed in access to healthcare to stop more girls dying (MDG 4); to prevent girls from missing out on school because of persistent illness (MDG 6); and to establish pre-school education so that girls and their families become more engaged in their education (MDG 2 and 3). The critical moment for these girls is now.

## WHO IS IN THE SAMPLE?

The study is following a core group of 130 largely randomly selected girls from nine countries. From the original group of 142 families, eight have left the study due to migration and, sadly, five girls have died. Each country has a cohort of between 15 and 22 girls (see map page 156 for more details). The majority of the girls live either in rural settings or on the outskirts of large towns. Many will not have easy access to a secondary school or to a major hospital. The majority are from farming families, and some supplement their income by petty trading, particularly in El Salvador, Dominican Republic and Brazil. Others have taken to seasonal migration for work, for example in Benin and Togo.

The 'Real Choices, Real Lives' study is a relatively small sample study which allows Plan's researchers to examine, in detail, a range of issues affecting girls by using in-depth interviews, focus groups and questionnaires. In the first two years of the study, baseline information was gathered through structured interviews. By year three, researchers began to explore the families' lives further through semi-structured interviews with the girls' parents, grandparents and other relatives. In year four, the researchers focused on progress towards meeting the MDGs by examining how families generate an income and feed their families, choices they make about migration and the reality of trying to ensure their daughters' access to quality education. In addition to interviews with the older siblings, cousins and neighbours of the cohort families, we also held a series of discussions with a wider group of teenage girls and boys in Brazil, El Salvador, Philippines, Togo and Uganda to understand their view of the changing world around them.

There are some practical challenges to running this kind of study in a developing country. Individual family members or whole families may move to other regions, to larger towns or cities, providing little information about their whereabouts. In fact, eight of the girls are already reported as having moved away. Where literacy rates are low, it can be challenging to communicate the value of the families' continued involvement in a study like this one. Families may choose not to continue to be interviewed every year as a result – four families have chosen to leave the study so far and this year returns in two countries, El Salvador and the Dominican Republic, were low. The intrusion into family life has also to be carefully considered.

**ERADICATE
EXTREME POVERTY
AND HUNGER**

**Key targets:** *Reduce by half the number of people living on less than a dollar a day by 2015; and reduce by half the proportion of people who suffer from hunger by 2015*

Globally, the majority of people living on less than $1 a day are female. The reality of the female face of poverty has not been fully factored into the indicators and targets of the MDGs. Progress towards reducing income poverty is being measured, but without a full analysis of the gender component of poverty reduction.

A closer look at how the families taking part in the 'Real Choices, Real Lives' study spend their meagre household incomes shows the impact of poverty on long-term decisions they can make, and how these decisions affect their daughters. Several

*Cintia and her mother*

CLAUDIA CANUTO

families have already mentioned cost as a factor in their decision not to send their daughters to pre-school. The poorer the family, the larger the proportion of their income that is spent on food – more than 90 per cent is spent by the families in Benin and Togo. We also asked families to explain what they would do if there was an unexpected expenditure, such as a family member requiring medical treatment. More than 50 per cent of families in the seven countries where this data was gathered said they would have to borrow the money, either from a relative, a money lender or a credit union, indicating that their incomes are not sufficient for families to have savings.

Several families taking part in the study in Cambodia, Philippines and Brazil receive a small monthly grant from their governments to supplement their income, usually with the proviso that their children will be enrolled in school or will be vaccinated. This type of investment can make a big difference to the girls themselves, and can play a large part towards reducing the number of people suffering from hunger. The Brazilian government, for example, provides a package of social security allowances for low-income families. The foundation of this social security programme is called *Bolsa Familiar* (Family Package) – an allowance of about $40 a month per child, granted on condition that parents send their children to school and have them vaccinated. The government also provides a *Bolsa de PETI* (an ending child labour allowance) of $15 a month per child, to encourage children who are at risk of dropping out of school in order to work to remain in education.

### Cintia, Brazil

Our researchers have met Cintia's mother, Silvana, and her four brothers several times now. They live in a rural area in the north east of Brazil. Cintia's father works as a poorly paid agricultural labourer. The family qualifies for the Brazilian government's Bolsa Familiar scheme, and receives a grant of $70 each month. Although they grow vegetables in their garden, almost 90 per cent of this family's income is spent on food.

## Coping with poverty – migration to cities

One response to poverty is for family members – or sometimes whole families – to migrate to the nearest town, city or even to a city in another country. Although the vast majority of the girls taking part in our cohort study and their families currently live in rural areas, the dramatic changes described in this year's 'Because I am a Girl' report are certainly impacting on their families. Migration to cities is impacting on the lives of the families in Latin America (Brazil, Dominican Republic and El Salvador) and in West Africa (Benin and Togo) in particular. In Benin, for example, a third of all the families taking part in the study are separated by seasonal or long-term migration to nearby or capital cities.

The views of the mothers of the girls taking part in the cohort study in El Salvador capture this ambition for a better economic life. Most of them would like to migrate abroad to make a better life for themselves and their children. "The dream of everyone is to travel [migrate] to the United States." At home in El Salvador, work is seasonal and poorly paid. Those who can secure a permanent job are paid slightly more – between $2.50 and $3.00 per day.

Research from across West Africa confirms that the departure of girls and young women to cities can be perceived both as a 'relief' and as an extra source of income for the family.[1] And as one Brazilian mother says: "When our daughters leave home to move to cities, it is always for a better life... [they are] searching for new work or study opportunities, which will provide them with a better, more comfortable life."

### FOR A BETTER LIFE

The teenagers we interviewed in Uganda were motivated to move to cities and gave the following reasons:
- Lack of employment in their communities of origin
- To send money back home and support their elderly parents
- To live a more exciting life than they have in the village
- To reduce family expenditure at home
- To raise money in order to build a house in their village of origin
- To pay school fees of their siblings
- Ultimately to help other family members to get jobs in the city/town.

In the Philippines, teenagers we interviewed explained that the majority of those who move away to work are mothers, and that they have observed that when mothers move away, their daughters tend to marry soon after graduating from secondary school. The majority of the Brazilian teenagers felt that migration to cities had a negative impact on family members who remained. In El Salvador, two of the girls taking part in the study are being raised by their grandmothers, as their parents have migrated to the United States and to Italy. Others are being raised only by their mothers because their fathers have migrated to cities abroad. "In my case, my husband moved to the United States leaving me alone with six small creatures [children]," one mother told us.

In Brazil, at least half of the parents interviewed were considering moving to a city, and 75 per cent of the girls indicated that their fathers had left home at various times, seeking work opportunities. One girl gave this account:
*"My father left. He spent three years away from home to work. The family was sad; he didn't even see my brother when he was born, and when my brother died, my father couldn't even come home to see him..."*

**ACHIEVE UNIVERSAL PRIMARY EDUCATION**

**Key target:** *Ensure that all boys and girls complete a full course of primary education by 2015*

Achieving MDG 2 is largely reliant on real progress being made on the MDG 3 target to ensure gender parity in education enrolment. This target should have been met by 2005.

*Salimata and her family*

## REAL LIVES – MIGRATION IN TOGO

Migration within Togo and to its neighbouring countries is widespread. More than 40 per cent of the Togolese population already lives in an urban area. It is not uncommon for adolescent girls and boys to be sent to towns and cities to live with relatives and to work or to train as apprentices. Out of the 20 Togolese families taking part in the cohort study, at least 12 have reported that a close family member has moved in the past year. Aridjatou's older siblings live in Gabon. Maninani's mother works part of the year in Lomé, the capital of Togo. One of Maridiyatou's older siblings lives in Ghana; a second lives in Lomé. Salimata has an older sister who lives in Nigeria.

Several of the families taking part in the cohort study mentioned that in order for their daughters to pursue the kind of education they would like, they would have to move to Sekode, which has secondary and post-secondary education facilities. Sekode is the nearest town for many of the families. It is on the main road running north to south through Togo – one of the major child trafficking routes in West Africa – an added risk to counterbalance the educational advantages which the town has to offer.

In nearby Soutouboua we met with a group of older girls – their stories illustrate the pressures to migrate from this part of

Togo. Abide left her family at the age 15 to earn money in Nigeria:

*"I come from a poor family and we had no money. I had nothing to do so I thought I may as well go to Nigeria. I went with my sister. I expected to find material things, but when I arrived it was very different. I was working as a maid 18 hours a day from 4am to 10pm for 5,000 cprs [$10] per month. Now I am back home and have been training to be a seamstress for the past three years. The money is much better and it is safer. I know maids who were beaten by their employers or who were not fed."*

Robeline and Joceline are both orphans, now aged 18 and 20. Three years ago, they took the more traditional route of working in the Togolese capital of Lomé. Robeline first worked as a maid. Her employer did not treat her well, making her work 18 hours a day with no holidays, and paying her $10 per month. A neighbour helped Robeline find a better-paid job at $15 per month with a kindly employer. Soon after their father died, their mother became ill. There was no money for hospital bills so Joceline went to Lomé and became apprenticed to a hairdresser, where she earned $25 per month.

All three girls were now happy to be back home in a Plan-supported vocational training school for seamstresses. A trained seamstress can earn more than $1 per hour, providing them with a much better future.

But of the 113 countries that failed to achieve gender parity in both primary and secondary school enrolment by the target date of 2005, only 18 are likely to achieve the goal by 2015. Progress is slow and increased investment in specific initiatives that encourage girls both to enrol and to remain in school are crucial. These should include investing in pre-school facilities, as evidence from various studies shows that participation in quality early childhood care and development programmes, including pre-school, can have a positive effect on how girls and their families engage with primary education and beyond.[2]

Our study shows that despite a major shift in attitudes towards the importance of girls' education in all of the countries taking part, parents still face immense economic difficulty when it comes to providing for their families and investing in their children's education. Combined with attitudes that determine strict boundaries around gender roles and responsibilities in the home, it is as yet unclear how much progress the girls taking part in the study will actually make. The study shows that girls are expected to combine a heavy domestic workload together with their schoolwork, whereas boys have more time to study and to socialise.

Almost half of the girls – 46 per cent across the seven countries where this has been reported – have already started to attend pre-school. Riza's mother from the Philippines explains: "Angelica is now in grade 3, Angie Rhea is in grade 1, while Riza is enrolled in the day care centre. Education of my children is very important so that they will have a bright future ahead…"

Thi Kim Khanh's mother in Vietnam explains her motivation for enrolling her

*Angel and her mother*

daughter in school: "Education enables her to know the right things… she has to be educated to be able to work, not like us farmers."

### Sreytin, Cambodia

Sreytin has been enrolled in the community pre-school in her village, as part of an early childhood care and development programme supported by Plan. Sessions run from 7am to 10am and include a cooked breakfast. Her mother explained the immediate benefits for Sreytin: "She is braver than before. She knows how to respect people, especially older people. She knows many friends. She can sing songs and she likes singing and dancing very much."

### Angel, Uganda

Angel is attending a nursery school. She also meets regularly with her local play group. In the group, Angel likes singing songs. All of her older siblings are in school. Angel's mother explains: "Girls are good at bringing about change in society and, if educated, they can transform their family as well as their community." She goes on: "It's

*Sreytin and her mother*

**COMBAT HIV/AIDS, MALARIA AND OTHER DISEASES**

**Key target:** *Halt and begin to reverse the incidence of malaria and other major diseases*

It is widely acknowledged that children who face nutritional deficiencies in early childhood also face learning difficulties, leading to lower educational attainment.[5] We can already see from our questionnaires that illness has kept Brenam and Fridos Is. in Togo from what would have been their first year in school, and caused Reaksa in Cambodia to miss the formal school enrolment date, and therefore an entire school year. As the study progresses we will be looking more closely at the impact of persistent illness and poor nutrition on the girls taking part in the study.

In the countries with the lowest health indicators taking part in our study – Togo, Benin and Uganda – the girls are not only

*Gloria*

PLAN

facing a daily challenge of poor nutrition, but they are also battling a constant onslaught of illness and disease. Despite a high proportion of the girls receiving both first and second round basic immunisations – across six countries where it was reported, all of the girls were immunised as babies and 94 per cent have received their second round of immunisations – many still face persistent illness. Malaria, for example, continues to be a problem for the cohort in Uganda, Togo and Benin, with the majority of the girls being treated at various times over the year either at the local health centre or the nearest hospital. The call for governments to increase their investment in preventing and treating diseases like malaria cannot be louder.

**Anna Maria, Uganda**
In the last year, Anna Maria fell sick with malaria and was taken to Kamuli government hospital for treatment. The hospital is four kilometres away from Anna Maria's home – her mother carried her there on her back. Anna Maria has made a full recovery.

**Gloria, Uganda**
Gloria was also treated at Kamuli government hospital, where she was put on a drip after being diagnosed with malaria. The family took her to hospital on a motorbike, a three-kilometre journey. Gloria has also made a full recovery.

**Ruth, Uganda**
Ruth sometimes suffers from convulsive malaria. Her parents took her to the nearest hospital, where they made a note of the drugs she was prescribed. Whenever she shows the same symptoms, they purchase the drugs locally as the nearest health centre does not always have supplies.

## Towards 2015

Yassiminatou and Gastine's story of death and survival sheds light on the immediate investments required to make a difference in the lives, not only of the girls taking part in the study, but of the millions of girls facing 21st century challenges. The experiences of these two four year olds illustrate the sheer urgency of the need to increase investments in basic services, and girls' access to these services.

As we have seen, migration to a city may provide a window to a new life for a girl as she approaches her teens. It may help her to provide additional income for her family or afford her the opportunity to go to secondary school. But this new opportunity carries risks too. In the next five years there is a lot to do if the girls in our survey and their families are to make real progress and achieve the goals that they have talked to us about. The current rate of progress towards meeting the MDGs is simply too slow for a four year old in 2010.

*"We don't know yet what she wants when she grows up. Of course as a mother we will support whatever she wants and, hopefully, we will have a better income when she grows up so that we can support her and all our children."*
Mother of Girlie, Philippines

**155**

# Because We are Girls

## 'Real Choices, Real Lives' Cohort Study Update

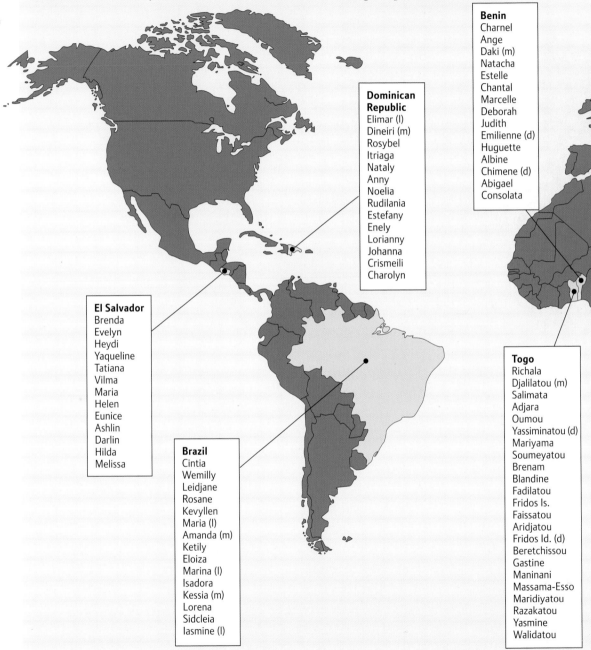

**Dominican Republic**
Elimar (l)
Dineiri (m)
Rosybel
Itriaga
Nataly
Anny
Noelia
Rudilania
Estefany
Enely
Lorianny
Johanna
Crismeili
Charolyn

**Benin**
Charnel
Ange
Daki (m)
Natacha
Estelle
Chantal
Marcelle
Deborah
Judith
Emilienne (d)
Huguette
Albine
Chimene (d)
Abigael
Consolata

**El Salvador**
Brenda
Evelyn
Heydi
Yaqueline
Tatiana
Vilma
Maria
Helen
Eunice
Ashlin
Darlin
Hilda
Melissa

**Brazil**
Cintia
Wemilly
Leidjane
Rosane
Kevyllen
Maria (l)
Amanda (m)
Ketily
Eloiza
Marina (l)
Isadora
Kessia (m)
Lorena
Sidcleia
Iasmine (l)

**Togo**
Richala
Djalilatou (m)
Salimata
Adjara
Oumou
Yassiminatou (d)
Mariyama
Soumeyatou
Brenam
Blandine
Fadilatou
Fridos Is.
Faissatou
Aridjatou
Fridos Id. (d)
Beretchissou
Gastine
Maninani
Massama-Esso
Maridiyatou
Razakatou
Yasmine
Walidatou

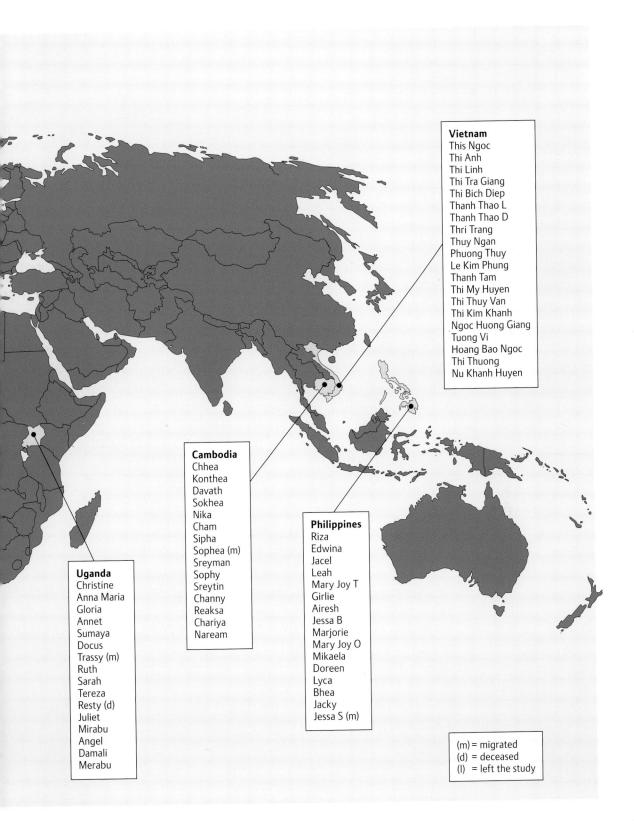

**Vietnam**
This Ngoc
Thi Anh
Thi Linh
Thi Tra Giang
Thi Bich Diep
Thanh Thao L
Thanh Thao D
Thri Trang
Thuy Ngan
Phuong Thuy
Le Kim Phung
Thanh Tam
Thi My Huyen
Thi Thuy Van
Thi Kim Khanh
Ngoc Huong Giang
Tuong Vi
Hoang Bao Ngoc
Thi Thuong
Nu Khanh Huyen

**Cambodia**
Chhea
Konthea
Davath
Sokhea
Nika
Cham
Sipha
Sophea (m)
Sreyman
Sophy
Sreytin
Channy
Reaksa
Chariya
Naream

**Philippines**
Riza
Edwina
Jacel
Leah
Mary Joy T
Girlie
Airesh
Jessa B
Marjorie
Mary Joy O
Mikaela
Doreen
Lyca
Bhea
Jacky
Jessa S (m)

**Uganda**
Christine
Anna Maria
Gloria
Annet
Sumaya
Docus
Trassy (m)
Ruth
Sarah
Tereza
Resty (d)
Juliet
Mirabu
Angel
Damali
Merabu

(m) = migrated
(d) = deceased
(l) = left the study

# Section 3

DINA TORRANS

# Plan's Because I am a Girl campaign

The Because I am a Girl campaign is Plan's campaign to promote girls' rights and lift millions of girls out of poverty. Across the world, girls face double discrimination due to their gender and age, leaving them at the bottom of the social ladder. For example, research has shown that girls are more likely to suffer from malnutrition; be forced into an early marriage; be subject to violence or intimidation; be trafficked, sold or coerced into the sex trade; or become infected with HIV. The 'State of the World's Girls' annual reports provide and will provide year after year tangible proof of the inequalities which still exist between boys and girls and will support the campaign with specific girl-oriented data.

The Because I am a Girl campaign will be geared towards equipping, enabling and engaging girls of all ages to acquire the assets, skills and knowledge necessary to succeed in life.

For more information visit:
*http://plan-international.org/what-you-can-do/campaigns/because-i-am-a-girl-campaign*

*Still in secondary school, Moyamba, Sierra Leone.*

NAZIA PARVEZ

# Introduction

In this section we highlight indicators that track the state of the world's girls, and through tailor-made maps provide a snapshot of the progress girls have made since the last report. What progress are we making towards helping girls realise their rights, and what are the areas that require further investment?

This year we have also introduced an analysis of the progress girls are making in the context of the Millennium Development Goals. Ten years after the Millennium Declaration rallied governments to finally end extreme poverty across the globe, we ask: what have these commitments meant for girls' lives? Are they better off? And where are the MDGs failing to reach the most vulnerable – adolescent girls? The maps in this section correlate with the five MDGs we focused on in Section 2 and provide a global backdrop to the lived experiences of our cohort girls.

Our final resource section provides a useful reference guide for information on organisations, campaigns, research and databases which are focused on girls' rights and well-being.

## The Millennium Development Goals and Girls

The Millennium Development Goals (MDGs) are eight goals set by the United Nations in an attempt to eradicate extreme poverty by 2015. The Goals were drawn from the Millennium Declaration, which was adopted by 189 nations at the United Nations Millennium Summit in September 2000. The eight goals are broken down into 21 quantifiable targets and measured by 60 indicators to monitor their progress.

These maps prove that although global investment in poverty reduction has remained high, this is not being translated into improvements in girls' lives. More needs to be done by donors, national governments and civil society organisations so girls don't get left behind, uncounted and unvalued.

*Trying to ignore the rubbish on a Cairo street.*

JEFF BLACK / IRIN

**161**

# Proportion of girls under-5 years that are underweight

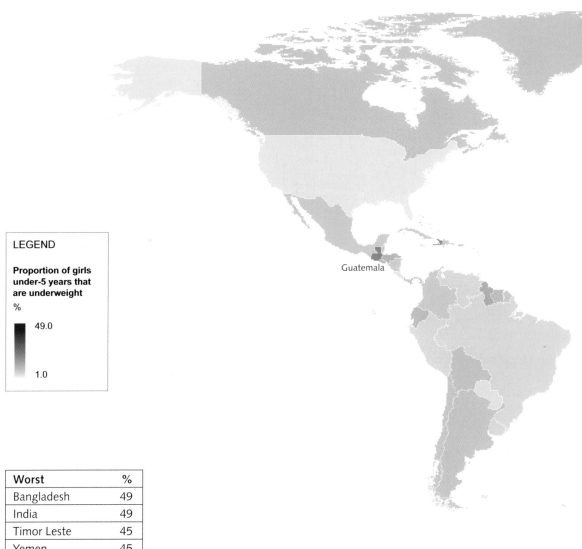

LEGEND

**Proportion of girls under-5 years that are underweight**
%

49.0

1.0

Guatemala

| Worst | % |
|---|---|
| Bangladesh | 49 |
| India | 49 |
| Timor Leste | 45 |
| Yemen | 45 |
| Niger | 45 |
| Afghanistan | 40 |
| Nepal | 40 |
| Eritrea | 39 |
| Ethiopia | 38 |
| Laos | 30 |

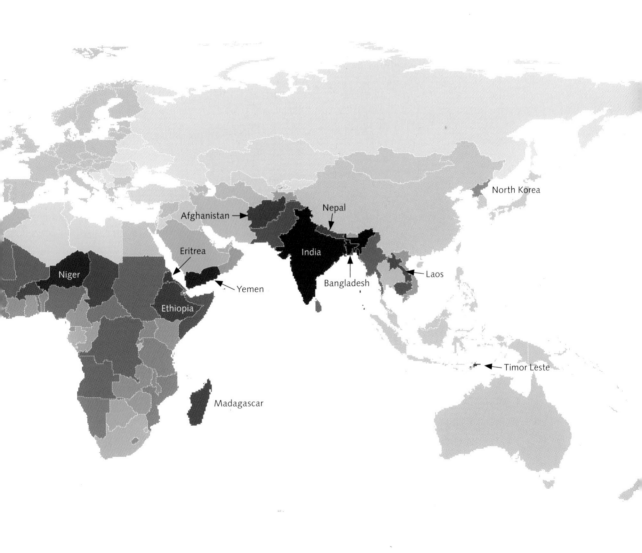

Afghanistan ➝
Eritrea
Niger
Ethiopia
Yemen
India
Nepal
Bangladesh
Laos
North Korea
Timor Leste
Madagascar

**ACHIEVE UNIVERSAL PRIMARY EDUCATION**

# Girls' gross primary school graduation rate

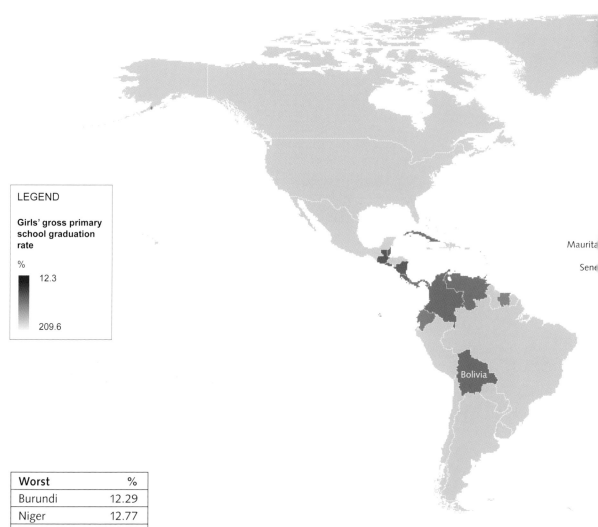

LEGEND

**Girls' gross primary school graduation rate**

%

12.3

209.6

Maurita

Sene

Bolivia

| Worst | % |
|---|---|
| Burundi | 12.29 |
| Niger | 12.77 |
| DR Congo | 16.68 |
| Burkina Faso | 21.91 |
| Djibouti | 22.68 |
| Malawi | 23.40 |
| Mauritania | 24.10 |
| Mozambique | 27.30 |
| Benin | 30.20 |
| Senegal | 33.10 |

Gross primary school graduation rate: the number of children graduating from primary school in any one year divided by the number of children in the age group at which primary school completion should occur.

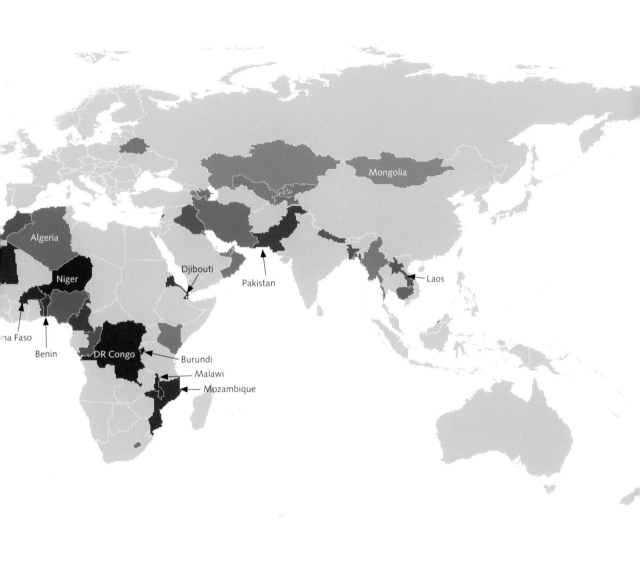

Algeria

Niger

na Faso

Benin

DR Congo

Djibouti

Pakistan

Mongolia

Laos

Burundi

Malawi

Mozambique

**PROMOTE GENDER EQUALITY AND EMPOWER WOMEN**

# Proportion of girls aged 15-19 years married by age 15

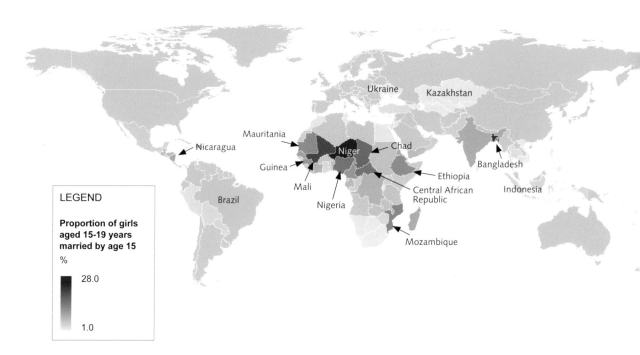

**LEGEND**

**Proportion of girls aged 15-19 years married by age 15**

%

28.0

1.0

| Highest | % |
|---|---|
| Niger | 28 |
| Bangladesh | 26.3 |
| Mali | 22.8 |
| Chad | 17.9 |
| Central African Republic | 16.1 |
| Nigeria | 16.1 |
| Mozambique | 14 |
| Mauritania | 13.4 |
| Ethiopia | 12.7 |
| Guinea | 12.2 |

# Female transition from primary to secondary education

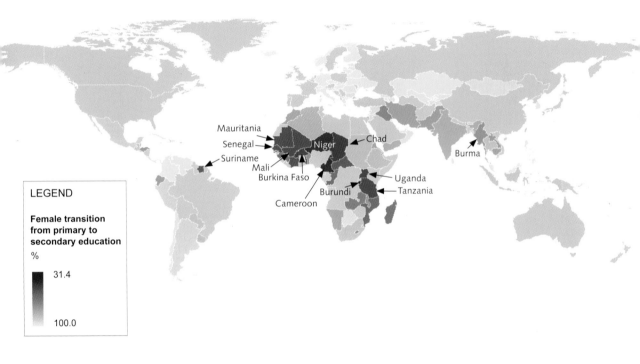

LEGEND

**Female transition from primary to secondary education**

%

31.4

100.0

| Worst | % |
|---|---|
| Burundi | 31.39 |
| Cameroon | 36.77 |
| Niger | 37.48 |
| Chad | 41.81 |
| Uganda | 43.30 |
| Burkina Faso | 43.60 |
| Tanzania | 45.20 |
| Mali | 46.80 |
| Mauritania | 47.20 |
| Senegal | 47.70 |

**PROMOTE GENDER EQUALITY AND EMPOWER WOMEN**

# Estimated female earned income (PPP*, US$)

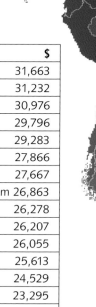

Mexico

Guayana

Guinea-Bissau

Sierra Leone

Liberia

Bolivia

LEGEND

PPP, US$

191

31,663

| Worst | $ |
|---|---|
| DR Congo | 191 |
| Liberia | 222 |
| Burundi | 291 |
| Guinea-Bissau | 315 |
| Eritrea | 349 |
| Sierra Leone | 396 |
| Timor Leste | 428 |
| Palestinian Territories | 432 |
| Niger | 437 |
| Togo | 478 |
| Central African Republic | 517 |
| Malawi | 596 |
| Mozambique | 663 |
| Rwanda | 696 |
| Madagascar | 723 |
| Uganda | 735 |
| Cote d'Ivoire | 787 |

| Best | $ |
|---|---|
| Norway | 31,663 |
| Hong Kong | 31,232 |
| Sweden | 30,976 |
| Denmark | 29,796 |
| Iceland | 29,283 |
| Australia | 27,866 |
| Finland | 27,667 |
| United Kingdom | 26,863 |
| Switzerland | 26,278 |
| Netherlands | 26,207 |
| Canada | 26,055 |
| USA | 25,613 |
| France | 24,529 |
| Ireland | 23,295 |
| Greece | 21,181 |
| Spain | 20,174 |
| Israel | 19,653 |

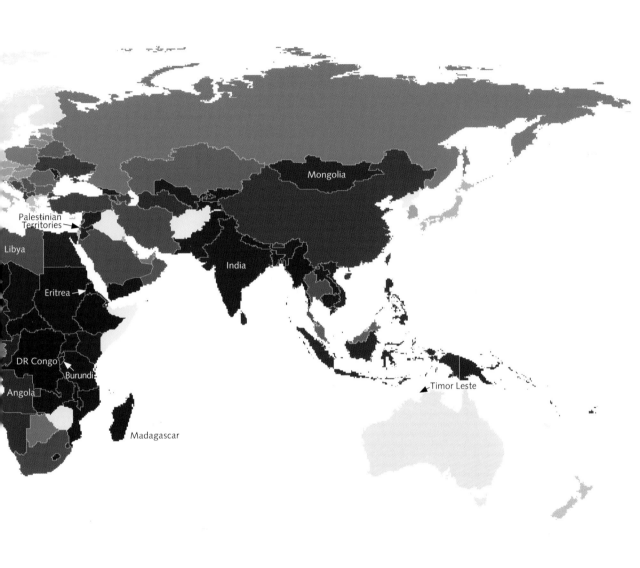

Palestinian
Territories →

Libya

Eritrea →

Mongolia

India

DR Congo
Burundi

Angola

Timor Leste

Madagascar

*PPP is the cost of buying a similar basket of goods (such as
a Big Mac) in different countries, calculated in local currency
and expressed in US dollars using purchasing power parity.

**REDUCE
CHILD MORTALITY**

# Infant mortality rates /
# Proportion of young women aged 20-2

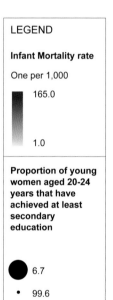

LEGEND

**Infant Mortality rate**

One per 1,000

165.0

1.0

**Proportion of young
women aged 20-24
years that have
achieved at least
secondary
education**

6.7

• 99.6

Honduras

Peru

Paraguay

Sierra Leo

## Infant mortality rates

| Worst | Out of 1,000 births |
|-------|---------------------|
| Afghanistan | 165 |
| Democratic Republic of Congo | 126 |
| Chad | 124 |
| Sierra Leone | 123 |
| Somalia | 119 |
| Guinea Bissau | 117 |
| Central African Republic | 115 |
| Mali | 103 |
| Liberia | 100 |

# ars that have achieved at least secondary education

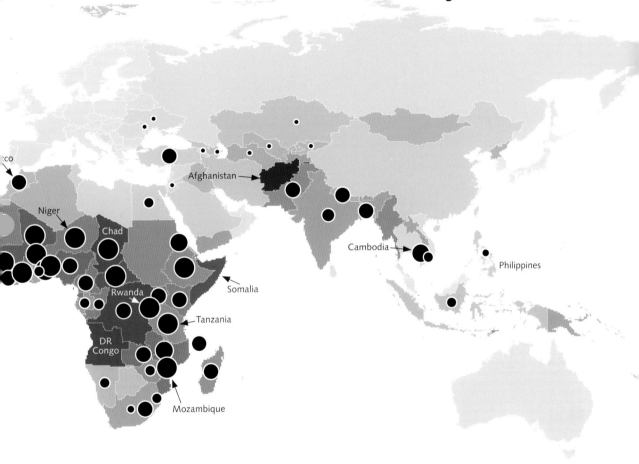

Proportion of young women aged 20-24 years that have achieved at least secondary education

| Worst | % |
| --- | --- |
| Niger | 6.7 |
| Chad | 9.2 |
| Tanzania | 10.4 |
| Mozambique | 10.6 |
| Rwanda | 10.7 |
| Burkina Faso | 12.3 |
| Mali | 12.8 |
| Senegal | 14.8 |
| Guinea | 15.6 |
| Ethiopia | 17.3 |

# Ratio of young women to young men living with HIV

**COMBAT HIV/AIDS, MALARIA AND OTHER DISEASES**

6

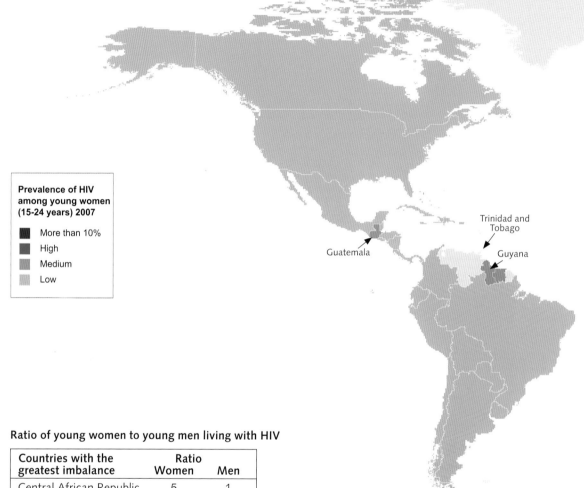

**Prevalence of HIV among young women (15-24 years) 2007**

- More than 10%
- High
- Medium
- Low

Trinidad and Tobago

Guatemala

Guyana

**Ratio of young women to young men living with HIV**

| Countries with the greatest imbalance | Ratio | |
|---|---|---|
| | Women | Men |
| Central African Republic | 5 | 1 |
| Swaziland | 3.9 | 1 |
| Cameroon | 3.6 | 1 |
| Malawi | 3.5 | 1 |
| Guyana | 3.4 | 1 |
| Sudan | 3.3 | 1 |
| Trinidad and Tobago | 3.3 | 1 |
| Burundi | 3.3 | 1 |
| Ghana | 3.3 | 1 |
| Liberia | 3.3 | 1 |
| Eritrea | 3.3 | 1 |

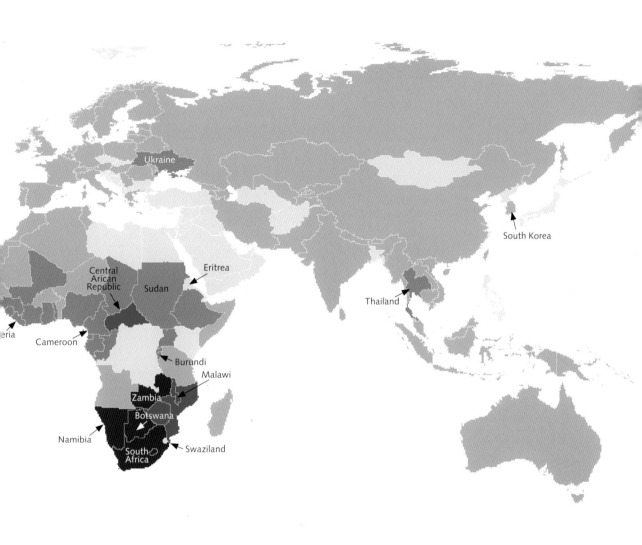

Ukraine

Central
Arican
Republic

Sudan

Eritrea

Thailand

South Korea

eria

Cameroon

Burundi

Malawi

Zambia

Botswana

Namibia

South
Africa

Swaziland

# References

## Introduction, Section 1: Chapter 1

### Introduction

1 Plan International. Interview with Precious for the Street Children's World Cup in Durban, South Africa, March 2010.
2 Jejeebhoy, Shireen J., and Sarah Bott. Non-consensual Sexual Experiences of Young People: A Review of the Evidence from Developing Countries. New Delhi, India: Population Council, 2003.
3 Plan Netherlands. "Safety in Cities". An online survey commissioned for the 'Because I am a Girl' report 2010.
4 "Chat-wise, street-wise". Internet forum in the United Kingdom, March 2001.
5 Plan and the Child Protection Partnership "Brazilian Adolescent Girls in a Virtual World". Original research commissioned for the 'Because I am a Girl' report 2010.
6 EFA Global Monitoring Report 2009. Summary Overcoming Inequality: Why Governance Matters. UNESCO: Paris, France, 2008. http://unesdoc.unesco.org/images/0017/001776/177609e.pdf.
7 UN-Habitat. "State of the World's Cities 2008/2009". United Nations. http://www.unhabitat.org/content.asp?catid=7&cid=5964&subMenuId=0&typeid=46 (accessed June 2, 2010).
8 Plan International. Interview with street girl for the Street Child Africa in Accra, Ghana for the 'Because I am a Girl' report 2010.
9 http://www.guardian.co.uk/uk/2010/mar/08/peter-chapman-facebook-ashleigh-hall
10 Plan International. Transcripts from Interviews for the Street Children's World Cup, South Africa, May 2010.
11 UN-Habitat. "Interview with Hasina Hamza, Student." United Nations. http://www.unhabitat.org/content.asp?cid=6107&catid=531&typeid=4&subMenuId=0 (accessed June 9, 2010).

### SECTION 1
### Chapter 1

1 Plan International. Transcripts from Interviews for the Street Children's World Cup, South Africa, 2010.
2 Interview with Nikki van der Gaag, for Plan International, 'Because I am a Girl' report 2010.
3 Ethiopia Ministry of Youth and Sports, Population Council & UNFPA. "Programme Brief Berhane Hewan (Light for Eve)"; a programme to support married and unmarried adolescent girls in rural Amhara Region, Ethiopia. Population Council. http://www.popcouncil.org/projects/100_BerhaneHewanEthiopia.asp (accessed June 9, 2010).
4 Abt Enterprises LLC. "Rapid Situation Assessment of Street Children in Cairo and Alexandria: Final Report". Prepared for the U.N. Office for Drug Control and Crime Prevention, the World Food Program, and the U.N. International Children Emergency Fund (UNICEF), March 29, 2001, pp17, 18.
5 UNFPA. "Growing Up Urban, State of World Population 2007: Youth Supplement." UNFPA. http://www.unfpa.org/swp/2007/youth/english/story/preface.html (accessed June 9, 2010).
6 Lloyd, Cynthia B., ed. Growing up Global: The Changing Transitions to Adulthood in Developing Countries National Research Council and Institute of Medicine of the National Academies. Washington, D.C.: The National Academies Press, 2005, p78.
7 UNFPA. "Growing Up Urban, State of World Population 2007: Youth Supplement." UNFPA. http://www.unfpa.org/swp/2007/youth/english/story/preface.html (accessed June 9, 2010).
8 UNFPA. "Growing Up Urban, State of World Population 2007: Youth Supplement." UNFPA. http://www.unfpa.org/swp/2007/youth/english/story/preface.html (accessed June 9, 2010).
9 Benin Enquete Demographique et de Sante 2006, HIV/AIDS Survey Indicators Database. http://www.measuredhs.com/hivdata/ (accessed March 25, 2010)
10 UNFPA. "Growing Up Urban, State of World Population 2007: Youth Supplement." UNFPA. http://www.unfpa.org/swp/2007/youth/english/story/preface.html (accessed June 9, 2010).
11 "Adolescent Girls Most Vulnerable to Sexual Harassment". The Daily Star, February 18, 2010, http://www.thedailystar.net/newDesign/news-details.php?nid=126860.
12 Save the Children. 10 Essential Learning Points: Listen and Speak out against Sexual Abuse of Girls and Boys. Norway: The International Save the Children Alliance, 2005, p43. http://www.crin.org/docs/resources/publications/violence/Save_Alliance_Global_Submission.pdf.
13 García-Moreno, Claudia, et al. Multi-country Study on Women's Health and Domestic Violence Against Women Initial Results on Prevalence, Health Outcomes and Women's Responses. Switzerland: World Health Organisation, 2005.
14 Save the Children. 10 Essential Learning Points: Listen and Speak out against Sexual Abuse of Girls and Boys. Norway: The International Save the Children Alliance, 2005, p44. http://www.crin.org/docs/resources/publications/violence/Save_Alliance_Global_Submission.pdf.
15 Moore, A., et al. "Coercive First Sex among Adolescents in Sub-Saharan Africa: Prevalence and Context." Paper presented at the IUSSP XXV Conference on Population, Tours, France, July 18-23, 2005.
16 Ministry of Women and Child Development. Study on Child Abuse: INDIA 2007. Kriti, New Delhi: Government of India, 2007. http://www.indianet.nl/pdf/childabuseIndia.pdf.
17 Child Hope UK. http://www.childhope.org.uk (accessed June 9, 2010).
18 Plan International. "Girls Experiences Of Policing And Incarceration In The Philippines". Prepared by Justice For Girls International.
19 Adapted from A Safe City for Women and Girls is…. found in UNIFEM. Knowledge Asset on Safe Cities and Communities for Women and Girls to Live a Life Free of Violence. Women in Cities International and Red Mujer y Habitat de America Latina, November 2009.
20 World Bank. World Development Report 2007: Development and the Next Generation. Washington, D.C.: The International Bank for Reconstruction and Development, 2006.
21 International Telecommunication Union. Guidelines Proposed for Child Online Protection Initiative. Switzerland: ITU, 2009.
22 Lenhart, Amanda. "Cyberbullying and Online Teens". Pew Internet & American Life Project, June 27, 2007. http://www.pewinternet.org/~/media/Files/Reports/2007/PIP%20Cyberbullying%20Memo.pdf.pdf (accessed June 9, 2010).

## Chapter 2

1 Population Reference Bureau. "Human Population: Urbanization". United Nations. http://www.prb.org/Educators/TeachersGuides/HumanPopulation/Urbanization.aspx (accessed June 9, 2010).

2 UN-Habitat. Gender Equality for Smarter Cities. Challenges and Progress. Nairobi, Kenya: United Nations, 2010.

3 UNFPA. "State of the World Population 2007: Unleashing the Potential of Urban Growth." UNFPA, 2007. http://www.unfpa.org/swp/2007/presskit/pdf/sowp2007_eng.pdf (accessed June 9, 2010).

4 UN-Habitat. "State of the World's Cities 2008/2009". United Nations. http://www.unhabitat.org/content.asp?catid=7&cid=5964&subMenuId=0&typeid=46 (accessed June 2, 2010).

5 UN-Habitat. "State of the World's Cities 2008/2009". United Nations. http://www.unhabitat.org/content.asp?catid=7&cid=5964&subMenuId=0&typeid=46 (accessed June 2, 2010).

6 UNFPA. "Growing Up Urban, State of World Population 2007: Youth Supplement." UNFPA. http://www.unfpa.org/swp/2007/youth/english/story/preface.html (accessed June 9, 2010).

7 Women in Cities International and UN-Habitat Safer Cities. Working Discussion Paper on Gender and Urbanization, 2010, unpublished.

8 Youth Development. "Young Citizens. The Landmark Achievements of Brazil's Social Movement for Children's Rights." http://www.cydjournal.org/NewDesigns/ND_99Sum/Brandao.html (accessed June 9, 2010).

9 Women in Cities International and UN-Habitat Safer Cities. Working Discussion Paper on Gender and Urbanization, 2010, unpublished.

10 Plan International. Because I am a Girl The State of the World's Girls 2009: Girls in the Global Economy: Adding it all Up.

11 UNESCO and UN-Habitat. Urban Policies and the Right to the City: Rights, Responsibilities and CitizenshipCardiff, United Kingdom: Cardiff University, March 2009. http://unesdoc.unesco.org/images/0017/001780/178090e.pdf.

12 Women in Cities International and UN Habitat Safer Cities. Working Discussion Paper on Gender and Urbanization, 2010, unpublished.

13 Ruble, Blair, Joseph Tulchin, Diana Varat and Lisa Hanley, eds. "Youth Explosion in Developing World Cities: Approaches to Reducing Poverty and Conflict in an Urban Age." Washington, D.C: Woodrow Wilson International Center for Scholars, 2003.

14 Based on Czapska, Asia, Annabel Webb and Nura Taefi. More Than Bricks & Mortar: A Rights-Based Strategy to Prevent Girl Homelessness in Canada. Vancouver, Canada: Justice for Girls, 2008.

15 Justice for Girls. Submission to the United Nations Committee on Economic, Social and Cultural Rights at its 5th periodic review of Canada: http://www2.ohchr.org/english/bodies/cescr/docs/info-ngos/justice-girls-new.pdf (accessed: June 24, 2010)

16 Canadian Housing and Renewal Association. On Her Own: Young Women and Homelessness in Canada. Ottawa, Canada: Government of Canada Depository Services Program, March 2002.

17 McCreary Centre Society. "Adolescent Health Survey." http://www.mcs.bc.ca (accessed June 9, 2010).

18 Women in Cities International and UN Habitat Safer Cities. Working Discussion Paper on Gender and Urbanization, 2010, unpublished.

19 UN-Habitat. "State of the World's Cities 2008/2009". United Nations. http://www.unhabitat.org/content.asp?catid=7&cid=5964&subMenuId=0&typeid=46 (accessed June 2, 2010).

20 UNFPA. "Growing Up Urban, State of World Population 2007: Youth Supplement." UNFPA. http://www.unfpa.org/swp/2007/youth/english/story/preface.html (accessed June 9, 2010).

21 Urban World. A New Strategy to Close the Gender Divide. July 2009, p19.

22 UNFPA. "Growing Up Urban, State of World Population 2007: Youth Supplement." UNFPA. http://www.unfpa.org/swp/2007/youth/english/story/preface.html (accessed June 9, 2010).

23 UN-Habitat. "Global Urban Observatory." United Nations. http://www.unhabitat.org/categories.asp?catid=422 (accessed June 9, 2010).

24 UN-Habitat. "State of the Urban Youth 2010/2011: Leveling the Playing Field." United Nations, 2010.

25 Davis, Mike. "Planet of Slums: Urban Involution and the Informal Proletariat." New Left Review 26 (March-April 2004): 5-34.

26 Davis, Mike. "Planet of Slums: Urban Involution and the Informal Proletariat." New Left Review 26 (March-April 2004): 5-34.

27 World Urban Forum. Realizing the Potential of Urban Slums. March 2010.

28 Centre on Housing Rights and Evictions (COHRE). Women, Slums and Urbanization: Examining the Causes and Consequences. Geneva: COHRE, May 2008.

29 "At least half the world's slum population is under the age of 20" on Davis, Mike. "Planet of Slums: Urban Involution and the Informal Proletariat." New Left Review 26 (March-April 2004): 5-34.

30 UN-Habitat. "State of the Urban Youth 2010/2011: Leveling the Playing Field." United Nations, 2010.

31 UN-Habitat. Brochure on Istanbul +5. United Nations, 2001. http://ww2.unhabitat.org/istanbul+5/statereport.htm.

32 African Movement of Working Children and Youth (AMWCY). "Mobile children, from victims to actors - Early migration and child trafficking in Africa", 2009

33 Crivello, Gina. "Becoming Somebody: Youth Transitions Through Education and Migration – Evidence from Young Lives, Peru." Young Lives Working Paper No. 43, February 2009.

34 Anderson, Kristen for 'Because I am a Girl' Report 2010, Children's Legal Centre Essex.

35 Crivello, Gina. "Becoming Somebody: Youth Transitions Through Education and Migration – Evidence from Young Lives, Peru." Young Lives Working Paper No. 43, February 2009.

36 Plan Sierra Leone, Fadimata Alainchar, Country Director in correspondence for 'Because I am a Girl' 2010 report, April 2010.

37 Centre on Housing Rights and Evictions (COHRE). Women, Slums and Urbanization: Examining the Causes and Consequences. Geneva: COHRE, May 2008; and International HIV/AIDS Alliance: Children Living outside of Family Care: The Street, September 2009. http://www.ovcsupport.net/s/.

38  Humanitarian Futures Programme. Humanitarian Horizons: A Practitioners Guide to the Future. Medford, USA: Feinstein International Center, 2010. http://www. humanitarianfutures.org/main/sites/default/files/Final_ web_PGF.pdf

39  World Bank. World Development Report 2007: Development and the Next Generation. Washington, D.C.: The International Bank for Reconstruction and Development, 2006.

40  Plan USA. "Changing Lives through Savings and Loans: The Stories of West African Youth".

41  International Organization for Migration. "Gender and Migration." IOM. http://www.iom.int/jahia/Jahia/ gender-migration (accessed June 14, 2010).

42  International Organisation for Migration. "Gender and Migration." IOM. http://www.iom.int/jahia/Jahia/ gender-migration (accessed June 14, 2010).

43  International Organisation for Migration. "Gender Issues and Migration Policy." IOM. http://www.iom. int/jahia/Jahia/about-migration/developing-migration- policy/migration-gender/gender-issues-migration-policy (accessed June 14, 2010).

44  Centre on Housing Rights and Evictions (COHRE). Women, Slums and Urbanization: Examining the Causes and Consequences. Geneva: COHRE, May 2008; and International HIV/AIDS Alliance: Children Living outside of Family Care: The Street, September 2009. http://www.ovcsupport.net/s/.

45  Thorsen, Dorte. "If Only I Get Enough Money for a Bicycle! A Study of Childhoods, Migration and Adolescent Aspirations Against a Backdrop of Exploitation and Trafficking in Burkina Faso." Sweden: Nordic Africa Institute, September 2007.

46  Centre on Housing Rights and Evictions (COHRE). Women, Slums and Urbanization: Examining the Causes and Consequences. Geneva: COHRE, May 2008.

47  Actionaid. "Chennai Gets First Lesbian Helpline." The Times of India, February 8, 2009. http://www. actionaidusa.org/what/womens_rights/chennai_gets_ first_lesbian_helpline/ (accessed June 14, 2010).

48  Amnesty International. "Lesbian, Gay, Bisexual and Transgender (LGBT) Network." http://www.amnesty. org.uk/content.asp?CategoryID=876&ArticleID=876 (accessed June 14, 2010).

49  Thorsen, Dorte. "If Only I Get Enough Money for a Bicycle! A Study of Childhoods, Migration and Adolescent Aspirations Against a Backdrop of Exploitation and Trafficking in Burkina Faso." Sweden: Nordic Africa Institute, September 2007.

50  Crivello, Gina. "Becoming Somebody: Youth Transitions Through Education and Migration – Evidence from Young Lives, Peru." Young Lives Working Paper No. 43, February 2009.

51  Abt Enterprises LLC. "Rapid Situation Assessment of Street Children in Cairo and Alexandria: Final Report". Prepared for the U.N. Office for Drug Control and Crime Prevention, the World Food Program, and the U.N. International Children Emergency Fund (UNICEF), March 29, 2001, pp17, 18.

52  Centre on Housing Rights and Evictions (COHRE). Women, Slums and Urbanization: Examining the Causes and Consequences. Geneva: COHRE, May 2008.

53  New Internationalist. "Street children." New Internationalist No. 377 (April 2005). http://www. newint.org/issue377/rukshana.htm.

54  UNFPA. "Growing Up Urban, State of World Population 2007: Youth Supplement." UNFPA, p33. http://www. unfpa.org/swp/2007/youth/english/story/preface.html (accessed June 9, 2010).

55  Ethiopia Ministry of Youth and Sports, Population Council & UNFPA. "Programme Brief Berhane Hewan (Light for Eve)"; a programme to support married and unmarried adolescent girls in rural Amhara Region, Ethiopia. Population Council. http://www.popcouncil.org/projects/100_ BerhaneHewanEthiopia.asp (accessed June 9, 2010).

56  Erulkar, Annabel S., Tekle-Ab Mekbib, Negussie Simie and Tsehai Gulema. Adolescent Life in Low income and Slum Areas of Addis Abbaba, Ethiopia. Population Council/ UNICEF, 2004.

57  Centre on Housing Rights and Evictions (COHRE). Women, Slums and Urbanization: Examining the Causes and Consequences. Geneva: COHRE, May 2008.

58  Maplecroft, www.girlsdiscovered.org (accessed: 2 June 2010).

59  FGC involves the cutting off of the clitoris, and sometimes also the labia of a young girl. Its most extreme version, Type III, also involves sewing up the genitals, leaving only a small hole for urine to pass through. The practice can lead to severe psychological and physical complications and even death.

60  El-Zanaty, Fatma and Ann Way. Egypt Demographic and Health Survey 2008. Cairo, Egypt: Ministry of Health, El-Zanaty and Associates, and Macro International, 2009.

61  El-Zanaty, Fatma and Ann Way. Egypt Demographic and Health Survey 2008. Cairo, Egypt: Ministry of Health, El-Zanaty and Associates, and Macro International, 2009.

62  El-Zanaty, Fatma and Ann Way. Egypt Demographic and Health Survey 2008. Cairo, Egypt: Ministry of Health, El-Zanaty and Associates, and Macro International, 2009.

63  Erulkar, Annabel S., Tekle-Ab Mekbib, Negussie Simie and Tsehai Gulema. Adolescent Life in Low income and Slum Areas of Addis Abbaba, Ethiopia. Population Council/ UNICEF, 2004.

64  Erulkar, Annabel S., Tekle-Ab Mekbib, Negussie Simie and Tsehai Gulema. Adolescent Life in Low income and Slum Areas of Addis Ababa, Ethiopia. Population Council/ UNICEF, 2004.

65  Interview with Marie Staunton, Director of Plan UK

66  New Internationalist. "Street children, our lives our words." New Internationalist No. 377 (April 2005). http://www.newint.org/issue377/rukshana.htm.

67  Plan International Egypt, CAP (El Marg) programme documents.

68  UNFPA. "Growing Up Urban, State of World Population 2007: Youth Supplement." UNFPA. http://www.unfpa. org/swp/2007/youth/english/story/preface.html (accessed June 9, 2010).

69  UNFPA. "Growing Up Urban, State of World Population 2007: Youth Supplement." UNFPA. http://www.unfpa. org/swp/2007/youth/english/story/preface.html (accessed June 9, 2010).

70  Sabo, Donald, et al. The Women's Sports Foundation Report: Sport and Teen Pregnancy. New York: Women's Sports Foundation, 1998.

71  Brady, Martha and Arjmand Banu Khan. Letting Girls Play: The Mathare Youth Sports Association's Football Program for Girls. New York: Population Council, 2002, p14. http://www.popcouncil.org/pdfs/girlsplay.pdf.

72  UNICEF. "The State of the World's Children 2003." http://www.unicef.org/sowc03/specialtopics/panel4.html (accessed June 14, 2010).

73  Plan International. Transcripts from Interviews for the Street Children's World Cup, South Africa, 2010.

74  Interview with Nikki van der Gaag, for Plan International, 'Because I am a Girl' report 2010.

75  UNFPA. "Growing Up Urban, State of World Population 2007: Youth Supplement." UNFPA. http://www.unfpa.org/swp/2007/youth/english/story/preface.html (accessed June 9, 2010).

76  UN-Habitat. "State of the World's Cities 2008/2009". United Nations. http://www.unhabitat.org/content.asp?catid=7&cid=5964&subMenuId=0&typeid=46 (accessed June 2, 2010).

77  Quoted in World Bank. World Development Report 2007: Development and the Next Generation. Washington, D.C.: The International Bank for Reconstruction and Development, 2006.

78  Myat, Mon M. "When Hard Times Hit, Some Children Go to Factories." Inter Press Service, February 16, 2010. http://www.ipsnews.net/news.asp?idnews=50346

79  Quoted in World Bank. World Development Report 2007: Development and the Next Generation. Washington, D.C.: The International Bank for Reconstruction and Development, 2006.

80  Amin, Sajeda, Ian Diamond, Ruchira T. Naved, and Margaret Newby. "Transition to Adulthood of Female Garment-Factory Workers in Bangladesh." Studies In Family Planning 29,2 (1998): 185–200, p193.

81  Anderson, Kristen. 2010 Report. Essex: The Children's Legal Centre, 2010.

82  World Bank. World Development Report 2007: Development and the Next Generation. Washington, D.C.: The International Bank for Reconstruction and Development, 2006.

83  CAP Foundation. http://www.capfoundation.in/ (accessed June 14, 2010).

84  United Nations Development Programme. Egypt Human Development Report 2008. Egypt: UNDP and The Institute of National Planning, 2008.

85  International Labour Organisation. Global Employment Trends Report 2009. Geneva, Switzerland: ILO, 2009.

86  UN-Habitat. The Challenge of Slum Global Report on Human Settlements 2003. Nairobi, Kenya: UN-Habitat, 2003.

87  UN-Habitat. "State of the World's Cities 2008/2009 – Harmonious Cities". United Nations. http://www.unhabitat.org/content.asp?catid=7&cid=5964&subMenuId=0&typeid=46 (accessed June 15, 2010).

88  Plan International and Justice for Girls, 'Adolescent girls' experiences of detention and rehabilitation in the Philippines', 2010.

89  Plan International. Interview conducted by Street Child Africa for the 'Because I am a Girl' report 2010.

90  New Internationalist. "Street children, our lives our words." New Internationalist No. 377 (April 2005). http://www.newint.org/issue377/rukshana.htm.

91  UNFPA. "Growing Up Urban, State of World Population 2007: Youth Supplement." UNFPA. http://www.unfpa.org/swp/2007/youth/english/story/preface.html (accessed June 9, 2010).

92  New Internationalist. "Street children, our lives our words." New Internationalist No. 377 (April 2005). http://www.newint.org/issue377/rukshana.htm.

93  UN-Habitat. The Challenge of Slum Global Report on Human Settlements 2003. Nairobi, Kenya: UN-Habitat, 2003.

94  Plan Sierra Leone. Fadimata Alainchar, Country Director in correspondence for 'Because I am a Girl' 2010 report, April 2010.

95  Centre on Housing Rights and Evictions (COHRE). Defending the Housing Rights of Children. Geneva: COHRE, June 2006, p58.

96  Centre on Housing Rights and Evictions (COHRE). Defending the Housing Rights of Children. Geneva: COHRE, June 2006.

97  Interact Worldwide, Aoife Nic Charthaigh, in correspondence with Plan International for 'Because I am a Girl' report 2010.

98  Plan International. "Adolescent Sexual Health in West Africa, Rights, Realities Responses." Case Study 1, December 2009.

99  Rahman, M. "Determinants Of Knowledge And Awareness About AIDS: Urban-Rural Differentials In Bangladesh." Journal of Public Health and Epidemiology Vol. 1(1) (October 2009): 14-21.

100 Demographic And Health Surveys. http://www.measuredhs.com/ (accessed June 9, 2010).

101 UN-Habitat. "State of the Urban Youth 2010/2011: Leveling the Playing Field." United Nations, 2010.

102 Interact Worldwide, Rutti Goldberger in correspondence with Plan International for the 'Because I am a Girl' report 2010.

103 The World Bank. World Development Report 2007: Development and the Next Generation. Washington, D.C.: The International Bank for Reconstruction and Development, 2006.

104 UN-Habitat. "State of the Urban Youth 2010/2011: Leveling the Playing Field." United Nations, 2010.

105 Centre on Housing Rights and Evictions (COHRE). Defending the Housing Rights of Children. Geneva: COHRE, June 2006.

106 Alford, Sue, Nicole Cheetham and Debra Hauser. Science & Success in Developing Countries: Holistic Programs that Work to Prevent Teen Pregnancy, HIV & Sexually Transmitted Infections. Washington, D.C.: Advocates for Youth, 2005. http://www.advocatesforyouth.org/storage/advfy/documents/sciencesuccess_developing.pdf

107 Kumar, Maya, Kirsty McNay and Adriana Castaldo. "Migration Affects The Health Of Mothers And Children In Rajasthan's Slums." Eldis. http://www.eldis.org/go/home&id=48196&type=Document (accessed June 15, 2010).

108 UN-Habitat. The Challenge of Slum Global Report on Human Settlements 2003. Nairobi, Kenya: UN-Habitat, 2003.

109 UN-Habitat. "State of the Urban Youth 2010/2011: Leveling the Playing Field." United Nations, 2010.

110 Interview with Nikki van der Gaag, for Plan International, 'Because I am a Girl' report 2010.

111 World Bank. Ready for Work? Increasing Economic Opportunity for Adolescent Girls and Young Women. Washington D.C.: World Bank, 2008, p4.

112 ID 21 Health. "Reducing Maternal Mortality in Matlab, Bangladesh." www.id21.org/health/h8mec1g1.html (accessed May 19, 2009). See also: Ellis, A., et al. Gender and Economic Growth in Uganda: Unleashing the Power of Women. Washington, DC: World Bank, 2006. See also: DFID. "DFID 's Gender Equality Action Plan (GEA P): First Progress Report 2007/2008." http://www. dfid.gov.uk (accessed June 14, 2010). See also: Plan International. Because I am a Girl The State of the World's Girls 2009: Girls in the Global Economy: Adding it all Up.

113 Nike Foundation. "The Girl Effect: Not Just about Girls: Engaging Men and Boys is Key to Girls' Ability to Achieve their Full Potential." www.nikefoundation.com/media_ room.html (accessed May 19, 2009).

114 Bazan, Cesar. Learn Without Fear. Hamburg: Plan International, November 14, 2009.

115 UN-Habitat. "State of the Urban Youth 2010/2011: Leveling the Playing Field." United Nations, 2010.

116 UN-Habitat. "State of the Urban Youth 2010/2011: Leveling the Playing Field." United Nations, 2010.

117 UN-Habitat. "State of the World's Cities 2006/2007 – Urban Features: Children, Slums' First Casualties." United Nations. http://www.unhabitat.org/downloads/ docs/5637_49115_SOWCR%2016.pdf (accessed June 14, 2010).

118 UN-Habitat. "State of the World's Cities 2008/2009 – Harmonious Cities". United Nations. http://www. unhabitat.org/content.asp?catid=7&cid=5964&subMen uId=0&typeid=46 (accessed June 15, 2010).

119 UN-Habitat. "State of the World's Cities 2006/2007 – Urban Features: Children, Slums' First Casualties." United Nations. http://www.unhabitat.org/downloads/ docs/5637_49115_SOWCR%2016.pdf (accessed June 14, 2010).

120 Speech to the 1st World Conference of Ministers Responsible for Youth, Lisbon, Portugal, 1998, quoted in World Bank. World Development Report 2007: Development and the Next Generation. Washington, D.C.: The International Bank for Reconstruction and Development, 2006.

121 World Bank. World Development Report 2007: Development and the Next Generation. Washington, D.C.: The International Bank for Reconstruction and Development, 2006.

122 World Bank. World Development Report 2007: Development and the Next Generation. Washington, D.C.: The International Bank for Reconstruction and Development, 2006.

123 Perlman, Janice E., and Sarah E. Anthony. "Citizenship and Youth in the Favelas of Rio de Janeiro." Background paper for the WDR 2007, 2006.

124 UN-Habitat. Lucia Kiwala, Director, Gender Mainstreaming Unit in correspondence with Plan International for 'Because I am a Girl' Report 2010.

125 World Bank. World Development Report 2007: Development and the Next Generation. Washington, D.C.: The International Bank for Reconstruction and Development, 2006.

126 World Bank. World Development Report 2007: Development and the Next Generation. Washington, D.C.: The International Bank for Reconstruction and Development, 2006.

127 UNIFEM. Knowledge Asset on Safe Cities and Communities for Women and Girls to Live a Life Free of Violence. Women in Cities International and Red Mujer y Habitat de America Latina, November 2009, p11.

128 World Health Organization. World Report on Violence and Health. Geneva: WHO, 2002.

129 New Internationalist. "Street children, our lives our words." New Internationalist No. 377 (April 2005).

130 We will be using the following definition of violence: Use of power, by an individual or group that results in or has a high likelihood of resulting in actual or potential harm to a girl's health, survival, development or dignity (amended from Pinheiro, 2006: 4).

131 United Nations Development Fund for Women. "Violence against Women." UNIFEM. http://www.unifem.org/ gender_issues/violence_against_women/ (accessed June 14, 2010).

132 García-Moreno, Claudia, et al. Multi-country Study on Women's Health and Domestic Violence Against Women Initial Results on Prevalence, Health Outcomes and Women's Responses. Switzerland: World Health Organisation, 2005.

133 García-Moreno, Claudia, et al. Multi-country Study on Women's Health and Domestic Violence Against Women Initial Results on Prevalence, Health Outcomes and Women's Responses. Switzerland: World Health Organisation, 2005.

134 Moore, A., et al. "Coercive First Sex among Adolescents in Sub-Saharan Africa: Prevalence and Context." Paper presented at the IUSSP XXV Conference on Population, Tours, France, July 18-23, 2005.

135 Jejeebhoy, Shireen J., and Sarah Bott. Non-consensual Sexual Experiences of Young People: A Review of the Evidence from Developing Countries. New Delhi, India: Population Council, 2003.

136 Moore, A., et al. "Coercive First Sex among Adolescents in Sub-Saharan Africa: Prevalence and Context." Paper presented at the IUSSP XXV Conference on Population, Tours, France, July 18-23, 2005.

137 "Adolescent Girls Most Vulnerable To Sexual Harassment." The Daily Star, February 18, 2010. http://www.thedailystar.net/newDesign/news-details. php?nid=126860

138 UNFPA. "State of the World Population 2007: Unleashing the Potential of Urban Growth." UNFPA, 2007. http:// www.unfpa.org/swp/2007/presskit/pdf/sowp2007_eng. pdf (accessed June 9, 2010).

139 Centre on Housing Rights and Evictions (COHRE). Defending the Housing Rights of Children. Geneva: COHRE, June 2006.

140 Karim, Fazlul, Nayma Qayum, Ziauddin Hyder and Kazi Nazrul Fattah. Human Rights Violation in Bangladesh: Lessons Learned from the Information Gathering System of BRAC Social Development Program. BRAC, October 2009.

141 Urban World. A New Strategy to Close the Gender Divide. July 2009, p19.

142 Women in Cities International. Results of FGDs carried out by Jagori in the framework of the Action Research Project on Women's Rights and Access to Water and Sanitation in Asian Cities. Canada's International Development Research Centre (IDRC), 2009.

143 Centre on Housing Rights and Evictions (COHRE). Women, Slums and Urbanization: Examining the Causes and Consequences. Geneva: COHRE, May 2008.

144 Centre on Housing Rights and Evictions (COHRE).

145 Centre on Housing Rights and Evictions (COHRE). Women, Slums and Urbanization: Examining the Causes and Consequences. Geneva: COHRE, May 2008.

146 Centre on Housing Rights and Evictions (COHRE). Women, Slums and Urbanization: Examining the Causes and Consequences. Geneva: COHRE, May 2008.

147 Stanford, Peter. "'They Like Us Naïve': How Teenage Girls are Groomed for a Life of Prostitution by UK Gangs." The Independent, January 31, 2010. http://www.independent.co.uk/news/uk/crime/they-like-us-naive-how-teenage-girls-are-groomed-for-a-life-of-prostitution-by-uk-gangs-1880959.html.

148 Findings from Hallman, K. and J. Diere. "Social Isolation and Economic Vulnerability: Adolescent HIV and Pregnancy Risk Factors in South Africa." Poster presentation at the Annual Meeting of the Population Association of America, Boston, MA, 2005.

149 Stanford, Peter. "'They Like Us Naïve': How Teenage Girls are Groomed for a Life of Prostitution by UK Gangs." The Independent, January 31, 2010. http://www.independent.co.uk/news/uk/crime/they-like-us-naive-how-teenage-girls-are-groomed-for-a-life-of-prostitution-by-uk-gangs-1880959.html.

150 Mabala, Richard. "From HIV Prevention to HIV Protection: Addressing the Vulnerability of Girls and Young Women in Urban Areas." Environment and Urbanization 18 (2006): 407.

151 Although this study draws primarily from research with 13-20 year olds, the issues discussed affect a larger age groupThe use of "young women and girls" indicates this overlap in issues that affect adolescent girls and other young women.

152 Dowdney, L. Neither War nor Peace: International Comparisons of Children and Youth in Organised Armed Violence. Rio de Janeiro: Viva Rio, ISER, IANSA, 2005.

153 Rodgers, Dennis. "Joining the Gang and Becoming a Broder : The Violence of Ethnography in Contemporary Nicaragua", Bulletin of Latin American Research, Vol. 26, No. 4, pp444–461, 2007Brooks World Poverty Institute, University of Manchester, UK.

154 Soares, B. M. "Retrato das Mulheres Presas no Estado do Rio de Janeiro - 1999/2000." Boletim Segurança e Cidadania. Rio de Janeiro: CESeC 01(01), 2002.

155 Goldstein, D. M. Laughter Out of Place: Race, Class, Violence, and Sexuality in a Rio Shantytown. London: University of California Press, 2003.

156 Wilding, Polly. "'New Violence': Silencing Women's Experiences in the Favelas of Brazil." Journal of Latin American Studies, forthcoming.

157 Erulkar, Annabel S., Tekle-Ab Mekbib, Negussie Simie and Tsehai Gulema. Adolescent Life in Low income and Slum Areas of Addis Ababa, Ethiopia. Population Council/UNICEF, 2004.

158 Safe Spaces Nairobi, Kenya. http://www.youtube.com/watch?v=h7VqazOij1k (accessed June 15, 2010).

159 UN-Habitat. "Causes of the Increase in Delinquency." http://www.unhabitat.org/content.asp?typeid=19&catid=375&cid=1437 (accessed June 14, 2010).

160 "Who's at Risk: Factors Associated with Intimate Partner Violence in the Philippines." SocialScience and Medicine 55(8) (2002): 1385-1399.

161 UNIFEM. Knowledge Asset on Safe Cities and Communities for Women and Girls to Live a Life Free of Violence. Women in Cities International and Red Mujer y Habitat de America Latina, November 2009, p3.

162 Plan Netherlands, 'Safety in Cities: an online survey", conducted for Plan International 'Because I am a Girl' Report 2010.

163 Plan Sudan, Don McPhee, Country Director in correspondence for 'Because I am a Girl' Report March 2010.

164 UNFPA. "Growing Up Urban, State of World Population 2007: Youth Supplement." UNFPA. http://www.unfpa.org/swp/2007/youth/english/story/preface.html (accessed June 9, 2010).

165 UNFPA. "Growing Up Urban, State of World Population 2007: Youth Supplement." UNFPA. http://www.unfpa.org/swp/2007/youth/english/story/preface.html (accessed June 9, 2010).

166 García-Moreno, Claudia, et al. Multi-country Study on Women's Health and Domestic Violence Against Women Initial Results on Prevalence, Health Outcomes and Women's Responses. Switzerland: World Health Organisation, 2005. www.who.int/gender/violence/who_multicountry_study/summary_report/summary_report_English2.pdf).

167 Steele, Cynthia. Empower. http://www.empowerweb.org (accessed June 15, 2010). See also: Instituto Sou Da Paz. http://www.soudapaz.org/ (accessed June 15, 2010).

168 Kruger, Jill S. and Louise Chawla. "We Know Something Someone Doesn't Know: Children Speak Out on Local Conditions in Johannesburg." Environment & Urbanization Vol. 14 No. 2 (October 2002). See also: UNESCO. "Growing Up in Cities." A UNESCO – MOST Project. http://www.unesco.org/most/guic/guicpubframes.htm (accessed June 15, 2010).

169 UNFPA. "Growing Up Urban, State of World Population 2007: Youth Supplement." UNFPA. http://www.unfpa.org/adolescents/docs/urban_eng.pdf (accessed June 15, 2010).

170 Women cops on trains for security of female passengers, Thaindian News, http://www.thaindian.com/newsportal/uncategorized/women-cops-on-trains-for-security-of-female-passengers_100325508.html

171 From Laura Mack, Girls Getting to Secondary School Safely: Combating Gender-based Violence in the Transportation Sector in Tanzania AED/Center for Gender Equity 2009.

## Chapter 3

1 Plan International. Transcripts from Interviews for the Street Children's World Cup, South Africa, 2010.

2 Plan International. Transcripts from Interviews for the Street Children's World Cup, South Africa, 2010.

3 UN-Habitat. "State of the Urban Youth 2010/2011: Leveling the Playing Field." United Nations, 2010.

4 Anderson, Kristen for 'Because I am a Girl' Report 2010, Children's Legal Centre Essex.

5 Plan International. Interview conducted by Street Child Africa for the 'Because I am a Girl' report 2010.

6 United Nations. CESCR. "The Right to the Highest Attainable Standard of Health (article 12 of the International Covenant on Economic, Social and Cultural Rights)." UN Doc. E/C.12/2000/4, August 11, 2000. http://www.unhchr.ch/tbs/doc.nsf/(symbol)/E.C.12.2000.4.En. Open Document, quoted in COHRE. Defending the Housing Rights of Children. Geneva: COHRE, June 2006.

7 "Amount of Street Children Rises." Tempo Interactive, February 5, 2007. http://www.streetchildren. uk/_uploads/Publications/5_amount_of_street_children_rises.pdf.

8 "Amount of Street Children Rises." Tempo Interactive, February 5, 2007. http://www.streetchildren.org. uk/_uploads/Publications/5_amount_of_street_children_rises.pdf.

9 Payne, Ruth. "Voices from the Street: Street Girl Life in Accra, Ghana." CEDAR Research Papers Number 40, January 2004. http://www.streetchildren.org. uk/_uploads/Publications/3.Voices_from_the_Street_-_Street_Girl_Life_in_Accra%2C_Ghana.pdf.

10 National Coalition for the Homeless (NCH). "Homelessness Families with Children." NCH Fact Sheet No. 7, June 28, 2004. http://www.nationalhomeless.org.

11 Believe in Children Barnardo's. "The Children's Society's Still Running II." http://www.barnardos.org.uk/news_and_events/media_centre/press_releases.htm?ref=52474 (accessed June 14, 2010).

12 Compiled by the Consortium for Street Children, January 2009

13 Compiled by the Consortium for Street Children, January 2009.

14 Interviewed by Patrick Shanahan, Street Invest, for 'Because I am a Girl' Report, March 2010.

15 Plan International. Interview with street girl for the Street Child Africa in Accra, Ghana for the 'Because I am a Girl' report 2010.

16 Consortium for Street Children. http://www. streetchildren.org.uk/ (accessed June 15, 2010).

17 World Health Organisation, Department of Mental Health and Substance Dependence. "Module 1: A Profile of Street Children. Working with Street Children: A Training Package on Substance Use, Sexual and Reproductive Health, including HIV/AIDS and STDs." WHO/MSD/MDP/00.14. Geneva: WHO, 2000. http://whqlibdoc.who.int/hq/2000/WHO_MSD_MDP_00.14_Module1.pdf. Quoted in COHRE and CordAid. Defending the Housing Rights of Children. Geneva: COHRE, June 2006.

18 Girl participant. CRADLE / USK / CSC National Workshop on Street Children and Juvenile Justice. Nairobi, Kenya: March 6-7, 2003.

19 Wernham, Marie. An Outside Chance: Street Children and Juvenile Justice – An International Perspective. The Consortium for Street Children, May 2004.

20 New Internationalist. "Brave New World – Housing and Homelessness." New Internationalist Issue 276 (February 1996). http://www.newint.org/issue276/scared.htm

21 Plan International. Transcripts from Interviews for the Street Children's World Cup, South Africa, March 2010.

22 Empower. Interview with Cynthia Steele, Chief Executive. www.empowerweb.org (accessed June 14, 2010).

23 Interview with Nikki van der Gaag, for Plan International, 'Because I am a Girl' report 2010.

24 In correspondence with Nikki van der Gaag, for Plan International, 'Because I am a Girl' report 2010.

25 Puzon, Marco Paa. Painted Gray Faces, Behind Bars and in the Streets: Street Children and Juvenile Justice System in the Philippines. University of the Philippines in partnership with the Consortium for Street Children, 2003.

26 ChildLine UK. Case Notes. http://www.

nspcc.org.uk/Inform/publications/casenotes/CLcasenotesrunningaway_wdf53960.pdf (accessed: June 24 2010)

27 New Internationalist. "Street children, Our Lives Our Words." New Internationalist No. 377 (April 2005). www.newint.org/issue377/rukshana.htm.

28 Buncombe, Andrew. "All Aboard Delhi's Beggar Express." The Independent, March 3, 2010. http://www.independent.co.uk/news/world/asia/all-aboard-delhis-beggar-express-1914922.html

29 Hamza, Waqar. "Young Beggar Girls May End Up as Prostitutes: Survey." The Nation, May 11, 2009. http://www.nation.com.pk/pakistan-news-newspaper-daily-english-online/Regional/Karachi/11-May-2009/Young-beggar-girls-may-end-up-as-prostitutes-survey

30 Plan International. Interview with street girl for the Street Child Africa for the 'Because I am a Girl' report 2010, (Interviewer; Allabiah Kunje).

31 Samoun, S. "Violence Against Women in Urban Areas: An Analysis of the Problem from a Gender Perspective." Urban Management Programme Working Paper Series No. 17. Nairobi, Kenya: UN-Habitat, 2000, pp29-30.

32 Justice for Girls. Submission to the United Nations Committee on Economic, Social and Cultural Rights at its' 5th periodic review of Canada: http://www2.ohchr.org/english/bodies/cescr/docs/info-ngos/justice-girls-new.pdf (accessed: June 24, 2010) 33 Ministry of Women and Child Development.

33 Ministry of Women and Child Development. Study on Child Abuse: INDIA 2007. Kriti, New Delhi: Government of India, 2007. http://www.indianet.nl/pdf/childabuseIndia.pdf.

34 Ministry of Women and Child Development. Study on Child Abuse: INDIA 2007. Kriti, New Delhi: Government of India, 2007. http://www.indianet.nl/pdf/childabuseIndia.pdf.

35 UNICEF. "Girls' Education Campaigns." http://www.unicef.org/girlseducation/campaign_21877.html (accessed June 15, 2010).

36 Child Hope UK. http://www.childhope.org.uk/ (accessed June 15, 2010).

37 Plan International. Street Child Africa survey for the 'Because I am a Girl' report 2010.

38 World Vision International, Gender and Development Department and World Vision. "Hope for the Girl Child." A Briefing Paper to the United Nations Commission on the Status of Women at its 51st Session, February 2007.

39 World Bank. World Development Report 2007: Development and the Next Generation. Washington, D.C.: The International Bank for Reconstruction and Development, 2006.

40 New Internationalist. "Street Children." New Internationalist No. 377 (April 2005).

41 New Internationalist. "Street Children." New Internationalist No. 377 (April 2005). http://www.newint.org/features/2005/04/01/harare-zimbabwe/

42 UNICEF. Executive Board Annual Session 2006, Item 13 of the Provisional Agenda, May 18, 2006.

43 UNICEF. Violence Related To Children and Adolescents in Conflict with the Law: Oral Report. May 18, 2006.

44 Wernham, Marie. An Outside Chance: Street Children and Juvenile Justice – An International Perspective. The Consortium for Street Children, May 2004.

45 Bari, Shoshur. Street Children in Conflict with the Law, Juvenile Justice Panel. UK: Save the Children UK, 2000.

46 Human Rights Watch, "Children's Rights: Street Children". http://www.hrw.org/en/category/topic/children%E2%80%99s-rights/street-children (accessed: June 24 2010)

47 Human Rights Watch, "Children's Rights: Street Children". http://www.hrw.org/en/category/topic/children%E2%80%99s-rights/street-children (accessed: June 24 2010)

48 Amnesty International. Children in South Asia: Securing Their Rights. London: Amnesty International, 1998.

49 Anderson, Kristen. 2010 Report. Essex: The Children's Legal Centre, 2010.

50 Dean, Amber R. "Locking Them Up to keep them 'Safe': Criminalized Girls in British Columbia." Canada: Justice for Girls, 2005.

51 Bari, Shoshur. Street Children in Conflict with the Law, Juvenile Justice Panel. UK: Save the Children UK, 2000.

52 Human Rights Watch. "Charged with Being Children." Human Rights Watch, February 18, 2003. http://www.hrw.org/en/node/12360/section/4 (accessed June 15, 2010).

53 Bari, Shoshur. Street Children in Conflict with the Law, Juvenile Justice Panel. UK: Save the Children UK, 2000.

54 Amnesty International. Document - Nigeria: Rape, the Silent Weapon. Amnesty International, November 2006. http://www.amnesty.org/en/library/asset/AFR44/020/2006/en/d9dcf48c-d3e9-11dd-8743-d305bea2b2c7/afr440202006en.html

55 Amnesty International. Document - Nigeria: Rape, the Silent Weapon. Amnesty International, November 2006. http://www.amnesty.org/en/library/asset/AFR44/020/2006/en/d9dcf48c-d3e9-11dd-8743-d305bea2b2c7/afr440202006en.html

56 Human Rights Watch. Children of Bulgaria, Police Violence and Arbitrary Confinement. Human Rights Watch, September 1996.

57 Human Rights Watch. Still Making Their Own Rules: Ongoing Impunity for Police Beatings, Rape and Torture in Papua New Guinea. Human Rights Watch, Vol. 18, No. 13, October 29, 2006.

58 Puzon, Marco Paa. Painted Gray Faces, Behind Bars and in the Streets: Street Children and Juvenile Justice System in the Philippines. University of the Philippines in partnership with the Consortium for Street Children, 2003.

59 Rurevo, R. and M. Bourdillon. Girls on the Street. Harare, Zimbabwe: Weaver Press, 2003.

60 De Benítez, Sarah Thomas. "State of the World's Street Children: Violence." Consortium for Street Children, 2007.

61 Women Educational Researchers of Kenya (WERK). The Story of Children Living and Working on the Streets of Nairobi. Kenya: SNV Kenya and GTZ PROSYR, 2002.

62 Puzon, Marco Paa. Painted Gray Faces, Behind Bars and in the Streets: Street Children and Juvenile Justice System in the Philippines. University of the Philippines in partnership with the Consortium for Street Children, 2003.

63 Child Hope. "Bangladesh." www.childhope.org.uk/article.asp?id=520 (accessed June 15, 2010). See also: BBC Lifeline Appeal for Childhope – BBC One. www.youtube.com/watch?v=E8ln4UsrXOw (accessed June 15, 2010).

64 Wernham, Marie. An Outside Chance: Street Children and Juvenile Justice – An International Perspective. The Consortium for Street Children, May 2004.

65 Puzon, Marco Paa. Painted Gray Faces, Behind Bars and in the Streets: Street Children and Juvenile Justice System in the Philippines. University of the Philippines in partnership with the Consortium for Street Children, 2003.

66 Movimiento Nacional de Meninos e Meninas de Rua (MNMMR). Street Children Latin America and the Caribbean. Brazil: National Movement of Street Boys and Girls, October 18, 2004. http://pangaea.org/street_children/latin/mnmmr.htm

67 Butterflies Programme with Street and Working Children. "Child Workers Union / Bal Mazdoor Union." http://www.butterflieschildrights.org/union.asp (accessed June 15, 2010).

68 ENDA, Fabrizio Terenzio in corredpondence with Nikki van der Gaag for Plan International 'Because I am a Girl' Report 2010.

69 Plan International. "Each and every child".

70 Casa Alianza. "Street Children Programmes in Central America and Mexico." http://www.casa-alianza.org.uk/northsouth/CasaWeb.nsf/3/Honduras_Cherub_Home?OpenDocument (accessed June 15, 2010).

71 Perez, Hilda M. "Shelter Allows Girls to Escape Exploitation." CRS. http://crs.org/honduras/cherub-home/ (accessed June 15, 2010).

72 This research design was implemented and facilitated in collaboration with Plan Philippines, with many NGOs in the country generously assisting us in gaining access to research sites and participants. The interview sample consisted of 22 participants, 5 boys and 17 girls ranging between the ages of 9 and 18 years of age. We also spoke with key informants from community organisations and social workers.

73 Save the Children UK. Breaking the Rules: Children in Conflict with the Law and the Juvenile Justice System. The experience in the Philippines. Philippines: Save the Children UK, 2004. http://vac.wvasiapacific.org/downloads/SAVE5.pdf

74 Save the Children UK. The Right Not To Lose Hope: Children in Conflict with the Law. Save the Children, 2005. http://www.savethechildren.org.uk/en/54_2172.htm

75 Save the Children UK. Breaking the Rules: Children in Conflict with the Law and the Juvenile Justice System. The experience in the Philippines. Philippines: Save the Children UK, 2004. http://vac.wvasiapacific.org/downloads/SAVE5.pdf

76 Department of Social Welfare and Development. "Number of Children in Conflict with the Law Served, by Program/Project/Service, by Sex, by Age by Region-CY2009." www.dswd.gov.ph (accessed March 1, 2010).

77 Save the Children UK (2004). Breaking the rules: Children in conflict with the law and the juvenile justice system. The experience in the Philippines. Retrieved, December 28, 2009, from http://vac.wvasiapacific.org/downloads/SAVE5.pdf

78 Council for the Welfare of Children. "Situationer on Filipino Children: Children in Need of Special Protection." www.cwc.gov.ph/downloads.php (accessed January 21, 2010).

79  Save the Children UK. The Right Not To Lose Hope: Children in Conflict with the Law. Save the Children, 2005. http://www.savethechildren.org.uk/en/54_2172.htm
80  Council for the Welfare of Children. "Situationer on Filipino Children: Children in Need of Special Protection." www.cwc.gov.ph/downloads.php (accessed January 21, 2010).
81  Coalition to Stop Child Detention through Restorative Justice. Philippines: 2009.
82  Save the Children UK. Breaking the Rules: Children in Conflict with the Law and the Juvenile Justice System. The experience in the Philippines. Philippines: Save the Children UK, 2004. http://vac.wvasiapacific.org/downloads/SAVE5.pdf
83  Key informant, Justice for Girls and Plan International, 'Adolescent girls' experiences of detention and rehabilitation in the Philippines', 2010.
84  Queen Rania Al-Abdullah, Women in the World, Accessed online: http://www.thedailybeast.com/video/item/women-in-the-world-queen-rania
85  World Bank Development Report 2007: Development and the Next Generation. Accessed online: http://www.wds.worldbank.org/external/default/WDSContentServer/WDSP/IB/2006/0 9/13/000112742_20060913111024/Rendered/PDF/359990WDR0complete.pdf
86  Child Protection Partnership and Plan International, original research undertaken in Brazil for the 2010 'Because I am a Girl' Report (March 2010)
87  George, Peter (2009). "A Kyrgyz local hero fights to protect the rights of street children in Bishkek". Accessed online: http://www.unicef.org/protection/kyrgyzstan_50946.html
88  UNESCO and UN Habitat (2009), Urban Policies and the Right to the City: Rights, responsibilities, and citizenship, http://unesdoc.unesco.org/images/0017/001780/178090e.pdf
89  Plan International, Learn Without Fear Campaign. Accessed online: http://plan-international.org/learnwithoutfear/learn-without-fear
90  UNIFEM Launches Safe Delhi for Women Initiative in India. (2009). Accessed online: http://www.unifem.org/news_events/story_detail.php?StoryID=997
91  Shakeel, Anjum. 'Training of cops on child rights, civic issues starts.' The News, March 31 2010,
92  Creed, C. ( 2007). 'A Place for Everyone? Gender Equality and Urban Planning".
93  Adopt a Light. Accessed oline: http://www.adopt-a-light.com/ Kenya
94  See UNIFEM, Knowledge Asset, 2010-www.endvawnow.org
95  UNESCO, 'Growing up in Cities'. Accessed online: http://www.unesco.org/most/guic/guicaboutframes.htm
96  UNICEF. "Child Friendly Cities". Accessed online: http://www.childfriendlycities.org/
97  UNICEF. "Child Friendly Cities". Accessed online: http://childfriendlycities.org/building-a-cfc
98  Lambrick, Melanie & Travers, Kathryn. UN Habitat. "Women's Safety Audits. What Works and Where?" 2008. Accessed online: www.womenincities.org
99  Lambrick, Melanie & Travers, Kathryn. UN Habitat. Women's Safety Audits. "What Works and Where?" 2008. Accessed online: www.womenincities.org

## Chapter 4

1  BarCampSwaziland June 2009. Interview with Tibusiso Msibi in Swaziland, Africa. Youth Assets. http://www.youtube.com/watch?v=E5h_OjhiPFs (accessed June 15, 2010).
2  World Bank. "Frequently Asked Questions." Engendering ICT Toolkit. http://go.worldbank.org/Z0FVJM0HF0 (accessed June 15, 2010).
3  The Independent: http://www.independent.co.uk/news/business/sustainit/closing-the-digital-divide-1640433.html (accessed: June 24 2010)
4  Statement to the World Summit on the Information Society, Geneva, December 10, 2003.
5  World Bank. Information and Communication for Development: Extending Reach and Increasing Impact. World Bank: 2009.
6  Giriharadas, Anand. "In Many Parts of the World, a Cell Phone is Sufficient". New York Times, April 18, 2010.
7  International Telecommunication Union. Measuring the Information Society – the ICT Development Index 2009. Geneva, Switzerland: ITU, 2009, p4. http://www.itu.int/ITU-D/ict/publications/idi/2009/material/IDI2009_w5.pdf.
8  International Telecommunication Union. Measuring the Information Society – the ICT Development Index 2009. Geneva, Switzerland: ITU, 2009, p5. http://www.itu.int/ITU-D/ict/publications/idi/2009/material/IDI2009_w5.pdf.
9  Youth of the Bresee Foundation together with The Children's Partnership"Why Does Technology Matter For Youth? Community Technology Programs Deliver Opportunities to Youth." The Children's Partnership, 2007. http://www.childrenspartnership.org/AM/Template.cfm?Section=Home&TEMPLATE=/CM/HTMLDisplay.cfm&CONTENTID=11243 (accessed June 15, 2010).
10  World Bank. World Development Report 2007: Development and the Next Generation. Washington, D.C.: The International Bank for Reconstruction and Development, 2006.
11  Hafkin, Nancy and Nancy Taggart. Gender, Information Technology, and Developing Countries: An Analytic Study. AED/LearnLink for the Ofiice of Women in Development, USAID, 2001.
12  International Telecommunication Union. Measuring the Information Society – the ICT Development Index 2010. Geneva, Switzerland: ITU, 2010. http://www.itu.int/ITU-D/ict/publications/idi/2010/Material/MIS_2010_without%20annex%204-e.pdf (accessed June 15, 2010).
13  Cherie Blair Foundation. Women & Mobile: A Global Opportunity. A study on the mobile phone gender gap in low and middle-income countries. London: GSMA London, February 2010.
14  Cherie Blair Foundation. Women & Mobile: A Global Opportunity. A study on the mobile phone gender gap in low and middle-income countries. London: GSMA London, February 2010.
15  Schonfeld, Erick. "Facebook is Now the Fourth Largest Site in the World." TechCrunch, August 4, 2009. http://techcrunch.com/2009/08/04/facebook-is-now-the-fourth-largest-site-in-the-world/
16  Cherie Blair Foundation. Women & Mobile: A Global Opportunity. A study on the mobile phone gender gap

in low and middle-income countries. London: GSMA London, February 2010. http://vitalwaveconsulting.com/pdf/Women-Mobile.pdf

17  Freedom House. "Special Report Section. Freedom on the Net: A Global Assessment of Internet and Digital Media. Egypt." http://www.freedomhouse.org/template.cfm?page=384&key=200&parent=19&report=79 (accessed June 15, 2010).

18  Cherie Blair Foundation. Women & Mobile: A Global Opportunity. A study on the mobile phone gender gap in low and middle-income countries. London: GSMA London, February 2010. http://vitalwaveconsulting.com/pdf/Women-Mobile.pdf

19  Society for International Development and UNESCO. Women in the Digital Age—Using Communication Technology for Empowerment: A Practical Handbook. Society for International Development and UNESCO, 1998.

20  World Bank. World Development Report 2007: Development and the Next Generation. Washington, D.C.: The International Bank for Reconstruction and Development, 2006.

21  Spicer, Kate and Abul Taherreport. "Girls and Young Women are Now the Most Prolific Web Users." The Sunday Times, March 9, 2008. http://technology.timesonline.co.uk/tol/news/tech_and_web/the_web/article3511863.ece

22  Gadio, Coumba. Exploring the Gender Impacts of World Links in Some Selected Participating African Countries: A Qualitative Approach. WorldLinks, December 2001.

23  Lee, Dayoung. The Impact of Mobile Phones on the Status of Women in India. Stanford: Department of Economics, Stanford University, May 2009.

24  Gadio, Coumba. Exploring the Gender Impacts of World Links in Some Selected Participating African Countries: A Qualitative Approach. WorldLinks, December 2001.

25  Studies Centre for Handicapped Research (SCHR). http://www.caihand.org (accessed June 15, 2010).

26  Plan International, Keshet Bachan for Because I am a Girl Report 2010.

27  'IT's Hot for Girls! ICTs as an instrument in advancing girls' and women's capabilities in school education in Africa' in Isaacs, Shafika. Information and Communication Technologies and their Impact on and Use as an Instrument Forth Advancement and Empowerment of Women. Seoul, Republic of Korea: United Nations Division for the Advancement of Women Expert Group Meeting, November 11-14, 2002.

28  Kulsoom Ally, Michael Quesnell, Community Involvement, Nokia Group.

29  Abdoun, Safaa. "A 'Plan' to change the world." The Daily News, Egypt, May 22, 2009.

30  Abdoun, Safaa. "A 'Plan' to change the world." The Daily News, Egypt, May 22, 2009.

31  Take Back the Tech. "Take Control of Technology to End Violence Against Women." www.takebackthetech.net (accessed June 15, 2010).

32  Cherie Blair Foundation. Women & Mobile: A Global Opportunity. A study on the mobile phone gender gap in low and middle-income countries. London: GSMA London, February 2010.

33  Cherie Blair Foundation. Women & Mobile: A Global Opportunity. A study on the mobile phone gender gap in low and middle-income countries. London: GSMA

London, February 2010.

34  Youth of the Bresee Foundation together with The Children's Partnership "Why Does Technology Matter For Youth? Community Technology Programs Deliver Opportunities to Youth." The Children's Partnership, 2007. http://www.childrenspartnership.org/AM/Template.cfm?Section=Home&TEMPLATE=/CM/HTMLDisplay.cfm&CONTENTID=11243 (accessed June 15, 2010).

35  Jocelyn DeJong, Bonnie Shepard, Farzaneh Roudi-Fahimi, Lori Ashford. Young People's Sexual and Reproductive Health in the Middle East and North Africa, Population Reference Bureau http://www.prb.org/pdf07/MENAyouthreproductivehealth.pdf

36  Learning About Living. "Self Esteem. Learning to Like Myself." http://www.learningaboutliving.com/south/young_people/personal_skills/self_esteem (accessed June 15, 2010). See also: One World UK. "Learning about Living." http://uk.oneworld.net/article/archive/9789 (accessed June 15, 2010).

37  Gadio, Coumba. Exploring the Gender Impacts of World Links in Some Selected Participating African Countries: A Qualitative Approach. WorldLinks, December 2001.

38  Oksman, Virpi and Pirjo Rautiainen. "'I've Got My Whole Life in My Hand.' Mobile Communication in the Everyday Life of Children and Teenagers in Finland." Estudios de Juventud 57, No. 2 (2002): 28.; Fortunati and Magnanelli. "Young People and the Mobile Telephone." p74.; Vershinskaya. "Mobile Communication. Use of Mobile Phones as a Social Phenomenon--the Russian Experience." p144.

39  Cherie Blair Foundation. Women & Mobile: A Global Opportunity. A study on the mobile phone gender gap in low and middle-income countries. London: GSMA London, February 2010.

40  Anderson, Kristen for 'Because I am a Girl' Report 2010, Children's Legal Centre Essex.

41  For example, Article 2 of the Convention on the Rights of the Child and Article 2 of the International Covenant on Civil and Political Rights.

42  Beijing Declaration and Platform for Action, para. 1. Available at: http://www.un.org/womenwatch/daw/beijing/platform/declar.htm (accessed June 15, 2010).

43  Beijing Declaration and Platform for Action, section J. Available at: http://www.un.org/womenwatch/daw/beijing/platform/declar.htm (accessed June 15, 2010).

44  Further actions and initiatives to implement the Beijing Declaration and Platform for Action, A/RES/S-23/3, 2000, para. 29. Available at: www.un.org/womenwatch/daw/followup/ress233e.pdf (accessed June 15, 2010).

45  Report of the Secretary-General on the review of the implementation of the Beijing Declaration and Platform for Action and the outcome of the twenty-third special session and its contribution to shaping a gender perspective in the realization of the Millennium Development Goals, 318 E/CN.6/2010/2.

46  See generally, Geneva Declaration of Principles, WSIS-03/GENEVA/DOC/0004 (2003); Geneva Plan of Action, WSIS-03/GENEVA/DOC/0005 (2003); Tunis Commitment WSIS-05/TUNIS/DOC/7 (2005); and Tunis Agenda for the Information Society, WSIS-05/TUNIS/DOC/6 (rev. 1) (2005), all available at: http://www.itu.int/wsis/documents/index1.html (accessed June 15, 2010).

47  IDEA. "Women's Card." http://www.ideacellular.com/
    IDEA.portal?_nfpb=true&_pageLabel=IDEA_Page_Ad
    vertisements&displayParam=main_womens_card.html
    (accessed June 15, 2010).

48  Donner, Jonathan and Shikoh Gitau. New Paths: Exploring
    Mobile-Centric Internet Use in South Africa. Chicago,
    Illinois: Pre-conference workshop at the International
    Communication Association, May 20-21, 2009.
    http://mobileactive.org/files/file_uploads/final-paper_
    donner_et_al.pdf

49  Spicer, Kate and Abul Taherreport. "Girls and Young
    Women are Now the Most Prolific Web Users." The
    Sunday Times, March 9, 2008. http://technology.
    timesonline.co.uk/tol/news/tech_and_web/the_web/
    article3511863.ece

50  Plan International, Chitra Iyre in correspondence for
    'Because I am a Girl' 2010 report.

51  Spicer, Kate and Abul Taherreport. "Girls and Young
    Women are Now the Most Prolific Web Users." The
    Sunday Times, March 9, 2008. http://technology.
    timesonline.co.uk/tol/news/tech_and_web/the_web/
    article3511863.ece

52  Spicer, Kate and Abul Taherreport. "Girls and Young
    Women are Now the Most Prolific Web Users." The
    Sunday Times, March 9, 2008. http://technology.
    timesonline.co.uk/tol/news/tech_and_web/the_web/
    article3511863.ece

53  CHI. "Girls Don't Waste Time": Pre-Adolescent Attitudes
    toward ICT. Montreal, Quevebc, Canada: CHI, April
    22-27, 2006. http://userpages.umbc.edu/~lutters/
    pubs/2006_CHI_LBR_Hou,Kaur,Komlodi,Lutters,Boot,M
    orrell,Cotten,Ozok,Tufekci.pdf

54  Polak, Michele. "It's a gURL Thing: Community versus
    Commodity in Girl-Focused Netspace" in Buckingham,
    David and Rebekah Willett. Digital Generations: Children,
    Young People and the New Media. Laurence Erlbaum
    Associates, 2006.

55  Watten et al. http://www.seminar.net/current-issue/
    gender-profiles-of-internet-and-mobile-phone-use-
    among-norwegian-adolescents.

56  Microsoft Canada Co and Youthography Internet Safety
    Survey, Results from Jan 2009 Poll of 1,065 Canadian
    Youth aged 9-17.

57  Spicer, Kate and Abul Taherreport. "Girls and Young
    Women are Now the Most Prolific Web Users." The
    Sunday Times, March 9, 2008. http://technology.
    timesonline.co.uk/tol/news/tech_and_web/the_web/
    article3511863.ece

58  IBGE (Brazilian Institute of Geography and Statistics).
    http://www.ibge.gov.br/servidor_arquivos_est/
    (accessed June 15, 2010).

59  Spicer, Kate and Abul Taherreport. "Girls and Young
    Women are Now the Most Prolific Web Users." The
    Sunday Times, March 9, 2008. http://technology.
    timesonline.co.uk/tol/news/tech_and_web/the_web/
    article3511863.ece

60  Cherie Blair Foundation. Women & Mobile: A Global
    Opportunity. A study on the mobile phone gender gap
    in low and middle-income countries. London: GSMA
    London, February 2010.

61  Ribak, Rivka and Hiyam Omari-Hijazi. "The Mobile
    Phone in the Lives of Palestinian-Israeli Young Women:
    Notes on the Domestication of a Mobile Communication

Technology." Paper presented at the annual meeting
    of the NCA 93rd Annual Convention, TBA, Chicago, IL,
    November 15, 2007. http://www.allacademic.com/meta/
    p191426_index.html.

62  Gill, Kirrin, Kim Brooks, Janna McDougall, Payal Patel
    and Aslihan Kes. Bridging the Gender Divide: How
    Technology can Advance Women Economically. ICRW,
    2010.

63  Castaño, Cecilia. The Second Digital Divide and Young
    Women. Universidad Complutense de Madrid, 2008.

64  The Cherie Blair Foundation. Women & Mobile: A Global
    Opportunity. A study on the mobile phone gender gap
    in low and middle-income countries. London: GSMA
    London, February 2010.

65  World Bank. World Development Report 2007:
    Development and the Next Generation. Washington,
    D.C.: The International Bank for Reconstruction and
    Development, 2006.

66  Murphy, Caryle. "Saudi Women Revel in Online Lives
    - Internet Gives Saudi Women a Rare Outlet for Social
    Interaction." GlobalPost, February 4, 2010. http://www.
    globalpost.com/dispatch/saudi-arabia/100203/internet-
    women?page=0,0.

67  Hafkin, Nancy and Nancy Taggart. Gender, Information
    Technology, and Developing Countries: An Analytic
    Study. AED/LearnLink for the Office of Women in
    Development, USAID, 2001.

68  Interview with Nikki van der Gaag, for Plan International,
    'Because I am a Girl' report 2010.

69  'IT's Hot for Girls! ICTs as an instrument in advancing
    girls' and women's capabilities in school education in
    Africa' in Isaacs, Shafika. Information and Communication
    Technologies and their Impact on and Use as an
    Instrument Forth Advancement and Empowerment
    of Women. Seoul, Republic of Korea: United Nations
    Division for the Advancement of Women Expert Group
    Meeting, November 11-14, 2002.

70  Interview with Nikki van der Gaag, for Plan International,
    'Because I am a Girl' report 2010.

71  Castaño, Cecilia. The Second Digital Divide and Young
    Women. Universidad Complutense de Madrid, 2008.

72  Gadio, Coumba. Exploring the Gender Impacts of World
    Links in Some Selected Participating African Countries: A
    Qualitative Approach. WorldLinks, December 2001.

73  Gadio, Coumba. Exploring the Gender Impacts of World
    Links in Some Selected Participating African Countries: A
    Qualitative Approach. WorldLinks, December 2001.

74  Cisco, Kreetta Ryodi, in correspondence with Plan
    International for 'Because I am a Girl' Report.

75  Omamo, Salome, Okwach Abagi and Olive Sifuna.
    "Professional Women in ICT Careers in Kenya: What
    Successful ICT Journeys Entail." GRACE. http://www.grace-
    network.net/publications.php (accessed June 15, 2010).

76  Spicer, Kate and Abul Taherreport. "Girls and Young
    Women are Now the Most Prolific Web Users." The
    Sunday Times, March 9, 2008. http://technology.
    timesonline.co.uk/tol/news/tech_and_web/the_web/
    article3511863.ece

77  Association of Women Educators. "Policy on Girls and
    Information and Communication Technologies." AWE,
    Australia. http://www.awe.asn.au/ (accessed June 15,
    2010).

78  Association of Women Educators. "Girls and Information

and Communication Technologies." AWE Policy. http://
www.awe.asn.au/documents/AWEGirlsICTs.doc
(accessed June 15, 2010).

79 Seybert, Heidi. "Gender Differences in the Use of
Computers and the Internet." EUROSTAT. http://epp.
eurostat.ec.europa.eu/cache/ITY_OFFPUB/KS-SF-07-119/
EN/KS-SF-07-119-EN.PDF (accessed June 15, 2010).

80 Higher Education Statistics Agency, quoted in Spicer, Kate
and Abul Taherreport. "Girls and Young Women are Now
the Most Prolific Web Users." The Sunday Times, March
9, 2008. http://technology.timesonline.co.uk/tol/news/
tech_and_web/the_web/article3511863.ece

81 Derbyshire, Helen. "Gender Issues in the Use of
Computers in Education in Africa." Desk review of
Imfundo, January 2003.

82 Gill, Kirrin, Kim Brooks, Janna McDougall, Payal Patel and
Aslihan Kes. Bridging the Gender Divide: How Technology
can Advance Women Economically. ICRW, 2010.

83 Spicer, Kate and Abul Taherreport. "Girls and Young
Women are Now the Most Prolific Web Users." The
Sunday Times, March 9, 2008. http://technology.
timesonline.co.uk/tol/news/tech_and_web/the_web/
article3511863.ece

84 Seybert, Heidi. "Gender Differences in the Use of
Computers and the Internet." EUROSTAT. http://
epp.eurostat.ec.europa.eu/cache/ITY_OFFPUB/KS-
SF-07-119/EN/KS-SF-07-119-EN.PDF (accessed June 15,
2010).

85 Insight Blog. "ICT Gender Gap: Stereotyped Thinking
Countinues to Impact Females' Choice for Teach
Careers." http://blog.eun.org/insightblog/2009/06/
ict_gender_gap_stereotyped_thi.html (accessed June 15,
2010).

86 Hafkin, Nancy and Nancy Taggart. Gender, Information
Technology, and Developing Countries: An Analytic
Study. AED/LearnLink for the Ofiice of Women in
Development, USAID, 2001.

87 Mitter, S. "Teleworking and Teletrade in India." loc.
cit.; Teleworking and Development in Malaysia, Vol. I
Integrated Report. United Nations University/Institute for
New Technologies Policy Research Project in partnership
with MIMOS Bhd. and UNDP, April 1999, p2247.

88 Ng. "Teleworking and Gender in the Information Age:
New Opportunities for Malaysian Women?" http://
gendevtech.ait.ac.th/gasat/papers/ngp.htm (accessed:
June 24 2010).

89 UNIFEM and UNU/INTECH. "Gender and
Telecommunications: An Agenda for Policy." UNIFEM.
http://www.unifem.undp.org/conferen.htm (accessed
June 15, 2010).

90 Plan India

91 Kulsoom Ally & Michael Quesnell, Community
Involvement, Nokia.

92 Hafkin, Nancy and Nancy Taggart. Gender, Information
Technology, and Developing Countries: An Analytic
Study. AED/LearnLink for the Ofiice of Women in
Development, USAID, 2001.

93 Global Learning. "Online Mentoring Narrowing the Gap
Between Rich and Poor." AED Connections, 2009. http://
www.aed.org/aedconnections/Spring%202009/pdfs/glg.
pdf (accessed June 15, 2010).

94 Samuel, Jonathan, Niraj Shah, and Wenona Hadingham.
Mobile Communications in South Africa, Tanzania and

Egypt: Results from Community and Business Surveys.
Newbury, Berkshire, U.K.: Vodafone Policy Paper Series 2,
2005.

95 Hughes, Donna. "The Use of New Communications
and Information Technologies for Sexual Exploitation of
Women and Children." Hastings Women's Law Journal
Vol. 13:1: 129-148.

96 UNICEF. From Invisible to Indivisible Promoting and
Protecting the Right of the Girl Child to be Free from
Violence. UNICEF, 2008.

97 García-Moreno, Claudia, et al. Multi-country Study
on Women's Health and Domestic Violence Against
Women Initial Results on Prevalence, Health Outcomes
and Women's Responses. Switzerland: World Health
Organisation, 2005.

98 Palfrey, John and Urs Gasser. Born Digital: Understanding
the First Generation of Digital Natives. Basic Books, 2009.

99 ECPAT International to World Congress III against
Sexual Exploitation of Children and Adolescents, ECPAT
International, Bangkok, 2008

100 CEOP in correspondence with Plan International for
'Because I am a Girl' report, 2010

101 Council of Europe. Trafficking in human beings: Internet
recruitment. Misuse of the Internet for the recruitment
of victims of trafficking in human beings. EG-THB-INT
(2007).

102 Internet Watch Foundation. See: Council of Europe.
Trafficking in human beings: Internet recruitment. Misuse
of the Internet for the recruitment of victims of trafficking
in human beings. EG-THB-INT (2007).

103 Sonia Randhawa, 'Cambodia, Malaysia, Pakistan and
the Philippines: Cross-country Study on Violence against
Women and Information Communication Technologies',
Association for Progressive Communications Women's
Networking Support Programme http://www.genderit.
org/resources/APC_WNSP_MDG3_VAW_ICT_asia_en_
jan2010_2.pdf

104 Council of Europe. Trafficking in human beings: Internet
recruitment. Misuse of the Internet for the recruitment
of victims of trafficking in human beings. EG-THB-INT
(2007).

105 Council of Europe. Trafficking in human beings: Internet
recruitment. Misuse of the Internet for the recruitment of
victims of trafficking in human beings. EG-THB-INT (2007).

106 Communication with CEOP for this report.

107 Council of Europe. Trafficking in human beings: Internet
recruitment. Misuse of the Internet for the recruitment of
victims of trafficking in human beings. EG-THB-INT (2007).

108 Michelet, Isabelle. 'Our Children at Risk Online: The
example of Thailand.' ECPAT International 2003

109 'Child Online Protection' ITU 2009

110 End Child Prostitution, Child Pornography and the
Trafficking of Children, 'Violence against Children in
Cyberspace', (2005), p.69, Available at: http://www.
ecpat.net/EI/Publications/ICT/Cyberspace_ENG.pdf.

111 A/RES/54/263, opened for signature 25 May 2000 and
entered into force 18 January 2002. As of March 2010,
- 136 state parties. Available at: http://www2.ohchr.org/
english/law/pdf/crc-sale.pdf.

112 A/RES/54/263, opened for signature 25 May 2000 and
entered into force 18 January 2002. As of March 2010,
- 136 state parties. Available at: http://www2.ohchr.org/
english/law/pdf/crc-sale.pdf.

113  E.g. Convention on the Rights of the Child Article 34.

114  Anderson, Kristen for 'Because I am a Girl' Report 2010, Children's Legal Centre Essex.

115  Council of Europe. "Misuse of the Internet for the recruitment of victims of trafficking in human beings." Seminar Proceedings, Strasbourg 7-8 June 2007. Available at: www.coe.int/t/dghl/monitoring/trafficking/Source/eg-thb-int-2007_Proceedings.pdf

116  Communication with CEOP for this report.

117  UNICEF Innocent Research Centre and the Government of the Netherlands. A Study on Violence against Girls: Report on the International Girl child Conference. 9-10 March 2009, The Hague, Netherlands.

118  Chat-wise, street-wise, Internet Forum in the United Kingdom, March 2001

119  UN General Assembly, Report of the independent expert for the United nations study on violence against children, A/61/299, 29 August 2006, C.80.

120  Hughes, Donna. "The Use of New Communications and Information Technologies for Sexual Exploitation of Women and Children". Hastings Women's Law Journal (Vol. 13:1, pp. 129-148).

121  Internet Watch Foundation. See: Council of Europe. Trafficking in human beings: Internet recruitment. Misuse of the Internet for the recruitment of victims of trafficking in human beings. EG-THB-INT (2007, pg. 28).

122  Donna Hughes, in: Maltzahn, Kathleen. Digital Dangers: Information and Communication Technologies and Trafficking in Women. APC Issue Paper, August 2006.

123  Council of Europe. Trafficking in human beings: Internet recruitment. Misuse of the Internet for the recruitment of victims of trafficking in human beings. EG-THB-INT (2007).

124  UNICEF Innocenti Research Centre and the Government of the Netherlands. A Study on Violence against Girls: Report on the International Girl child Conference. 9-10 March 2009, The Hague, Netherlands.

125  Girls' Net, Women's Net, UNIFEM. "Keep your chats exactly that!" http://www.womensnet.org.za/sites/womensnet.org.za/files/resources/Brochure_design-1.pdf (accessed: 24 June 2010)

126  Beeby, Nicolle. Texting and Sexting : Keep your Chats Safe. SA NGO Net. Available at: http://www.ngopulse.org/article/texting-and-sexting-keep-your-chats-safe

127  UN.GIFT. The Vienna Form to fight Human Trafficking, February 2008, "017 Workshop: Technology and Human Trafficking", pg. 12-13.

128  Council of Europe. Trafficking in human beings: Internet recruitment. Misuse of the Internet for the recruitment of victims of trafficking in human beings. EG-THB-INT (2007).

129  UN.GIFT. The Vienna Form to fight Human Trafficking, February 2008, "017 Workshop: Technology and Human Trafficking", pg. 12-13.

130  Council of Europe Group of specialists on the impact of the use of New Information Technologies on Trafficking in Human beings for the purpose of Sexual exploitation Strasbourg 17 February 2003, Document EG-S-NT (2002)

131  Hughes, Donna. "The Use of New Communications and Information Technologies for Sexual Exploitation of Women and Children". Hastings Women's Law Journal (Vol. 13:1, pp. 129-148).

132  Council of Europe. "Trafficking in human beings: Internet recruitment. Misuse of the Internet for the recruitment

133  of victims of trafficking in human beings". EG-THB-INT (2007)

133  Background paper for workshop: 'Technology and human trafficking' The Vienna Forum to fight Human Trafficking"." February 2008

134  Hughes, Donna. "The Use of New Communications and Information Technologies for Sexual Exploitation of Women and Children". Hastings Women's Law Journal (Vol. 13:1, pp. 129-148).

135  ASTRA Anti-Trafficking Action. "Human (Child) Trafficking, A look through the internet window". Belgrade, 2006. Available at: http://www.astra.org.rs/eng/wp-content/uploads/2009/09/internet-research-eng.pdf . p72-3.

136  Skinner, Robyn., and Maher, Catherine. "Child Trafficking and Organized Crime: Where have all the Young Girls Gone?" Youth Advocacy International (YAPI) Resource Paper. Available at: www.yapi.org

137  Now Public. "A fundamental assault on liberties – Human Trafficking". http://www.nowpublic.com/world/fundamental-assault-liberties-human-trafficking (accessed February 25, 2009).

138  'Technology and Human Trafficking 'Vienna Forum to Fight Human Trafficking, February 2008

139  Council of Europe. Trafficking in human beings: Internet recruitment. Misuse of the Internet for the recruitment of victims of trafficking in human beings. EG-THB-INT (2007).

140  UN.GIFT. The Vienna Forum to fight Human Trafficking, February 2008, "017 Workshop: Technology and Human Trafficking".

141  Maltzahn, Kathleen. Digital Dangers: information and communication technologies and trafficking in women, APC issue paper. 2006.

142  International Organization for Migration: http://www.iom.int/jahia/jsp/index.jsp (accessed: 24 June 2010)

143  ECPAT, Online Child Sexual Abuse: The Law Enforcement Response, 2008, 18, available at: http://www.ecpat.net/WorldCongressIII/PDF/Publications/ICT_Law/Thematic_Paper_ICTLAW_ENG.pdf

144  Carter, Helen. "Teenage girl is first to be jailed for bullying on facebook". Guardian, UK. August 21, 2009. Available at: http://www.guardian.co.uk/uk/2009/aug/21/facebook-bullying-sentence-teenage-girl

145  http://www.dailymail.co.uk/femail/article-1217289/Facebook-bullies-ruined-life-As-internet-bully-sent-jail-story-terrify-parent.html

146  Ministers' Declaration, "Reinforcing the International Fight Against Child Pornography", G-8 Justice and Home Affairs Ministers, May 24th, 2007, p. 2.

147  International Telecommunications Union, Draft Guidelines for Industry on Child Online Protection (2005), available at: http://www.itu.int/osg/csd/cybersecurity/gca/cop/guidelines/Draft/INDUSTRY.pdf.

148  Anderson, Kristen for 'Because I am a Girl' Report 2010, Children's Legal Centre Essex.

149  United Nations Standard Minimum Rules for the Administration of Juvenile Justice ("The Beijing Rules").G.A. res. 40/33, annex, 40 U.N. GAOR Supp. (No. 53) at 207, U.N. Doc. A/40/53 (1985); United Nations Guidelines for the Prevention of Juvenile Delinquency (The Riyadh Guidelines), G.A. res. 45/112, annex, 45 U.N. GAOR Supp. (No. 49A) at 201, U.N. Doc.

A/45/49 (1990); United Nations Rules for the Protection of Juveniles Deprived of their Liberty. G.A. res. 45/113, annex, 45 U.N. GAOR Supp. (No. 49A) at 205, U.N. Doc. A/45/49 (1990); UN Economic and Social Council 1997/30. Administration of juvenile justice. 36th plenary meeting. July 21, 1997.

150 UN Convention on the Rights of the Child, Article 40(1). Available at: http://www2.ohchr.org/english/law/crc.htm

151 International Center for Missing and Exploited Children. "Child Pornography: Model Legislation and Global Review" (2008), p. iii, available at: http://www.icmec. org/en_X1/English__5th_Edition_.pdf.

152 Donovan, Helen. Law Council of Australia, Proof Committee Hansard. 9 March 2010, p. 6. cited in Legal and Constitutional Affairs Legislation Committee, Crimes Legislation Amendment (Sexual Offences Against Children) Bill 2010 [Provisions], (2010), page 31, available at: http://www.aph.gov.au/Senate/committee/legcon_ ctte/crimessexualoffences/report/report.pdf

153 Legal and Constitutional Affairs Legislation Committee, Crimes Legislation Amendment (Sexual Offences Against Children) Bill 2010 [Provisions], (2010), page 31, available at: http://www.ema.gov.au/ www/ministers/oconnor.nsf/Page/Speeches_2010_ FirstQuarter_11February2010-CrimesLegislationAmendm ent(SexualOffencesAgainstChildren)Bill2010.

154 Legal and Constitutional Affairs Legislation Committee, Crimes Legislation Amendment (Sexual Offences Against Children) Bill 2010 [Provisions], (2010), page 31, available at: http://www.ema.gov.au/ www/ministers/oconnor.nsf/Page/Speeches_2010_ FirstQuarter_11February2010-CrimesLegislationAmendm ent(SexualOffencesAgainstChildren)Bill2010

155 Legal and Constitutional Affairs Legislation Committee, Crimes Legislation Amendment (Sexual Offences Against Children) Bill 2010 [Provisions], (2010), page 29-31, available at: http://www.aph.gov.au/Senate/committee/ legcon_ctte/crimessexualoffences/report/report.pdf

156 Anderson, Kristen for 'Because I am a Girl' Report 2010, Children's Legal Centre Essex, Legal and Constitutional Affairs Legislation Committee, Crimes Legislation Amendment (Sexual Offences Against Children) Bill 2010 [Provisions], (2010), page 30, available at: http:// www.aph.gov.au/Senate/committee/legcon_ctte/ crimessexualoffences/report/report.pdf

157 Knight, Kathryn. "Facebook bullies ruined my life: As the first internet bully is sent to jail, the story that will terrify every parent". Mail Online. Oct. 1, 2009. Available at: http://www.stopcyberbullying.org/what_is_ cyberbullying_exactly.html

158 Summary for Children and Young People, Byron Review, (2008) UK. Available at: http://www.dcsf. gov.uk/byronreview/pdfs/A%20Summary%20for%20 Children%20and%20Young%20People%20FINAL.pdf

159 BBC News. "Alarm bells ring over 'sexting'. May 15, 2009. Available at: http://news.bbc.co.uk/1/hi/world/ americas/8043490.stm

160 Microsoft Canada News Center. "Fact Sheet: Microsoft Canada and Youthography Internet Safety Survey". Available at : http://news.microsoft.ca/corporate/ archive/2009/02/25/fact-sheet-microsoft-canada-and- youthography-internet-safety-survey.aspx

161 Beeby, Nicolle. Texting and Sexting : Keep your Chats

Safe. SA NGO Net. Available at: http://www.ngopulse. org/article/texting-and-sexting-keep-your-chats-safe

162 Li, Qing. "Cyberbullying in Schools A Research of Gender Differences". School Psychology International (2006), Vol. 27(x).

163 Pew Internet & American Life Project. Lenhart, Amanda. (2007) "Cyberbullying and Online Teens". Available at: http://www.pewinternet.org/~/media//Files/ Reports/2007/PIP%20Cyberbullying%20Memo.pdf.pdf

164 Noora Ellonen et al, 2008: Violence against Children and Adolescents in Finland. Police College of Finland.

165 Plan Finland, Anna Kononen in correspondence for 'Because I am a Girl' Report 2010

166 According to Sergeant Forss IRC-Galleria can be compared to e.g. Facebook, Hyves (Netherlands), Lunarstorm (Sweden), Skyrock (France), Orkut (Brazil and India), ShulerVS (Germany). In 2009, IRC-Galleria had over 0.5 million users and contains over 9 million photos. Over 80 % of the Finnish girls were registered to IRC- Galleria. The biggest user group was 14–20 years. 2/3 of the users registered daily, 80 % weekly.

167 Award given by the Ministry of Transport and Communication in Finland.

168 The site has had 70,000 visitors a year. The website also includes useful information about the Police work especially for the children and youth.

169 Cox Communications Teen Online & Wireless Safety Survey, in Partnership with the National Center for Missing & Exploited Children® (NCMEC) and John Walsh. May 2009. http://www.cox.com/takeCharge/includes/ docs/2009_teen_survey_internet_and_wireless_safety.pdf

170 Logrono, Julieta. Plan Ecuador. "Dimensions of Sexual Abuse of Adolescent Boys and Girls, Cultural Practices and Mechanisms of Protection", 2009

171 CBS News. "Sexting" Shockingly Common Among Teens." Jan. 15, 2009. Available at : http://www. cbsnews.com/stories/2009/01/15/national/ main4723161.shtml

172 BBC News. "Alarm bells ring over 'sexting'. May 15, 2009. Available at: http://news.bbc.co.uk/1/hi/world/ americas/8043490.stm

173 The Chicago Tribune, Sexting bill passes Illinois Senate, 18 March 2010. Available at: http://www. chicagotribune.com/news/local/ct-met-illinois-sexting- bill-0319-20100318,0,552959.story

174 Burney, Linda. "Safe Sexting: No Such Thing." Media Release. May 3, 2009. Available at: http://www. community.nsw.gov.au/docswr/_assets/main/lib100039/ safe_sexting.pdf

175 Women's Net. "Girl's Net: Empowering Girls." http://www. womensnet.org.za/node/863. (accessed : 24 June 2010)

176 Beeby, Nicolle. Texting and Sexting : Keep your Chats Safe. SA NGO Net. Available at: http://www.ngopulse. org/article/texting-and-sexting-keep-your-chats-safe

177 Buckingham, David, Willett, R. 'Digital Generation: Children, Young People, and New Media'. New Jersey: Lawrence Erlbaum, 2006

178 ibid

179 GirlScouts LMK: http://lmk.girlscouts.org/Meet-the-girls. aspx (accessed 26 April 2010)

180 Byron Review. "Safer children in a digital world: the report of the Byron Review". UK, 2008. Available at: http:// www.dcsf.gov.uk/byronreview/actionplan/index.shtml

181 Byron Review. "Safer children in a digital world: the report of the Byron Review". UK, 2008. Available at: http://www.dcsf.gov.uk/byronreview/actionplan/index.shtml

182 Devitt, Kerry and Roker, Debi. 'The Role of Mobile Phones in Family Communication'; Mobile phone ownership and usage among pre-adolescents." Journal of Telematics and Informatics.

183 Madanda, Aramanzan, Ngolobe, Berna and Goretti Zavuga Amuriat. "Uganda: Violence against Women and Information and Communication Technologies." Association for Progressive Communications (APC) 2009. Available at: http://www.genderit.org/resources/uganda_APC_WNSP_MDG3_VAW_ICT_ctryrpt.pdf

184 All the above statistics from 'Child Online Protection' ITU 2009

185 Michelet, Isabelle. 'Our Children at Risk Online: The example of Thailand.' ECPAT International, 2003.

186 'Byron Review, Children's Call for Evidence 2008, http://publications.dcsf.gov.uk/default.aspx?PageFunction=productdetails&PageMode=publications&ProductId=DCSF-00333-2008& (accessed: June 24 2010)

187 'Byron Review, Children's Call for Evidence 2008, http://publications.dcsf.gov.uk/default.aspx?PageFunction=productdetails&PageMode=publications&ProductId=DCSF-00333-2008& (accessed: June 24 2010)

188 Virtual Global Taskforce. "A global response to child sexual exploitation." Pg. 2, available at: http://www.virtualglobaltaskforce.com/pdfs/VGTLeaflet120308.pdf.

189 Virtual Global Taskfroce. "A global response to child sexual exploitation." Pg. 2, available at: http://www.virtualglobaltaskforce.com/pdfs/VGTLeaflet120308.pdf.

190 Kristen Anderson, Children's Legal Centere, Essex University . Virtual Global Taskforce. Available at: http://www.virtualglobaltaskforce.com/index.asp.

191 International Telecommunication Union. Child Online Protection. http://www.itu.int/osg/csd/cybersecurity/gca/cop/

192 UNIFEM. Say no- unite, end violence against women. http://www.saynotoviolence.org/

193 Steenson, Molly Wright. "Mobile Space is Women's Space: Reframing Mobile Phones and Gender in an Urban Context.' April 2006 Yale School of Architecture.

194 All research in this box IBGE Instituto Brasileiro de Geografia e Estatística December 2009

195 Accessed online : http://lmk.girlscouts.org/Meet-The-Girls/Rockstars/Ada.aspx

196 Child Protection Partnership and Plan International, original research undertaken in Brazil for the 2010 'Because I am a Girl' Report (March 2010)

197 Article 13, CRC: The child shall have the right to freedom of expression; this right shall include freedom to seek, receive and impart information and ideas of all kinds, regardless of frontiers, either orally, in writing or in print, in the form of art, or through any other media of the child's choice.

198 Article 16, CRC: No child shall be subjected to arbitrary or unlawful interference with his or her privacy, family, home or correspondence, nor to unlawful attacks on his or her honour and reputation. The child has the right to the protection of the law against such interference or attacks.

199 Article 17, CRC: States Parties recognize the important function performed by the mass media and shall ensure that the child has access to information and material from a diversity of national and international sources, especially those aimed at the promotion of his or her social, spiritual and moral well-being and physical and mental health.

200 ITU News. April 2010. Accessed online: http://www.itu.int/net/itunews/issues/2010/03/07.aspx

201 Akhtar Badshah, Community investment, Microsoft Corporation

202 Based on: Cisco, 'White Paper: Women and ICT: Why are girls still not attracted to ICT studies and careers?' accessed online http://newsroom.cisco.com/dlls/2009/ekits/Women_ICT_Whitepaper.pdf

203 Based on: Working Group of Canadian Privacy Commissioners and Child and youth Advocates, 'There Ought to be a Law: Protecting Children's Online Privacy in the 21st Century', Discussion Paper, November 19, 2009

204 ibid

205 Accessed online: www.letmeknow.girlscouts.org

206 Child Protection Partnership and Plan International, original research undertaken in Brazil for the 2010 'Because I am a Girl' Report (March 2010)

207 Council of Europe, Trafficking in human beings: Internet recruitment. Misuse of the Internet for the recruitment of victims of trafficking in human beings. EG-THB-INT (2007).

208 Working Group of Canadian Privacy, 'There Ought To be A Law: Protecting Children's Online Privacy in the 21st Century', A discussion Paper, November 2009.

209 SkyNews, 'Facebook to add panic button to CEOP'. Accessed online: http://news.sky.com/skynews/Home/UK-News/Facebook-Will-Add-A-Panic-Button-Link-To-Ceop-After-Public-Outcry-Over-Ashleigh-Hall-Murder/Article/201005415639276.

210 ECPAT International, Report of the World Congress III against Sexual Exploitation of Children and Adolescents, September 2009.

211 UNICEF Innocenti Research Centre and the Government of the Netherlands. A Study on Violence against Girls: Report on the International Girl child Conference. 9-10 March 2009, The Hague, Netherlands.

212 ECPAT International. Report of the World Congress III against Sexual Exploitation of Children and Adolescents, September 2009

213 Anderson, Kristen. 2010 Girls Report. Children's Legal Centre, Essex.

**SECTION 2**

1 Mobile Children: From Victims to Actors, Early Migration and Trafficking in West Africa, 2009, African Movement of Working Children and Youth/Enda Tiers.

2 Save the Children. State of the World's Mothers: Investing in the Early Years. 2009.

3 UNFPA. State of World Population 2007. Growing Up Urban.

4 Sweetman, Caroline. Gender and the Millennium Development Goals, Gender and Development Journal, June 2005 (accessed online: http://tiny.cc/5e2mv)

5 Young Lives, 2008. "Children and the Food Price Crisis". Young Lives Policy Brief 5, An International Study of Childhood Poverty. Oxford:UK.

# Girls online

A list of links to websites, reports, research institutions, databases and agencies working on gender-based discrimination, with a particular focus on girls and young women.

## Business Sector

**The Girl Effect** is a shared initiative by the Nike Foundation and the NoVo Foundation to create opportunities for girls. It maps the 'girl effect', showing how a girl's empowerment can impact the girl, her community and humanity at large; and also provides tools and information for private employers, NGOs, IGOs and policymakers on how to empower girls. The '**Your Move'** **report can be found at:** *www.girleffect.org/ downloads/Girl_Effect_Your_Move.pdf*

**Goldman Sachs 10,000 Women** is an initiative that works to provide under-served women with business and management educations and expanding entrepreneurial talent in developing countries. Its goal is to provide 10,000 women with a business and management education over the next five years. '10,000 Women' works with development, NGO and educational actors. **More information on the initiative can be found at:** *www.10000women.org/index.html*

**HP Global Social Innovation** For 60 years, Hewlett Packard has supported innovation in education, granting cash, HP technology and other resources to learning institutions around the world. They are especially concerned with fostering entrepreneurship and developing IT skills. *www.hp.com/hpinfo/grants/*

**Standard Chartered Bank – 'Goal'** works to empower women in their communities in India through netball in order to help work towards the MDGs. Working with grassroots NGOs, it reach 3,500 young women in Delhi. To find out more about Standard Chartered's MDG projects **see here:** *www.standardchartered.com/sustainability/ our-approach/millennium-development- goals/en/index.html*

**United Nations Global Compact** is a policy initiative for businesses that are committed to aligning their organisation with the humane principles in the area of human rights, anti-corruption, labour and environment. By implementing this, businesses can ensure that market and commerce benefit economies and societies everywhere. An important part of the programme is concerned with empowering women in the workplace. More information can be found here: *www.unglobalcompact.org/Issues/human_ rights/equality_means_business.html*

**World Economic Forum** runs a Women Leaders and Gender Parity Programme which strives to promote female leadership and close the gender gapIt produces a Global Gender Gap Report which includes a full ranking of 128 countries from both the developing and developed world. It also monitors the change in rank from previous years to map improvements in the gender gap**The 2009 report can be found here:** *www.weforum.org/pdf/gendergap/ rankings2009.pdf*

## Civil Society Organisations

**Amnesty International (Stop Violence Against Women)** is a campaign which strives to end violence against women and girls in times of peace as well as war. Its main themes are the empowerment of women, violence against women perpetrated by the state and the implementation of existing laws on rape and sexual violence. **For more information visit:** *www.amnesty.org/en/campaigns/stop-violence-against-women.*

**Campaign for Female Education (CAMFED)** is an organisation which strives to eradicate poverty in Africa through girls' education and female empowerment. Its model has four stages. Girls complete primary and secondary school, then receive business training for their own economic empowerment and finally are able to lead change in their community. For more information visit: *www.camfed.org*

**Centre on Housing Rights and Evictions (CoHRE)** is a Geneva-based organisation campaigning for adequate housing for the world's population and promoting compliance with international standards, and has special consultative status with the Economic and Social Council of the United Nations. **Of particular interest** is their extensive research on the impact of poor housing and forced evictions on women, as well as the right to marital property. Further information can be found at: www.cohre.org/women

**Clinton Global Initiative** CGI Annual Meetings bring together more than 125 current and former heads of state, 15 Nobel Peace Prize winners, hundreds of leading global CEOs, major philanthropists and foundation heads, directors of the most effective non-governmental organisations, and prominent members of the media. These CGI members have made nearly 1,700 commitments valued at $57 billion, which have already improved more than 220 million lives in 170 countries. Of particular interest is the action area on women and girls empowerment: www.clintonglobalinitiative. org/ourmeetings/2010/meeting_annual_ actionareas.asp?Section=OurMeetings &PageTitle=Actions%20Areas&Action_ Area=Empowering_Girls_Women

**Consortium for Street Children** is a leading international network committed to a better and sustainable future for the world's street children. It takes a collaborative, partnership-based approach to inform research and influence policy on street children. More information, including resources and membership details, can be found at: www.streetchildren.org.uk/default.asp

**Forum of African Women's Educationalists (FAWE)** is a pan-African NGO founded by five female ministers of education. It works to improve access and quality of education to girls in the region. It has national chapters in 35 African countries. **More information can be found at**: www.fawe.org

**Girls 20 Summit** is modelled after the G20 summit and was held in June 2010.

Girl representatives from each of the G20 countries aim to bring the economic prowess of women and girls to the attention of G20 leaders and place girls firmly on the G20 agenda. www.girlsandwomen.com/home-1.html

**Girls, Inc.** is a non-profit organisation dedicated to empowering girls. It provides educational opportunities to girls in the most vulnerable sections of society in the United States. **For more information visit**: www.girlsinc.org

**Girls in Tech** is an organisation dedicated to engagement, empowerment and success of women in the technology sector. They host conferences to foster innovation and entrepreneurship among women professionals working in technology. They also blog about issues concerning women working in this sector: http://girlsintech.net/

**Girls Learn International** is a US-based organisation which pairs American middle- and high-school chapters with schools in countries where girls have traditionally been denied education. It promotes cross-cultural awareness and understanding and trains girls to be leaders in the movement for positive social change. www.girlslearn.org/index. php?catid=1&over=1&color=White

**Ipas** is an organisation focused on increasing women's ability to assert their sexual and reproductive rights. It works in several areas, focusing on sexual violence and youth. It works in advocacy, research, training health workers in safe abortion technique and technologies and advocacy. **For more information visit:** www.ipas.org/Index.aspx

**Justice for Girls International** is a non-profit organisation that promotes freedom from violence, social justice and equality for teenage girls who live in poverty. Based in Canada, it works with girls on the streets and girls in conflict with the law. JFGI collaborated with the 'Because I am a Girl' 2010 report to document and analyse abuses against girls in conflict with the law in the Philippines: www.justiceforgirls.org/ international_hr/jfgi.html

**NGO Working Group on Girls' Rights** is an international network which aims to ensure domestic implementation of international standards relating to girls in all stages of their youth, as well as promote advocacy of girls' issues in international policy. **More information can be found at:** *www.girlsrights.org*

The **Population Council** is an international, nonprofit, nongovernmental organisation that seeks to improve the well-being and reproductive health of current and future generations around the world and to help achieve a humane, equitable and sustainable balance between people and resources. Of particular interest is their report on girls education: 'New Lessons: the Power of Educating Adolescent Girls' *www.popcouncil.org/pdfs/2009PGY_NewLessons.pdf*

**A Safe World for Women: The 2011 Campaign** focuses on ending all forms of abuse of women and girls. It is an online organisation that brings together NGOs, groups and individuals committed to a safer world. Their website contains useful information on the types of violence inflicted against women and girls. *http://asafeworldforwomen.org/*

**She's The First** is a media action campaign established by young women to promote girls' education by attracting donors to an online directory of schools with sponsorship programmes. *www.shesthefirst.org/about/*

**Soroptimist International** is an organisation for women in management and professions who work to advance women's status and human rights through advocacy, awareness and action. **For more information visit:** *www.soroptimistinternational.org/index.html*

**Street Child Africa** supports 12 partner organisations working with children in street situations in eight African countries by providing funding, capacity building, advocacy and awareness-raising. *www.streetchildafrica.org.uk*

**Vital Voices** is a global partnership that aims to empower women worldwide. Working in partnership with organisations in the business sector, it works to train women leaders and entrepreneurs around the world who can then go back and train women in their own communities. **Of particular interest** is its Vital Voices Radio which airs interviews with influential leaders in different sectors: *www.vitalvoices.org/desktopdefault.aspx?page_id=448*

**Womankind Worldwide** aims to promote women as a force for change in development. It works in 15 developing countries funding projects tied to women's legal rights and self-empowerment. Their publications which are available for download may be found at: *www.womankind.org.uk/publications.html* Their 'Respect 4 Us' campaign website provides interactive tools for young people to explore issues of violence. *www.respect4us.org.uk/container.html*

**Women in Cities International** is an organisation dedicated to the creation of an international exchange network on women's participation in the development of cities and communities as well as the consideration of a gender-based approach in municipal planning and management. Women in Cities International assisted the 'Because I am a Girl' 2010 report in the development of Chapter 2 – girls in cities, and endorsed our call to action (page 91): *www.womenincities.org/english/sets_en/set_intro_en.htm*

**Women in Development Europe (WIDE)** is an umbrella organisation of European women's organisations which monitors and influences economic and development policy from a feminist perspective. It produces a monthly e-newsletter on its activities and news relating to gender and development. **To sign up for the newsletter follow this link:** *www.wide-network.org/blocks/join.jsp*

**Women's World Summit Foundation** has consultative status with the UN and strives to alert governments and international bodies to take an active role in the empowerment of women and children. **More information can be found at:** *www.woman.ch*

**World Association of Girl Guides and Girl Scouts** works worldwide to provide a non-formal education through which girls can gain life skills and self-development. It reaches approximately 10 million girls through 145 member organisations. **For more information visit**: *www.wagggsworld.org/en/home*

**YWCA** is a global network empowering women around the world to enact social and economic change. It works with 25 million women and girls in 22,000 communities. It works in four priority areas: peace with justice, human rights, women's health and HIV/AIDS, and sustainable development. **For more information visit:** *www.worldywca.info*

## Foundations

**The Cherie Blair Foundation** works to provide entrepreneurship opportunities and access to technology for women worldwide. They provide finance, networking and business development support on the premise that economically empowered women not only have greater control over their own lives and the lives of their children, but also signal a brighter future for their communities and economies. Their recent report *'Women and Mobile: A Global Opportunity'* highlights the need to increase mobile phone ownership by women in the developing world in order to advance gender, social and economic goals. The report may be accessed here: *www.cherieblairfoundation.org/uploads/ pdf/women_and_mobile_a_global_ opportunity.pdf*

**Girls Action Foundation** runs innovative girls' empowerment programmes across Canada, investing in girls and young women at both a local and national level. The programmes foster community leadership skills and inspire action to change the world. Many of the girls enrolled in the programmes are from remote, marginalised and urban communities. Find out more at: *www.girlsactionfoundation.ca/en*

**UN Foundation** The Foundation's Women and Population section has been working to empower women and girls worldwide, on the premise that they are essential to eradicating poverty and achieving social justice. They place a particular focus on reproductive and sexual health and rights, as well as investing in and advocating for, adolescent girls **More information can be found at:** *www.unfoundation.org/global-issues/ women-and-population/* The UN Foundation provides a vehicle through which donors can support the UN's work on girls – The Girl Fund *www.thegirlfund.org*

**Girl Up** is the United Nations Foundation awareness-raising campaign to harness girls' energy and enthusiasm as a powerful force for change. *http://girlup.org/*

## Multi-Laterals

**Organisation for Economic Cooperation and Development (OECD)** is an organisation which brings together governments committed to democracy and the market economy. Its **OECD Development Centre** has created **Wikigender,** a pilot project for the OECD Global Project on Measuring the Progress of Societies which provides a free forum through which to exchange and collect information on gender issues. **For more information visit:** *www.wikigender.org*

**World Bank** works closely with other development organisations towards improving girls' education. It finances projects in developing countries as well as providing technology and financial assistance to countries with high gender disparities in education. **Other excellent resources from the World Bank on girls' empowerment can be found at:** *http://go.worldbank.org/B9VQI8YJT0*

## Partnerships

**Girl Hub** is a collaboration between the UK government Department for International Development (DFID) and Nike Foundation. Girl Hub aims to form a global network of girls' experts and advocates and link them with development programmes and policymakers to promote girls' rights, and work to include girls in policy design and implementation. *www.girlhub.org/about/*

**The Coalition for Adolescent Girls** is a partnership between the United Nations Foundation and the Nike Foundation, and is committed to driving public and private investment in adolescent girls. **Check out:** *www.coalitionforadolescentgirls.org*

**World Bank Adolescent Girls Initiative** is an initiative hoping to improve girls' employment prospects tomorrow with training and education today. It works in partnership with the governments of Australia, the United Kingdom, Denmark, Sweden and Norway, and private sector firms including Cisco, Standard Chartered Bank and Goldman Sachs. The initiative also offers incentives to employers to hire and train girls. **For more information visit:** *http://go.worldbank.org/I5PX4JETM0.*

## Practitioner Blogs on Aid / Development / Gender

**AidWatch** A project of New York University's Development Research Institute, the blog centres on the idea of monitoring aid to ensure that it reaches the poor.
*http://aidwatchers.com/*

**Blood and Milk** examines the effectiveness of international assistance and development programmes as well as issues regarding employment in the development sector.
*http://bloodandmilk.org/*

**Tales From the Hood** is an insider's perspective on life in the humanitarian aid industry.
*http://talesfromthehood.wordpress.com/*

**Wait…What?** A personal blog written by an NGO worker on her involvement in integrating ICTs and social media in to community development programmes and increasing youth participation at local, national and global levels..
*http://lindaraftree.wordpress.com/*

**Wronging Rights** is a group blog written by lawyers and is dedicated to writing about and critiquing issues of human rights and justice.
*http://wrongingrights.blogspot.com/*

## Research

**Asia Pacific Women's Watch** is a regional network of women's organisations. It works to improve women's rights by working with other NGOs, national governments and the UN. **More information can be found at:** *www.apww.isiswomen.org*

**Association for Women's Rights in Development (AWID)** is an international organisation working for women's rights, gender equality and development. It works to build alliances and influence international institutions to advance women's issues. AWID provides current and up-to-date information on women's rights in the news; as well as profiling recent research and information on a multitude of topics, themes and countries. **See:** *www.awid.org*
Also, a profile of the 'Young Feminist Activism Program' can be found here: *www.awid.org/eng/About-AWID/AWID-Initiatives/Young-Feminist-Activism-Program*

**Centre for Global Development (CGDev)** is a non-profit policy research organisation focusing on reducing poverty. Of **particular interest** is its report 'Start with a Girl: A New Agenda for Global Health' (2009): *www.cgdev.org/content/publications/detail/1422899*

**Child Rights Information Network (CRIN)** is a global network of children's organisations which coordinates and promotes information on child rights. It has a membership of 2,000 organisations, and its search facilities can be narrowed down by region or theme with extensive information concerning children's legal rights. For more information concerning child rights mechanisms see *www.crin.org/docs/CRINmechs.pdf*

**International Centre for Research on Women (ICRW)** is an organisation which works on research, technical support for capacity building and advocacy. Its research focus includes: adolescence, HIV/AIDS, food security and nutrition, economic development, reproductive health and violence against women. Regarding girls, it works towards improving sexual and reproductive rights and combating child

marriage. **Its many publications on the subject can be found at:** *http://catalog.icrw.org/pubsearch.htm*
**International Women's Rights Action Watch (IWRAW) Asia Pacific** works to promote domestic implementation of international human rights standards. It focuses on the CEDAW, facilitating a flow of information from the international to the domestic, ensuring that women worldwide are aware of their rights. **More information can be found at:** *www.iwraw-ap.org*

**The Population Council** is an international non-governmental organisation conducting research into population issues worldwide. It is merging its research areas into three headings: HIV and AIDS; Poverty, Gender and Youth; and Reproductive Health. Their publications and resources can be found here: *www.popcouncil.org/publications/index.asp*

## Resources and Databases

**DevInfo** is a powerful database combining three databases to review the implementation of the Millennium Development Goals. Of particular interest is its 'Facts. You decide' page which shows statistics on each of the MDGs. **It can be found here:** *www.devinfo.org/facts.htm?IDX=13*
**Institutions and Development Database (GID-DB)** represents a new tool for researchers and policymakers to determine and analyse obstacles to women's economic development. It covers a total of 160 countries and comprises an array of 60 indicators on gender discrimination. The database has been compiled from various sources and combines in a systematic and coherent fashion the current empirical evidence that exists on the socio-economic status of women. *www.oecd.org/document/16/0,3343,en_26 49_33935_39323280_1_1_1_1,00.html*
Another of their projects is the **SIGI** (Social Institutions and Gender Index), a new composite measure of gender discrimination based on social institutions in 102 non-OECD countries. Users may build their own gender index by changing the priority of the social institutions in the SIGI. *www.genderindex.org*

**Girls Discovered** is a comprehensive, interactive resource of data relating to the welfare, health and education and opportunities of girls worldwide. It enables users to choose from over 200 datasets and view, compare and analyse their data on maps or download it as a spreadsheet. *www.girlsdiscovered.org/create_your_own_map/*

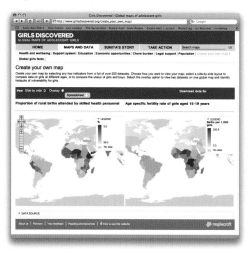

**WomenWatch** provides information and resources on gender equality and female empowerment. **The girl child is one of its critical areas of concern**. It is a useful source of information as it provides clear and easy access to the various UN conventions, bodies and activities relating to gender in a user-friendly way. **Information specifically related to the girl child can be found at:** *www.un.org/womenwatch/directory/the_girl_child_3012.htm*

**Young Feminist Wire** is an exciting new online community for young feminist activism, to showcase the work of young feminists, bring them together to enhance their effectiveness, and offer resources. *http://yfa.awid.org/*

## UN Agencies

**International Organisation for Migration (IOM)** provides research, advocacy and services in aid of migrants and migrant communities all over the world. Their core principle is that humane and orderly migration benefits both migrants and society. A quarterly bulletin on the *intersection of gender and migration* issues can be found here: *www.iom.int/jahia/Jahia/about-iom/organizational-structure/iom-gender/key-documents*

**Say NO to Violence** is presented by UNIFFEM, and records what individuals, governments and organisations are doing to end violence against women worldwide and count the actions taken towards that goal, with a view to reaching a count of one million actions by November 2010. They provide free resources and publications to download at: *www.saynotoviolence.org/issue/publication*

**United Nations Children's Fund (UNICEF)** focuses on child development, education and gender equality, HIV/AIDS, child protection and policy advocacy. **Of particular interest to girls** is the 2007 'State of the World's Children Report – Women and Children: the Double Dividend of Gender Equality': *www.unicef.org/sowc07/docs/sowc07.pdf* and the 2009 State of the World's Children Report: 'Maternal and Newborn Health': *www.unicef.org/sowc09/docs/SOWC09-FullReport-EN.pdf.*

**UN Commission on the Status of Women** is a commission of the Economic and Social Council dedicated to gender equality and the advancement of women. The 54th session of the commission, which reviewed the implementation of the Beijing Declaration and its contribution towards the realisation of the Millennium Development Goals, can be found here: *www.un.org/womenwatch/daw/beijing15/index.html*
The 2011 session will focus on issues relevant to this report, with the title being: 'Access and participation of women and girls to education, training, science and technology, including for the promotion of women's equal access to full employment and decent work.' *www.un.org/womenwatch/daw/csw/55sess.htm*

**United Nations Development Fund for Women (UNIFEM)** works on global gender issues in four different areas: reducing feminised poverty, ending violence against women, reversing the spread of HIV/AIDS among women and girls and achieving gender equality in democratic governance in times of peace as well as war. A number of their publications can be downloaded or purchased at *www.unifem.org*. Their website *http://endvawnow.org/* offers a knowledge centre for training with programming, resources for implementation, an expertise database and learning and training sessions.

**United Nations Development Programme (UNDP)** is the UN's development organisation and works on the ground in 166 countries. Its yearly Human Development Report monitors development on a national, regional and international level, and can be found at: *http://hdr.undp.org/en/reports/.* **Of particular interest**: Its Human Development Index (HDI) measures a country's development by considering education, life expectancy and income, but it also produces indices specific to gender: the Gender Development Index and the Gender Empowerment Index which **can be found at:** *http://hdr.undp.org/en/statistics/indices/gdi_gem/.*
It also runs a **Millennium Campaign** to support and promote awareness of the MDGs. The campaign produces 'The Millennium Goals Report' which summarises the data and achievements of all the MDGs. **It can be found at:** *www.un.org/millenniumgoals/pdf/The%20Millennium%20Development%20Goals%20Report%202008.pdf.*

**United Nations Girls Education Initiative (UNGEI)** aims to ensure that by 2015 the gender gap in primary and secondary education will have narrowed and all children complete primary education. Its 'Gender Achievement and Prospects' in Education (GAP) projects works to assess progress towards MDG 2 (universal primary education by 2015) and identify obstacles and innovations. The GAP Report can be found at: *www.ungei.org/gap/pdfs/unicef_gap_low_res.pdf*

The **E4 conference**, held in April-May 2010, aimed to promote partnerships for girls' education against the obstacles that violence poverty, climate change, health and educational quality can pose. The 'Dakar Declaration on accelerating Girls' Education and Gender Equality' was unanimously adopted by the participants at the conference: *www.ungei.org/index_2527.html*

**UN-Habitat** works to promotes socially and environmentally sustainable towns and cities, and improve the lives of the world's 100 million slum dwellers. **Of particular interest to this report** is the '2008/2009 State of the World's Cities' Report: *www. unhabitat.org/pmss/listItemDetails. aspx?publicationID=2562* as well as the forthcoming report on young people in urban areas: *www.unhabitat.org/pmss/ listItemDetails.aspx?publicationID=2928* They recently launched a co-operative initiative of community bodies to sponsor inclusive, safe cities for women and girls, for them to live in and have access to city services. Their global assessment report on women's safety in cities can be found here: *www.unhabitat.org/pmss/listItemDetails. aspx?publicationID=2848*

**United Nations Population Fund (UNFPA)** uses population data to ensure that every man, woman and child has the right to a healthy life. It produces a yearly 'State of the World's Population' report, several of which have focused on gender. 2006 focused on 'Women and International Migration'. *(www.unfpa.org/upload/lib_pub_file/650_ filename_sowp06-en.pdf)*

**UN Programme on Youth** is the UN's focus centre on youth. It produces a biannual World Youth Report. One of its areas of concern is girls and young women. **Information regarding its work on girls and young women can be found at:** *www.un.org/esa/socdev/unyin/wpaygirls.htm.*

# About Plan International

**Plan**
Be a part of it.

Founded over 70 years ago, Plan is one of the oldest and largest international development agencies in the world. We work in 48 developing countries across Africa, Asia and the Americas. Plan directly supports more than 1.5 million children and their families, and indirectly supports an estimated further 9 million people who live in communities that are working with Plan. We make long-term commitments to children in poverty and assist as many children as possible, by working in partnerships and alliance with them, their families, communities, civil society and government, building productive relationships and enabling their voices to be heard and recognised in issues that affect them. Plan is independent, with no religious, political or governmental affiliations.

## Our vision

Plan's vision is of a world in which all children realise their full potential in societies that respect people's rights and dignity.

## Our mission

Plan aims to achieve lasting improvements in the quality of life of deprived children in developing countries, through a process that unites people across cultures and adds meaning and value to their lives, by:

- enabling deprived children, their families and their communities to meet their basic needs and to increase their ability to participate in and benefit from their societies;
- building relationships to increase understanding and unity among peoples of different cultures and countries;
- promoting the rights and interests of the world's children.

**www.plan-international.org**

*Getting an education in a Ghana school.*

MARK PENGELLY

# Plan Offices

Plan International Headquarters
Christchurch Way
Woking
Surrey GU21 6JG
United Kingdom
Tel: (+44)1483 755 155
Web: www.plan-international.org

Plan Asia Regional Office
18th Floor, Ocean Tower 2 Building
75/24 Sukhumvit 19 Rd.
Klongtoey Nua, Wattana
Bangkok 10110, Thailand
Tel: +66 (0) 2 204 2630-4
Email: Aro.ro@plan-international.org

Plan East and South Africa Regional Office
Grevillea Grove, off Brookside Grove,
Westlands,
PO Box 14202-00800,
Nairobi, Kenya
Tel +254-20-4443462/3/4/5
Email: Regis.nyamakanga@plan-international.org

Plan Regional Office of the Americas
Ciudad del Saber,
Building 112, Ciudad del Saber,
Clayton, Panamá
Apartado 0819-05571
Panamá, Republica de Panamá
Tel: +507 317 1700
Email: melanie.swan@plan-international.org

Plan West Africa Regional Office
Amitié II Villa 4023,
BP 21121, Dakar,
Senegal
Tel: +221 33 869 7430
Email: waro.ro@plan-international.org

Plan International Australia
Level 18, 60 City Road
Southbank VIC 3006
Australia
Tel: +61-(0)3-9672-3600
Email: info@plan.org.au

Plan Belgium
Galerie Ravenstein 3 B 5
1000 Brussels
Belgium
Tel: +32 (0)2 504 60 00
Email: info@planbelgie.be/
info@planbelgique.be

Plan Canada
95 St. Clair Avenue West
Suite 1001
Toronto, Ontario M4V 3B5
Canada
Tel: +1 416-920-1654
Email: info@plancanada.ca

Plan Denmark
Rosenoerns Allé 18, 2.sal
1634 Copenhagen V
Denmark
Tel: +45-35-300800
Email: plan@plandanmark.dk

Plan Finland
Pasilanraitio 5, 2nd floor
00240 Helsinki
Finland
Tel: +358-9-6869-800
Email: anna.kononen@plan.fi

Plan France
11 rue de Cambrai
75019
Paris
France
Tel: +33-144-899090
Email: fno.office@plan-int.org

Plan Germany
Bramfelder Strasse 70
D-22305 Hamburg
Germany
Tel: +49-40-611400
Email: info@plan-deutschland.de

Plan Hong Kong
Unit 1104
11/F Cameron Centre
458 Hennessy Road
Causeway Bay
Hong Kong
Tel: +852-3405-5300
Email: info-hk@plan.org.hk

Plan Ireland
126 Lower Baggot Street
Dublin 2
Ireland
Tel: +353-1-6599601
Email:
Damien.queally@plan-international.org

Plan Japan
11F Sun Towers Center Building
2-11-22 Sangenjaya
Setagaya-Ku
Tokyo 154-8545
Japan
Tel: +81-3-5481-0030
Email: hello@plan-japan.org

Plan Korea
2nd Floor, Cheongwoo BD, 58-4
Samsung-dong, Gangnam-gu, Seoul
Korea 135-870
Tel:+82-2-790-5436
Email: kno@plan-international.org

Plan Netherlands
Van Boshuizenstraat 12
1083 BA, Amsterdam
Netherlands
Tel: +31-20-549-5555
Email: info@plannederland.nl

Plan Norway
Tullins Gate 4C
Postboks 1 St. Olavs Plass
0130 Oslo
Norway
Tel: +47-22-031600
Email: info@plan-norge.no

Plan Spain
C/ Pantoja 10
28002 Madrid
Spain
Tel: +34-91-5241222
Email: info@planespana.org

Plan Sweden
Box 92150
Textilgatan 43
SE -120 08, Stockholm
Sweden
Tel: +46-8-58 77 55 00
Email: info@plansverige.org

Plan Switzerland
Toedistrasse 51
CH-8002 Zurich
Switzerland
Tel: +41-44-288-9050
Email: info@plan-schweiz.ch

Plan United Kingdom
Finsgate
5-7 Cranwood Street
London EC1V 9LH
United Kingdom
Tel: +44 (0) 20 7482 9777
Email: mail@plan-international.org.uk

Plan USA
155 Plan Way
Warwick
Rhode Island
02886-1099 USA
Tel: +1-401-7385600
Email: donorrelations@planusa.org

Plan European Union (EU) Liaison Office
Galerie Ravenstein; 27/4
1000 Brussels
Belgium
Tel: +32-2-504-6050
Email: info-eu@plan-international.org